Gender and the Violence(s) of War and Armed Conflict

EMERALD STUDIES IN CRIMINOLOGY, FEMINISM AND SOCIAL CHANGE

Series Editors
Sandra Walklate, School of Social Sciences, Monash University, Australia.
Kate Fitz-Gibbon, School of Social Sciences at Monash University and Monash Gender and Family Violence Prevention Centre, Australia.
Jude McCulloch, Monash University and Monash Gender and Family Violence Prevention Centre, Australia.
JaneMaree Maher, Centre for Women's Studies and Gender Research, Sociology, Monash University, Australia.

Emerald Studies in Criminology, Feminism and Social Change offers a platform for innovative, engaged, and forward-looking feminist-informed work to explore the interconnections between social change and the capacity of criminology to grapple with the implications of such change.

Social change, whether as a result of the movement of peoples, the impact of new technologies, the potential consequences of climate change, or more commonly identified features of changing societies, such as ageing populations, inter-generational conflict, the changing nature of work, increasing awareness of the problem of gendered violence(s), and/or changing economic and political context, takes its toll across the globe in infinitely more nuanced and inter-connected ways than previously imagined. Each of these connections carry implications for what is understood as crime, the criminal, the victim of crime and the capacity of criminology as a discipline to make sense of these evolving interconnections. Feminist analysis, despite its contentious relationship with the discipline of criminology, has much to offer in strengthening the discipline to better understand the complexity of the world in the twenty-first century and to scan the horizon for emerging, possible or likely futures.

This series invites feminist-informed scholars, particularly those working comparatively across disciplinary boundaries to take up the challenges posed by social change for the discipline of criminology. The series offers authors a space to adopt and develop strong, critical personal views whether in the format of research monographs, single or co-authored books or edited collections. We are keen to promote global views and debates on these issues and welcome proposals embracing such perspectives.

Forthcoming titles in this series

The Emerald Handbook of Criminology, Feminism and Social Change
Sandra Walklate, Kate Fitz-Gibbon, Jude McCulloch and JaneMaree Maher (Eds)

Mothering from the Inside
Kelly Lockwood

Young Women's Carceral Geographies: Journeys In, Out, and Beyond Confinement
Anna Schliehe

Carceral Feminicidio: The Disappearance of Indigenous Women into Prisons
Gillian Balfour

Praise for Gender and the Violence(s) of War and Armed Conflict: More Dangerous to be a Woman?

'Banwell's careful scholarship challenges well-worn orthodoxies about gender, sexual violence, war and the state. A much needed addition to contemporary feminist criminology.'
　　　　-**Jennifer Fleetwood**, Senior Lecturer, Goldsmiths, University of London

'Banwell's book is truly imaginative. She draws on a wide range of interdisciplinary literature, constructs a framework that analyzes where and how gender is implicated in war and securitization. Taking a case study approach and adopting the assumptions of visual criminology, each chapter allows Banwell to demonstrate time and again her main arguments as well as the depth of her scholarship. This is a must read for students and academics alike. Chapter 1 ought to be on every undergraduate reading list for any criminological methods or theory course!'
　　　　-**Prof Jo Phoenix**, The Open University

'Rather than asking who suffers more in armed conflicts, Banwell explores the unique ways women and men experience war. Noting that gender is often deployed to justify war: think men as valient and women as fragile beings in need of protection, she urges criminologists to study the "new" wars. She is particularly focused on ways that these wars often blur categories in ways that make girls and women uniquely vulnerable to gender based violence.'
　　　　-**Meda Chesney-Lind**, University of Hawaii at Manoa

Gender and the Violence(s) of War and Armed Conflict: More Dangerous to Be a Woman?

BY

DR STACY BANWELL
University of Greenwich, UK

United Kingdom – North America – Japan – India – Malaysia – China

Emerald Publishing Limited
Howard House, Wagon Lane, Bingley BD16 1WA, UK

First edition 2020

Reprints and permissions service
Contact: permissions@emeraldinsight.com

British Library Cataloguing in Publication Data
A catalogue record for this book is available from the British Library

ISBN: 978-1-78769-116-2 (Print)
ISBN: 978-1-78769-115-5 (Online)
ISBN: 978-1-78769-117-9 (Epub)

An electronic version of this book is freely available, thanks to the support of libraries working with Knowledge Unlatched. KU is a collaborative initiative designed to make high quality books Open Access for the public good. More information about the initiative and links to the Open Access version can be found at www.knowledgeunlatched.org

ISOQAR certified Management System, awarded to Emerald for adherence to Environmental standard ISO 14001:2004.

ISOQAR
REGISTERED
Certificate Number 1985
ISO 14001

INVESTOR IN PEOPLE

Contents

Author Biography

Stacy Banwell, PhD, is a Principal Lecturer in Criminology at the University of Greenwich. She is also the Programme Leader of the MSc in Criminology, Gender and Sexualities at the University of Greenwich. Her research addresses gender and the violence(s) of war and armed conflict, as well as gender and economic foreign policy in warzones. She is one of the lead members of the Gender, Deviance and Society Research Group at the University of Greenwich. She is currently conducting empirical research on the reproductive healthcare needs of female war-affected populations. This research reviews US foreign policy on abortion under President Trump. She is also developing her research on the relationship between gender, the violence(s) of war/armed conflict and climate insecurity.

Acknowledgements

I would like to thank Taylor and Francis for granting me permission to reproduce parts of my previously published work.

Parts of Chapter 1 are based on the following article: Banwell, S. (2016). Rassenschande, genocide and the reproductive Jewish body: Examining the use of rape and sexualized violence against Jewish women during the Holocaust? *Journal of Modern Jewish Studies, 15*(2), 208–227. This was published by Taylor and Francis. The journal's website can be found here: www.tandfonline.com

Parts of Chapter 2 are based on the following article: Banwell, S. (2014). Rape and sexual violence in the Democratic Republic of Congo: A case study of gender-based violence. *Journal of Gender Studies, 23*(1), 45–58. This was published by Taylor and Francis. The journal's website can be found here: www.tandfonline.com

Parts of Chapter 3 are based on the following article: Banwell, S. (2015b) Globalisation masculinities, empire building and forced prostitution: A critical analysis of the gendered impact of the neoliberal economic agenda in post-invasion/occupation Iraq. *Third World Quarterly, 36*(4), 705–722. Copyright © Southseries Inc., www.thirdworldquarterly.com, reprinted by permission of Taylor & Francis Ltd, http://www.tandfonline.com on behalf of Southseries Inc., www.thirdworldquarterly.com

I would like to thank the USC Visual History Archive for the use of the Holocaust testimonies from their Shoah Foundation online archive. Thanks also to Maggie Paterson at Amnesty International for granting me permission to use the Amnesty International 2009 London Tube campaign.

For granting me space in my workload to write this book I would like to thank Sandra Clarke (University of Buckingham) and Professor Darrick Jolliffe (University of Greenwich).

I am grateful to Professor Sandra Walkate for passing on my details to Emerald Publishing when I first expressed an interest in publishing in their Feminism, Criminology and Social Change Series.

I would like to mention and thank the 2017/18 cohort of students on Crime in the City, Crime and the State for the debates we had about genocidal rape.

Thanks to Irene Barranco Garcia the Collaborations, Compliance and Copyright Manager at the University of Greenwich for her expertise and advice on copyright issues.

For making the publication of this book possible, I would like to thank the anonymous reviewers who reviewed the book proposal and offered constructive feedback on the outline of the book. Thanks to the supportive team at Emerald Publishing (Philippa Grand, Rachel Ward, Hazel Goodes, Katy Mathers, Alice Ford, Chris Tutill and Lauren Flintoft), it has been a pleasure working with you all. My particular thanks to Jules Willan and Helen Beddow for their guidance and reassurance throughout this whole process.

Thank you to my wonderful group of friends for your support and for checking in throughout this process (for the phone calls, and/or coffee/wine breaks, particular thanks to Opi, Mel and Emma).

Thanks to my friend and office pal Alex Fanghanel for her words of wisdom and her advice on how to write a book! And even though we never got around to it, knowing that you were on hand to cry over the sign, the signifier and signified kept me going!

I would like to give a special thanks to my incredible niece Jemima Duncalf, not least for reminding me to breathe, but for her encouragement and infectiously positive outlook on life.

For being there from the start (when I was anxiously awaiting the reviewer's comments on the draft proposal), right through to the final stages – even through the most difficult of times – I thank my oldest friend Lizzie Rutter. Your determination, resilience and selflessness are inspirational.

Most of all I would like to thank Michael Fiddler, not only for his support, advice and encouragement throughout this process, but for reading through drafts of this book. Thank you for your honesty and for holding no punches when it came to providing feedback on early drafts of the various chapters of this book. Your suggestions for further reading – which often pushed me outside of my comfort zone (yes, I'm referring to semiotics, postmodern memes and the sign, the signifier and signified!) – made this a much stronger piece of work.

You have always described us as a team. For this I feel blessed and grateful.

Introduction

Stacy Banwell

The Securitisation of Wartime Rape and Sexual Violence

The question that appears in the title of this book is taken from the following statement: 'it is perhaps more dangerous to be a woman than a soldier in armed conflict'. It was made by Major General Patrick Cammaert in a video clip on the *Stop Rape Now: UN Action against Sexual Violence in Conflict* website (Stop Rape Now, n.d.). He is the former United Nations force commander for the Eastern Democratic Republic of Congo (DRC). I will return to this statement shortly, for now let us review the *Stop Rape Now* website.

The site includes the 'GET CROSS!' campaign with the following caption: '[t]ake a stand against the use of sexual violence as a *tactic of war* by adding your crossed arm picture to our global campaign' (Stop Rape Now, n.d., emphasis added). This global campaign is visualised through an interactive map. This is populated with crosses where individuals have uploaded images of their crossed arms. Other images of individuals (including celebrities) crossing their arms flash across our screens. Celebrities, such as Charlize Theron and Nicole Kidman, also feature in the video clips included on the website. They inform us about the use of rape as a weapon of war against women and girls. They also encourage viewers to develop their knowledge further and take action.

Others have also written about the *Stop Rape Now* website (Grey & Shepherd, 2012; Meger, 2016b). Departing from this work, I draw on Visual Criminology to unpack this campaign. Briefly, and in simple terms (a more detailed review is provided in Chapter 5), Visual Criminology is interested in the visual representations of crime and punishment. It unpacks the visuality of hierarchical classifications such as race, class, gender and sexuality as they relate to these phenomena (Brown, 2014; Brown & Carrabine, 2017; Henne & Shah, 2016). Beyond this, Visual Criminology is interested in human lived experiences and in interrogating the ethical and moral consequences of looking at images (Brown, 2017; Brown & Carrabine, 2017; Gies, 2017). Of relevance for my discussion here is the argument that visuality need not only be visual, it also includes narratives which seek to reify

Gender and the Violence(s) of War and Armed Conflict:
More Dangerous to be a Woman?, 1–17
doi:10.1108/978-1-78769-115-520201002

and reproduce State power (Schept, 2016). In my analysis of this campaign, *Stop Rape Now,* a United Nations international organisation (comprising of 193 member States) is understood as a form of State power. And finally, on the subject of how power is conveyed through images, Hayward (2010, p. 5 as cited in Henne & Shah, 2016, p. 5) argues that images 'can be used as both a tool of control and resistance'. These ideas are teased out below.

Notwithstanding the literal display of resistance represented by the crossed arms; symbolising condemnation of the use of rape as a weapon of war, global advocacy such as the GET CROSS! campaign – which focuses narrowly on wartime rape against women and girls – reproduces 'master narratives' which are then 'presented as natural, universal, true, and inevitable' (Bal, 2003, p. 22 as cited by Henne & Shah, 2016, p. 18). I believe as a tool of control, the visuality of this campaign (the images of the crossed arms, the captions and the video clips that accompany them) – that is, the narrative it produces, results in the securitisation and fetishisation of wartime rape and sexual violence.

Securitisation, to paraphrase Hirschauer (2014, pp. 5–6), involves a process of applying a specific existential threat component to a social problem – in this instance, rape and sexual violence. The State, international bodies, non-governmental organisations (NGOs) and the media (referred to as securitisation actors) decide which groups are vulnerable to this security threat. Funding agencies, international institutions and donors are then persuaded, through discursive representations (by policymakers, activists and the news media), that exceptional measures are required to maintain peace and security.

Allied to securitisation is the fetishisation of wartime rape and sexual violence. This involves selective and sensationalist accounts of rape and sexual violence – particularly against women and girls – at the expense of other types of conflict violence. Here, rape and sexual violence are identified as the most dangerous forms of conflict violence (Meger, 2016a, 2016b). Not only does this obscure the complexity of wartime rape and sexual violence, and indeed the conflicts within which they occur, it also marginalises other types of violence taking place within and beyond conflict zones (Crawford, Green, & Parkinson, 2014). It also excludes the experiences of men and boys. This impedes wider efforts to address and combat the violence(s) of war and armed conflict (Baaz & Stern, 2013; Meger, 2016a, 2016b; Mertens & Pardy, 2017). Indeed, the statement made by General Patrick Cammaert is a perfect illustration of this gendered securitisation agenda: a policy narrative that prioritises the needs and experiences of women and girls while obscuring those of men and boys, thereby confirming the belief that it is they who are more at risk during war and armed conflict.[1]

---

[1]My criticism of this security paradigm should not be read as though I am suggesting that wartime rape and sexual violence are not worthy of attention (or recourses for that matter), nor do I want to diminish the impact these crimes have on victims and/or survivors. Rather, my goal is to draw attention to the implications of disproportionately focusing on rape and sexual violence at the expense of other types of conflict violence. At this point I would also like to acknowledge that the case studies and types of violence discussed in this book are based upon the experiences of those

Let us return to the visuality of the *Stop Rape Now* campaign and its role in reproducing hegemonic (read as western) discourses around violence and victimisation during conflict. Here, I will focus on the two video clips that are included on the website. In the first, we hear the story of a nameless victim who has been raped. We learn through Charlize Theron that the victim is female. She states: 'she could be your mother, your sister, your daughter'. The second video clip provides information regarding the prevalence and nature of wartime rape committed against women and girls. The brutal details of these acts are shared. While reference is made to the use of rape during the genocide in the former Yugoslavia, all other examples focus narrowly on wartime rape in Africa, omitting numerous other cases where rape has been used as part of warfare. In all of the examples, the victims are female.

I identify three elements within the visuality of this 'master narrative'. Firstly, this violence happens to 'other' women and girls. In order for us to empathise and take action, the victim has to be transformed from a generic marginalised 'other' to 'one of us'. Second, this violence happens elsewhere, specifically Africa, which evokes a colonial imagery '...of African backwardness and primitivism' (Dunn, 2003, p. 5 as cited in Mertens & Pardy, 2017, p. 958). The corollary of this: a powerful western organisation like the UN is needed to mobilise global support in order to 'rescue' these female victims and combat this violence. And third, by only referencing female victimisation, this campaign engages in 'visual essentialism': visual representations that reproduce essentialist depictions of gender and crime (Bal, 2003, p. 22 as cited in Henne & Shah, 2016, p. 18). This brief discussion of visual representations of the securitisation agenda acts as a preface to a more in-depth analysis provided in Chapter 4. For now, however, I want to unpack, in more detail, the implications of gender essentialism within existing accounts of war and armed conflict.

Gender Essentialism Within 'Stories' About War and Armed Conflict

In 2015, I was asked by the reviews editor of the *Journal of Gender Studies* to review *The Underground Girls of Kabul: The Hidden Lives of Afghan Girls Disguised as Boys* by Jenny Nordberg. The aim of Nordberg's book is to examine what it is like to be an Afghan woman after ten years of Operation Enduring Freedom in Afghanistan: 'America's longest war and one of the largest foreign aid efforts of a generation' (Nordberg, 2014, p. 9 as cited in Banwell, 2015a, p. 587). In contrast to the more visible efforts of the international community to address gender inequality in war-torn Afghanistan, the book reveals that Afghans are using more clandestine measures. In a deeply patriarchal, segregated society, women resort to presenting themselves, and their daughters, as men/boys. As I wrote in my review: these women 'do this in the context of a nation that has a

---

we might refer to as cisgender male and female - referred to throughout as boys, men, male(s) and girls, women, female(s). Elsewhere I have written about the experiences of LGBT+ individuals. See the chapter on *Sex and War* in the forthcoming book *Sex and Crime* by Fanghanel, Milne, Zampini, Banwell & Fiddler.

long history of war, conflict, invasion, nation building and outside attempts to effect gender parity' (Banwell, 2015a, p. 587). Nordberg's book follows the lives of five Afghan women or, *bacha posh;* a colloquial Dari term meaning 'dressed like a boy' (Nordberg, 2014, p. 67 as cited in Banwell, 2015a, p. 588).

In Afghanistan, having a son enhances a family's reputation. A baby boy is regarded as a 'triumph', while a baby girl is regarded as a 'humiliation' or a 'failure' (Banwell, 2015a, pp. 587–888). Indeed, in conflict-affected societies – where security and infrastructure are lacking – sons provide financial and social insurance. Presenting girls as boys offers girls freedom and opportunity. However, this is for a limited period only. Before reaching puberty, the girl must return to being female in order be married off and fulfil her childbearing responsibilities. Nordberg (2014) is convinced that this practice is not based on gender dysphoria, but rather is related to being female in the then war-torn Afghanistan. This then leads her to ask: would these women want to be male in other contexts?

This example can be interpreted in two ways. On a cursory level, it can be read as confirmation of male power, freedom and dominance, as well as the (perceived or otherwise) privilege and protection afforded to males. A more critical reading would argue that it is a reductive and essentialist comment on men and masculinity, specifically hegemonic masculinity. This is an interpretation that ignores the context specific ways in which *certain* men and *certain* masculinities are associated with power, freedom and authority. This first reading supports the gendered/essentialist assumption hinted at in the statement by Major General Patrick Cammaert: women are more vulnerable than men, especially during war and armed conflict. To be clear, my intention is not to diminish the oppressions and discrimination Afghan women faced (and indeed face), both at the individual and structural levels. Rather, my goal is to provide a nuanced understanding of women's victimisation, agency and resistance: one that challenges binary constructions of women as either always and exclusively victims or, as possessing complete agency for their actions. Both positions preclude an appreciation of the complexity and contradictions inherent within women's life choices and experiences.

The statement made by Major General Patrick Cammaert has been referred to a number of times so far in this Introduction. Below, as part of my review of the disproportionality thesis, I will dissect it in more detail.

Feminist writers within the fields of International Relations and International Security, and War Studies more broadly, have put forward the case that women are disproportionately affected by war and armed conflict (Alsaba & Kapilashrami, 2016; Cohn, 2013; Enloe, 2010; Lee-Koo, 2011; Raven-Roberts, 2013; Sjoberg, 2006a, 2006b; Sjoberg & Peet, 2011). This is also reiterated in numerous UN policy documents, most notably the eight UN Security Council Resolutions (UNSCR) that make up the Women, Peace and Security (WPS) agenda (see the special issue of *International Political Science Review* 2016 for a detailed examination of the WPS agenda). Furthermore, writers argue that pre-existing gender inequalities are exacerbated within and beyond the conflict zone, thus increasing females' vulnerability to various types of gender-based violence (GBV) (Baaz & Stern, 2013; Banwell, 2014, 2018; Davies & True, 2015; Henry, 2016; Leatherman, 2011; Manjoo & McRaith, 2011; Meger, 2010; Ohambe, Muhigwa, & Wa Mamba, 2005; Sjoberg, 2011, 2013; Skjelsbæk, 2001). For example, as Cohn

(2013) notes in relation to gendered divisions of labour, the domestic labour of rural women, such as fetching water or gathering firewood – activities that involve them travelling to isolated areas alone – increases their risk of attack in conflict-prone regions. Likewise, their role as primary caregivers for 'children, the sick and the elderly leaves [them] more vulnerable because they are too encumbered to flee quickly' (Cohn, 2013, p. 29).

Relatedly, this body of work has drawn attention to the ways in which pre-existing types of GBV are reproduced during war and armed conflict. As noted by the Peace and Security (GAPS) network:

> [...] sexual violence is only one of many related forms of gender-based violence in conflict situations and should not be addressed in isolation...this violence is linked to gender-based violence against women and girls in peace time and is driven by the same under-lying factors – namely women's unequal status in society. (GAPS UK 2013, 1, emphasis in the original as cited in Kirby, 2015a, p. 509)

In all of this work, women and girls are considered the main victims of GBV prior to, during and in the aftermath of war and armed conflict (United Nations General Assembly, 1993, United Nations High Commissioner for Refugees [UNHCR], 2003). This leads to the conviction that they are disproportionately affected by the violence(s) of war and armed conflict. However, it is worth pausing to unpack the 'taken-for-granted' premise of the disproportionality thesis in more detail.[2] If, as it is noted, there is a high prevalence of violence against women and girls in peacetime, what does it mean when we say they are disproportionately affected by war, disproportionate to what? Disproportionate to women's experiences of GBV during peacetime, which is already asymmetrical? On what basis do we make this claim and with whom, specifically, are we comparing them to/with? Do we make this claim because, making up the majority of civilians during war/armed conflict; compared with the higher numbers of male combatants, their suffering *is* disproportionate? Is it not logical then, based on their higher participation as fighters, to assume that males will make up the majority of casualties? In fact, '...statistics suggest that young men of military age are most likely to be killed in war, *whether as combatants or as civilians*' (Chinkin & Kaldor, 2013, p. 167 emphasis added). Does our preoccupation with the unequal experiences of women and girls during war and armed conflict diminish our ability to acknowledge the suffering of male civilians and combatants? How do we interpret their victimisation? Finally, is there a difference between increased vulnerability to certain types of GBV (which can happen to both males and females) and being disproportionately affected by war and armed conflict?

---

[2]In the interest of full disclosure, when I began writing about wartime rape and sexual violence against women and girls, I too was blinded by this focus on disproportionality. However, after spending more time researching, thinking and writing about this topic – expanding my analysis to include the experiences of men and boys – I began to see how shortsighted this quantitative, comparative endeavour was/is.

Rather than overwhelm readers with these questions, perhaps a more fruit-ful exercise is to examine the ways in which war and armed conflict are gen-dered. To rework (and reduce) the questions to the following: how is suffering gendered? how does gender inform experiences of war and armed conflict? rather than ask, who suffers more? As noted by Collins (2017, p. 62 emphasis added): '[u]ndeniably, all civilian populations suffer during conflict [,] but war leads to *specific gender-related harms* making women's experiences of conflict very dif-ferent from those of men...' For me the keyword here is different, not more (see also Cockburn, 2012). In this book, I trace the unique ways in which women and men experience war and armed conflict. Rather than pursue quantifiable, measurable differences, I am interested in unpacking the qualitative differences in how both genders experience war and armed conflict. I am more interested in understanding their material, lived experiences. To this end, where possible, I draw upon survivor testimonies[3] and first-hand accounts (details are provided in the individual chapters).

Drawing on examples of women and men as both victims and perpetrators of conflict violence, the aim of this book is to answer these revised questions and provide a thorough analysis of the ways in which women's experiences of war and armed conflict might be, and are, different to those of men. Before we continue, I want to outline the value of exploring war and armed conflict through a gen-dered lens; explain why I have chosen the term violence(s) and finally, clarify the difference between war and armed conflict.

Examining War and Armed Conflict Through a Gendered Lens

In this book, various examples of the violence(s) of war and armed conflict will be explored through a gendered lens. What does this mean? A gendered lens means viewing the world through the prism of gender where gender is under-stood relationally and hierarchically and is mapped onto the normative binary pair relations: male/female, masculine/feminine. The former is traditionally asso-ciated with agency and power, while the latter is associated with passivity and weakness (I offer a new way of thinking about gender binaries in the Conclusion). According to Steans (1998, p. 5 as cited in Gentry & Sjoberg, 2015, p.11):

> To look at the world through gender lenses is to focus on gender as a particular kind of power relation, or to trace out the ways in which gender is central to understanding international processes. Gender lenses also focus on the everyday experiences of women as *women* and highlight the consequences of their unequal social position.

---

[3]With regards to using the terms victim and/or survivor, I will use the terminology chosen by the individuals themselves and/or how they have been referred to in the literature.

Like many other writers, Steans (1998) appears to have conflated the term gender with women. A gendered lens should examine the everyday experiences of both males and females as they relate to the construction of masculinities and femininities in any given context. Applying this to the context of war and armed conflict, and to paraphrase Gentry and Sjoberg (2015, p. 137), a gender lens examines how gender is present, yet invisible in the lives of those who commit conflict violence and in the theories used to explain such violence. Below I offer two examples of the ways in which gender is used to (1) justify war and armed conflict and (2) inform the methods used during war and armed conflict.

Gendered Justificatory Narratives

Discourses that seek to legitimise war and armed conflict rely upon idealised and binary constructions of masculinity and femininity. This gender essentialism is crystalised through the immunity principle which draws upon notions of men as warriors and fighters and women as 'beautiful souls;' fragile beings who need protecting (Elshtain, 1982; Lobasz, 2008; Sjoberg, 2007; Sjoberg & Peet, 2011). This gendered interpretation of protection is used to encourage men to fight in 'just wars' (Sjoberg, 2011). Such gendered justificatory narratives have been used since the First World War (see Sjoberg, 2006a, 2006b, 2011 for other examples). They were also used during the Bush-administration's global war on terror[4] in Iraq and Afghanistan (Nayak, 2006; Shepherd, 2006; Sjoberg, 2006a; Stabile & Kumar, 2005; Steans, 2008). In both cases, President George W. Bush's overarching narrative '…linked the fight against terrorism to a battle for the rights and dignity of women' (Steans, 2008, p. 160). More recently, rape and sexual violence against women and girls in Syria has been used to inform such foreign policy agendas.

Gendered War-fighting

In terms of the methods used during war, men are celebrated and rewarded if they live up to the just warrior ideal and fight to protect their 'beautiful souls' – that is, their women. In both old and new wars (see below), women come to represent the nation, the centre of gravity (Cohn, 2013; Sjoberg & Peet, 2011). Men fight in wars to protect their nation. If men fail to fulfil this role, they are emasculated and feminised. Unpacking the logic of the woman-as-nation thesis, Sjoberg and Peet (2011, pp. 174–186) argue that wars are won by eliminating women who belong to the enemy group (see also Alison, 2007; Heit, 2009). This expulsion communicates to enemy masculinities that they have been incapable of protecting their women/nation. And while Sjoberg and Peet (2011) are not suggesting that it is only women who are attacked during war and armed conflict, they are suggesting a gendered dynamic to this victimisation. In their words:

---

[4]A foreign policy campaign created in response to the 9/11 terrorist attacks.

> Belligerents attack (women) civilians for the same reason they claim protection for their own – because the 'protection racket' is an underlying justification for [S]tates, governments, and their wars. Insomuch as women are indicators, signifiers, and reproduces of [S]tate and nation, belligerents attack *women* to attack the essence of [S]tate and nation. (Sjoberg & Peet, 2011, p. 186 emphasis in the original)

Why Violence(s)?

I use the term violence(s) to acknowledge the multiple, diverse and complex nature of the violence that takes place within and beyond the conflict zone. In this book, through various case studies, structural, institutional (the US military), interpersonal and State violence(s) are explored. I also address genocidal and reproductive violence and structural and interpersonal violence(s) that can be linked to extreme droughts caused by climate change. Examining this range of violence (through a gendered lens) broadens the diagnostic framework. This extends – thereby enriching – our understanding of the nature, causes and consequences of such acts. Details of these violence(s), and how they are addressed in the individual chapters of the book, are outlined below.

Why Use the Terms War and Armed Conflict?

Globally, there have been 252 conflicts since the Second World War (Themnér & Wallensteen, 2013). These are formed of 'interstate or internationalized intrastate conflicts' (also referred to as civil wars) (Themnér & Wallensteen, 2013, p. 510). As established, historically male combatants comprise the majority of casualties (Leiby, 2009). However, with the changing nature of wars and armed conflict – where the State often deliberately targets civilians – the majority of casualties are non-combatants, both male and female. Indeed, by the end of the 1990s, approximately 90% of all casualties of war were non-combatants (European Security Strategy, 2003).

New wars – as envisioned by Kaldor (1999, p. 2) – encompass the following:

> [...] a blurring of the distinctions between war (usually defined as violence between [S]tates or organized political groups for political motives), organized crime (violence undertaken by privately organized groups for private purposes, usually financial gain) and large-scale violations of human rights (violence undertaken by [S]tates or politically organized groups against individuals).

While there is considerable debate about the concept of new wars – for example see Rigterink (2013) for both a review of this literature and for an empirical test of Kaldor's (1999, 2013) theory – I find that it is a useful way to categorise the different elements of war and armed conflict discussed in this book. Let us unpack this concept in more detail.

New wars refer to 'internal or civil wars', as well as 'low-intensity conflict' (Kaldor, 1999, p. 2). The latter relates to guerilla warfare or terrorism and was coined during the Cold War (Kaldor, 1999). Often fought at the local level, new wars involve a complex network of transnational and international actors:

> [...] so that the distinction between internal and external, between aggression (attacks from abroad) and repression (attacks from inside the country), or even between local and global, are difficult to sustain. (Kaldor, 1999, p. 2)

New wars are often referred to as proxy wars as in the case of Syria (discussed in Chapter 4). Unlike new wars, where fighters include State and non-State actors, old wars were fought with armed soldiers of national military institutions (Chinkin & Kaldor, 2013). According to Chinkin and Kaldor (2013, p. 170), those fighting in new wars include fragments of official armed forces, paramilitary groups, private security companies, warlords and extremist terrorist groups as well as various criminal organisations (see also Kaldor, 2013). New wars are new in terms of their goals, methods and financing (Chinkin & Kaldor, 2013; Kaldor, 2013). I will examine each of these in more detail below.

Goals

In terms of their goals, distinguishing them from old wars – which were based on 'geopolitical and ideological goals' – new wars are fought in the name of ethnic, religious or tribal identities (Chinkin & Kaldor, 2013, p. 171; Kaldor, 1999, 2013, p. 2).

Methods

In terms of their methods, new wars use 'guerrilla warfare and counterinsurgency' methods of fighting (Kaldor, 1999, p. 7; see also Turshen, 2016). To paraphrase Kaldor (1999), while conventional war involves battles and the seizing of territory through military means, by contrast, guerrilla warfare avoids engaging in battle, rather, territory is captured through political suppression of the population. Counterinsurgency involves destabilisation and control of the population through expulsion (Kaldor, 1999). Those identified as 'them' (as different) are forcibly removed (Chinkin & Kaldor, 2013; Kaldor, 1999). This, as Kaldor (1999) points out, is why new wars are characterised by large increases in the number of refugees and Internally Displaced Persons (IDPs). Indeed, according to the UNHCR Global Trends report, by the end of 2016, 65.5 million people had been forcibly removed as a result of persecution, conflict, violence and/or human rights violations (UNHCR, 2016).

Financing

Whereas old war economies (e.g. the First and Second World Wars) were financed by taxation and were centralised, involving a labour force, '[n]ew war economies are decentralised and are open to the global economy' (Chinkin & Kaldor 2013, p. 175; Turshen, 2016). They do not rely as heavily on taxation; they involve high unemployment (Chinkin & Kaldor, 2013) and are funded by violent and criminal activities that include but are not limited to: the extraction, sale and illegal transport of valuable commodities to transnational corporations through regional and international criminal networks (Banwell, 2014); looting, pillaging and kidnapping; the exchange of stolen goods, money laundering and arms sales at cross-border points (Banwell, 2018; see also Richani, 2016). These activities form part of the informal global economy. Indeed, a key characteristic of new wars is the fragmentation and informalisation of the economy (Peterson, 2009; Banwell, 2015b, 2018). In its place, a new type of globalised informal economy emerges (this is discussed in Chapters 2, 3 and 4). Indeed, globalisation and neoliberalism are key facilitators of new (informal) war economies (Banwell, 2015b, 2018; Jacobson, 2013; Turshen, 2016).

In this book, war refers to traditional warfare, referred to in the literature as old wars. Obvious examples are the two World Wars. Armed conflict/conflict will be used when referring to new wars: the DRC, Syria and Darfur. This will include invasion and occupation (as in the case of Iraq). Unless referring to distinct examples of war (old wars) or armed conflict (new wars), I will use the term war/armed conflict to inform readers that the point I am making refers to both types of conflict. Although referred to as The Liberation War of 1971, the armed conflict between East Pakistan (now Bangladesh) and the then West Pakistan, does not fit the definition of a new war, nor is it an old war. Rather, this case study is understood as a violent uprising that resulted in genocide.

Before we arrive at the style and organisation of the book, two further themes are explored: the relationship between masculinities, femininities and war/armed conflict and GBV during war/armed conflict.

Masculinity/ies, Femininity/ies and War

In the statement made by General Cammaert, the gender of the solider is implicit: he is male. If we follow the logic of his assertion, the female is, necessarily, a civilian. If, however, we adopt the more critical reading of the *bacha posh* (dressed like a boy) outlined earlier, we can see that this approach essentialises men and masculinities (Al-Ali & Pratt, 2009a). With reference to men in the middle-east, Al-Ali and Pratt (2009a) remind us that it is not simply because of their biology or their sexual drives/frustrations that these men commit numerous acts of political, ethnic or domestic violence. Their use of violence is much more complex than this and can be attributed to: '...brutal occupations, states of lawlessness, economic crises, unemployment and political corruption' ...which can then be rooted in other factors such as 'class, nationality, religion, as well as gender' (Al-Ali & Pratt, 2009a, p. 10).

Another contributing factor is the construction of (heterosexual) militarised masculinity. Within the military institution, gender essentialism and the inherent maleness of war-making and war-fighting are reproduced. Within this institution, differentiated gender-role expectations are upheld. In terms of gendered expectations, militarised masculinity expects men to be tough and aggressive. The military is where male soldiers learn to fight and kill for their women/nation.

Conversely, idealised militarised femininity 'expects a woman to be as capable as a male soldier, but as vulnerable as a civilian woman' (Sjoberg & Gentry, 2007, p. 86). To elaborate:

> The militarized woman is…tough, but not violent…. She is brave, but not self-sufficient. She is masculine, but not above femininity. She is frail, but not afraid…She is a soldier and a participant, but, at bottom, innocent; a Beautiful Soul. (Sjoberg, 2007, p. 93)

As noted above, traditionally, within discourses of war/armed conflict, women are treated as passive, weak and in need of protection. Men within the military provide such protection (Sjoberg, 2007, p. 84). Recently, we have seen increasing numbers of women join the military. Like men, it would seem, they fight for and protect the nation. And yet, the expectation that women within the military perform idealised militarised femininity underscores that what is required of female soldiers is different from that which is expected of male soldiers. In this book, I examine female soldiers' use of sexualised violence and torture within the US military (see Chapter 5).

GBV During War/armed Conflict

The final theme I will address is the relationship between GBV and war/armed conflict. The subject of GBV in conflict and post-conflict situations has received increased attention from diverse audiences ranging from academics, NGOs, and policy makers to advocacy groups and the news media (Alsaba & Kapilashrami, 2016; Freedman, 2016; Manjoo & McRaith, 2011; Spencer et al., 2015; Tappis, Freeman, Glass, & Doocy, 2016; Wirtz et al. 2014). GBV is violence directed against an individual based on socially ascribed gender differences. The types of GBV committed in these contexts include: rape and sexualised violence, including sexual slavery and genital mutilation; forced abortion, forced sterilisation, forced nakedness, forced marriage, forced pregnancy, forced prostitution, forced labour and forced recruitment; sex-selective killing, kidnapping and trafficking. These map onto the structural, institutional, interpersonal, State, reproductive and genocidal violence(s) discussed above. All will be examined in the chapters to come. The impact of such violence, which can be physical, social, psychological, and/or economic, is severe. The consequences of such violence will be addressed in more detail in the individual chapters.

Numerous international bodies (e.g. The International Criminal Court, The United Nations, The International Court of Justice), international laws and instruments (e.g. International Criminal Tribunals, the Rome Statute, the Geneva Conventions; the Convention on the Elimination of all Forms of Discrimination against Women; the United Nations Declaration on the Elimination of Violence against Women), as well as UNSCRs (e.g. the eight UNSCRs on WPS: UNSCR 1325, 2000; UNSCR 1820, 2008; UNSCR 1888, 2009a; UNSCR 1889, 2009b;

UNSCR 1960, 2010; UNSCR 2106, 2013a; UNSCR 2122, 2013b and UNSCR 2242, 2015) have been put in place to combat the violence(s) of war and armed conflict. These will be addressed in the individual chapters as they relate to the case study under discussion. The remainder of this Introduction will address the style, contribution, analytical framework, case studies and organisation of the book.

Style

This book is eclectic in its approach. While it is largely informed by a feminist analysis, it adopts a multi-disciplinary approach and draws on theoretical and empirical research from a range of disciplines and sub-disciplines. Historically, the discipline of Criminology has inadvertently been western-centric. In order to redress this, in addition to drawing on the sub-disciplines of Critical, Feminist and Visual Criminology, this book engages with International Relations, Security Studies (including Environmental Security), Postcolonial Studies, Gender Studies and Political Geography. Combined, these subjects have enabled a nuanced and intricate exploration of gender and the violence(s) of war/armed conflict.

Contribution of the Book

In terms of war/armed conflict, criminologists have drawn attention to Criminology's surprising lack of engagement with topics such as genocide, murder, rape, torture, and the displacement and enslavement of war-affected populations (Maier-Katkin, Mears & Bernard, 2009; Pruitt, 2014). Despite some advances within the field (e.g. Hagan, Rymond-Richmond, & Parker, 2005; Haveman & Smeulers, 2008; Kramer & Michalowski, 2005; Mullins & Rothe, 2008), missing from this work is a gendered analysis of these issues (Collins' 2017 book is a notable exception). Whilst Mullins provides an excellent criminological analysis of sexual violence during the Rwandan genocide (Mullins, 2009a, 2009b) – and indeed, I too examine wartime rape and sexual violence during the course of this book – I extend Mullins' work in three ways: first, I examine structural forms of violence against women and girls (Chapters 3 and 4). Second, I consider female perpetrators of sexualised violence and torture (Chapter 5). And third, I examine GBV against men and boys, demonstrating how men and boys are also victims of reproductive and genocidal violence within the conflict zone (Chapter 6).

With regards to the feminist critique of mainstream Criminology, in her article, *Has Criminology awakened from its 'androcentric slumber'?*, Cook (2016, p. 340) reviews the 'social realities of gender' in relation to crime and victimisation. While there has been significant developments in this area – notable contributions include theories of 'doing gender', work on intersectionality and an understanding of gender as situated action (Cook, 2016, p. 343) – Cook (2016, p. 344) argues that 'there is room for their expansion within [C]riminology'. In Chapter 5 of this book, drawing on Feminist and Visual Criminology, I explore, among other issues, intersectionality and crime as resource for accomplishing gender in relation to women's involvement in sexualised violence and torture at Abu Ghraib.

As discussed earlier in relation to new wars, many crimes committed during armed conflicts are crimes committed by the State. There has been a growing body of criminological research on State crimes (e.g. Kramer & Michalowski 2005; Michalowski & Kramer, 2007; Rothe, 2009; Rothe & Mullins, 2011; Whyte, 2007). Criminologists have also addressed the subject of risk, moral panics, terrorism and the war on terror (see Aradau & van Munster 2009; Mythen & Walklate, 2006, 2008; Rothe & Muzzatti, 2004). Absent from this body of work is a gendered analysis of State crimes committed during armed conflict. Also missing is a gendered analysis of the 'war on terror'. In Chapters 2 and 3 of this book – drawing on international case studies relating to contemporary armed conflicts – I address State crimes from a gendered perspective. In Chapter 5, I provide a gendered analysis of the war on terror.

Two final contributions are worth highlighting:

Both within and outside of the discipline, traditional theories of genocide argue that in order for perpetrators to carry out atrocities they must dehumanise their victims first. I challenge the dehumanisation thesis and argue that the concept of 'essentialisation' (Chirot & McCauley, 2006) better explains the use of rape and sexualised violence by German men against Jewish women during the Holocaust, as well as by West Pakistani men against Bengali women. This is done in the first chapter in relation to the woman-as-nation thesis. I then revisit my anti-dehumanisation thesis in Chapter 5 when unpacking sexualised violence and torture against the enemy 'other'.

Finally, in Chapters 4 and 6, drawing on research from Political Geography and Environmental Studies, I expand the analytical framework to consider how climate variability, and the extreme weather events it leads to (such as droughts), is linked to the violence(s) of armed conflict.

Case Studies and the Five Key Messages of the Book

The case studies that I have chosen for analysis address all of the issues outlined in the preceding section. They include, The Holocaust, The 1971 Liberation War in Bangladesh, and the armed conflicts in the DRC, Iraq, Syria and Darfur. These case studies are central for illustrating the five key messages of this book:

1. The GBV(s) that take place during and in the aftermath of armed conflict cannot be reduced to visible acts of interpersonal violence, they also include, and are connected to, structural violence, State crimes and institutional organisations (Chapters 2, 3, 4 and 5).
2. As both symbolic and corporeal mothers of the nation, women are at risk of reproductive and genocidal violence during war/armed conflict (Chapter 1).
3. Gender essentialism – that is, the equation of maleness with war-fighting and femaleness with victimisation – obscures the experiences of male victims and female perpetrators (Chapters 5 and 6).

4. Climate variability intersects with gender to inform structural and interpersonal forms of violence within and beyond the conflict zone (Chapters 4 and 6).
5. The violence(s) of war/armed conflict take place at the interrelated macro-, meso- and micro-levels (all chapters).

The Analytical Framework of the Book

Throughout the book, gender and the violence(s) of war/armed conflict will be analysed at the macro-, meso- and micro-levels. This is the framing device for understanding and analysing the different types of violence across all case studies. The macro-level refers to large-scale, overarching social, cultural, political and/or economic processes, interactions and/or structures. These operate at both the global and State levels. The meso-level refers to institutions (e.g. the military) the law and (government) organisations. The micro-level deals with small-scale interactions and processes, often examining behaviour at the individual level. At the beginning of each chapter, I outline how these three interrelated levels map onto the case study under discussion.

As mentioned earlier, a key feature of new wars is the global informal economy. To assist in my discussion of this within the DRC, Iraq and Syria, I will draw upon the feminist political economy approach. This approach draws attention to the economic, political and gendered dimensions of armed conflict. It examines the macro- (global), meso- and micro- (local) contexts in which the violence(s) of armed conflict occur. It traces how GBV is both produced and reproduced within and beyond the conflict zone.

Organisation of the Book

Drawing on two historical case studies, the Holocaust and the 1971 Liberation War in Bangladesh, Chapter 1 explores the implications of the woman-as-nation thesis. Here, I explore how the female reproductive body, alongside discourses of biological motherhood, form part of women's experiences of sexualised, genocidal and reproductive violence during and in the aftermath of war/armed conflict. I draw on the concept of essentialisation (which opposes the dehumanisation thesis) to encapsulate the vulnerability of the maternal body. In both examples, it will be argued that rape has political, social and gendered motivations (Banwell, 2014, 2016). Furthermore, across both cases – and within the general literature on wartime rape and genocidal violence – I argue that such violence(s) take place at the macro-, meso- and micro-levels. In this chapter, I reimagine the woman-as-nation thesis to the following: woman-as-Jew, in the case of the Holocaust and, mother-as-nation, in the case of Bangladesh.

Chapter 2 draws upon the feminist political economy approach to examine rape and sexual violence in the DRC. It demonstrates how these violence(s) are perpetrated and facilitated at the macro-, meso- and micro-levels. At the macro-level, I outline the complex relationship between economic globalisation, hegemonic masculinity, global hyper-capitalism and conflict-related sexual violence in the Congo. Here, transnational corporations compete for access to minerals contained within the DRC. Fighters on the ground use rape to terrorise and displace the civilian population. This allows them access to these minerals. These are then sold to the various national and transnational companies involved in the trade. These actors, who rely on the chaos of the conflict to engage in these illegal transactions, are guilty of committing State crimes that include war crimes and crimes against humanity. At the meso-level, I explore how the military institution encourages men to adopt a violent and aggressive heterosexual masculinity. Pre-existing gendered inequalities, as reflected in Congolese law and cultural practices, are also explored at this level. And finally, at the micro-level, I argue that individual soldiers utilise rape and sexual violence to overcome their subordinate position within the gender hierarchy (Banwell, 2014).

These State corporate crimes are analysed with reference to the gender hierarchy and globalisation masculinities (Connell, 1998, 2005). Drawing on the concept of a 'feminist ethics of war' (Sjoberg, 2006b), the chapter closes with some suggestions for how we can address the crimes committed in the DRC.

The invasion and occupation of Iraq has been described by criminologists as a State crime, a crime of aggression and an illegal intervention under international law (Kramer & Michalowski, 2005, 2011). Utilising the feminist political economic approach, Chapter 3 explores this illegal intervention through a gendered lens, revisiting Connell's (1998) notion of globalisation masculinities.

In order to examine the gendered impact of this invasion and occupation, I compare pre-conflict security and gender relations in Iraq with the situation post-invasion/occupation. I also review men's and women's involvement in the illicit economy in Iraq following the intervention and the collapse of the formal economy. This analysis demonstrates how economic policies (specifically privatisation) imposed by the Global North on the Global South, resulted in women and girls either being forced into the illicit economy as a means of survival or, trafficked for sexual purposes by profit-seeking (male) criminal networks in post-invasion/occupation Iraq. While both are examples of GBV, forced prostitution is treated as a form of structural violence. A review of the different types of coerced sexual activities that occur during war/armed conflict – as well as the feminist debates that surround them – is also provided.

In Chapter 4, using the example of Syria, I argue that the securitisation of wartime rape and sexual violence against civilian women and girls obscures other forms of GBV that are taking place. Departing from this reductive tendency, and following on from Chapter 3, this chapter examines structural forms of GBV in Syria: denial of reproductive healthcare, specifically access to safe abortion; denial of education, exacerbated by the use of early marriage and denial of employment opportunities, leading to survival sex. Denial of reproductive healthcare is discussed in relation to President Trump's foreign policy on abortion, while diminished access to employment opportunities is attributed to environmental forces. Here, I explore the link between climate change and women's involvement in coerced sexual activities.

The feminist political economy approach (True, 2010, 2012) is used to demonstrate how women and girls' experiences of these three types of structural violence – taking place at the local level within and beyond the Syrian conflict zone – is informed by macro- and meso-level economic, cultural and political policies and practices: economic globalisation, neoliberalism and patriarchy.

In Chapter 5, I use Feminist and Visual Criminology to critically examine three women's involvement in the sexualised violence and torture at Abu Ghraib: Megan Ambuhl, Lynndie England and Sabrina Harman. This chapter provides a gendered analysis of the war on terror. It unpacks the three main narratives that emerge: 'the woman in need of rescue and protection,' 'the woman in danger' and 'the fallen woman.' At the meso-level, I consider women's role within the US military, replacing militarised femininity with my notion of 'war-on-terror femininity'. At the micro-level, I unpack the involvement of individual women (Lynddie England and Sabrina Harman) in the violence(s) that took place. All three levels are set against the backdrop of American exceptionalism.

In order to investigate women's involvement in these violence(s), four images from Abu Ghraib are analysed. This is done in three stages. In the first section, I use literature from Visual Criminology and scholarly work on war photography to explore the following: gender and sovereign violence; gender, ethics and appropriate responses to images of suffering (specifically the postmodern 'doing a Lynndie pose') and the limitations of images. Drawing on Feminist Criminology, the second section reviews mainstream media accounts of Lynndie England's involvement in sexualised violence and torture. With reference to the belief that crime is a resource for doing gender, the final section considers my notion of 'war-on-terror femininity'.

In Chapter 6, in order to redress the invisibility of male victimisation, I examine conflict-related sexual violence committed against men and boys. I focus in detail on the use of genocidal and reproductive violence (rape, sex-selective killing and acts of genital harm) against men and boys in Darfur. These sexual GBV(s), that are demarcated along environmental, institutional and interpersonal lines, are explored at the macro-, meso- and micro-levels. To facilitate this analysis, I replace Connell's notion of globalisation masculinities with my notion of glocalisation masculinities. The term glocalisation was used by Howe (2008) to capture the relationship and impact of macro-level systems and structures on experiences at the meso- and micro-levels. At the macro-level, I unpack how climate variability, and the severe droughts it led to, forms the backdrop to the genocidal violence that took place at the local level during the conflict in Darfur. At the meso-level, I unpack how State-led Arabisation policies were used to alter the gender hierarchy in Darfur for the purpose of marginalising African Darfuri men. Rape and sexual violence were the tools used to accomplish this subordination. Finally, at the micro-level, I examine genocidal and reproductive violence committed by the Janjaweed and the government of Sudan against Darfuri African men. Here, I explore individual and localised acts of conquest and expulsion.

I will close this Introduction by restating the main question I seek to answer in the remaining chapters of this book, namely: how does gender inform both the experiences of those who victimise and those who are victimised during war/armed conflict? In other words, how are the experiences of males and females (as victims and as perpetrators) distinct? This will be a qualitative endeavour rather than a quantitative, comparative analysis; one that is concerned with understanding the lived experiences of victims, survivors and perpetrators. The book explores the GBV(s) committed and experienced within and beyond the war/conflict zone, tracing how they are interrelated at the macro-, meso- and micro-levels. It does so through a gendered lens.

The overarching goal is to challenge the inherent gender essentialism within existing explanations and representations of gender and the violence(s) of war/armed conflict.

Chapter 1

Woman-as-nation

Introduction

As highlighted in the Introduction, wartime rape can be used to destroy the opponent's centre of gravity: their women. Thus, 'the rape of the women in a community can be regarded as the symbolic rape of the body of this community' (Seifert, 1994 as cited in Fein, 1999, p. 43). Indeed, in times of war/armed conflict, female bodies are regarded as the vessels through which national, ethnic, racial and religious identities are reproduced (Cohn, 2013, p. 14; see also Sharlach, 2000; Takševa, 2015). Rape in this context is used not only as an attack upon the individual female, but also as attack upon the nation (Alison, 2007; Baaz & Stern, 2009; Leiby, 2009). It is also, as Sjoberg (2013) notes, an attack against men and the masculine, specifically men belonging to the enemy group who have failed to protect women belonging to their group (we will revisit this in Chapter 6).

In this chapter, and elsewhere in this book (Chapters 4, 5 and in the Conclusion), drawing on a number of examples of war/armed conflict, I examine how State policies interact with discourses of biological motherhood and the (post-conflict) maternal body to form part of the landscape of physical and structural violence against women and girls. As noted above, according to the woman-as-nation thesis, women are understood as both symbolically and corporeally mothers of the nation. The implications of this coding are discussed in this chapter. Through an exploration of the Holocaust and the 1971 Bangladesh Liberation War, both the regulation (as was the case in Bangladesh) and the destruction of motherhood (which occurred during the Holocaust) are examined. In the case of Bangladesh, State regulation of motherhood was an attempt to recuperate the post-war maternal body. In the case of the Holocaust, the attack upon the maternal body (and its reproductive capabilities) formed part of the genocidal campaign. These historical case studies have been chosen because they both, albeit in different ways, exemplify the woman-as-nation thesis. They both highlight how women, as reproducers of the nation, are targeted during war/armed conflict.

Gender and the Violence(s) of War and Armed Conflict:
More Dangerous to be a Woman?, 19–42
Copyright © 2020 by Stacy Banwell. Published by Emerald Publishing Limited.
This work is published under the Creative Commons Attribution (CC BY 4.0) licence.
Anyone may reproduce, distribute, translate and create derivative works of this work
(for both commercial and non-commercial purposes), subject to full attribution to the original
publication and authors. The full terms of this licence may be seen at http://creativecommons.org/
licences/by/4.0/legalcode" Knowledge Unlatched Open Access
doi:10.1108/978-1-78769-115-520201003

In response to the question, 'is it more dangerous to be a woman than a soldier in armed conflict?', the two examples explored here unpack the *unique* ways in which women and girls experience war/armed conflict. Across both examples, we see how rape and sexual violence operate at the three interrelated levels: the macro-, meso- and micro- (these levels were defined in the Introduction).

I would like to close this Introduction by outlining my challenge to the dehumanisation thesis. Within mainstream analyses of genocide, it is argued that in order for ordinary individuals to carry out 'excessive' and brutal acts of violence their victims have to be 'transformed conceptually and psychologically into less-than-human creatures' (Lang, 2010, p. 227). Hagan and Rymond-Richmond (2008, p. 876) argue that collective dehumanisation places the targeted group 'outside the normative universe of moral protection', thereby leaving them vulnerable to genocidal violence. I believe that the logic of the woman-as-nation thesis (outlined above) necessarily negates the notion that the violence(s) enacted require persons to be dehumanised first. Let me explain in more detail.

Rape in warfare has been present throughout history. It has been used in both old and new wars. For example, Belgian women were raped during the First World War, Chinese women were raped during the invasion of Nanking in 1937 and the widespread rape of German women occurred at the end of the Second World War (Henry, 2016, p. 44). Henry (2016, p. 44) goes on to list the following recent examples: 'Vietnam, Bangladesh, Uganda, the former Yugoslavia, Rwanda, Sierra Leone, Peru, the DRC, Darfur, Libya, Iraq ... Syria.' To this, we can add Myanmar and Yemen. In modern civil conflicts, such as the former Yugoslavia, the DRC, Syria and Myanmar, rape is used as a systematic weapon against civilian populations.

According to Henry (2016, p. 44), a common theme among these examples '...is that rape is a product of warped (yet normalised) militarised hegemonic masculinity, which arguably is structurally embedded in pre-conflict gender inequality and unequal power relations'. In my own work, I have identified an additional theme within this literature: the assumption that, in order to commit such acts, perpetrators must dehumanise and objectify their victims first.

In contrast to this work, I argue that the concept of 'essentialisation' facilitates a more nuanced understanding of the use of rape and sexualised violence by German men against Jewish women during the Holocaust. According to Chirot and McCauley (2006), essentialisation involves the reduction and denigration of a diverse group into a single, redundant category, attributing them all with the same negative characteristics. They state:

> The idea of essence ... turns out to be a key psychological concept in examining violence against groups. Something about members of the targeted group is inherently disgusting – their habits ... their appearance – and this justifies the violence against them because their disgusting characteristics threaten to pollute the environment and must be eliminated. (Chirot & McCauley, 2006, p. 81)

As established through the woman-as-nation thesis: '...motherhood often starts with a conceptualization of the womb as a recruiting station in nationalist discourses... [W]omen serve their nation by "producing" children/soldiers [preferably sons] of the nation' (Åhäll, 2017, p. 22). Based on this, I argue that it was precisely because of their Jewishness (race) and their reproductive (gender) capabilities – the coding of woman-as-Jew – that Jewish women were targeted by German men during the Holocaust. My notion of woman-as-Jew has been adapted from Cohn's (2013, p. 14) 'nation-as-woman' and 'woman-as-nation' as, I would argue, in the case of Jewish women, Jews – along with Poles and Roma – would have been considered by the Nazis as a source of contamination to the German nation/bloodline, and thus more likely regarded as a counter-nation.

This notion of essentialisation can also be applied to my second case study. However, in my discussion of the 1971 Liberation War, and in contrast to what occurred during the Holocaust, I focus my attention on understanding genocidal rape as a form of social death when forced impregnation cannot be applied. My challenge to the dehumanisation thesis will be explored in more detail below. It will be revisited in Chapter 5 when I examine sexualised violence and torture against Iraqi prisoners at Abu Ghraib.

Outline of the Chapter

Drawing on two historical case studies, the Holocaust and the 1971 Liberation War in Bangladesh, this chapter will demonstrate how women were targeted based on the notion of woman-as-nation (Cohn, 2013). The chapter will begin with a gendered analysis of the Holocaust. It will then review the literature on wartime rape and genocidal rape, before examining the use of rape during the Nazi genocide. Essentialisation (the anti-thesis to dehumanisation) informs the discussion of sexualised and reproductive violence against Jewish women by German men. The chapter then moves on to unpack the second case study. This section begins with an overview of the 1971 conflict, including details of the systematic rape of Bengali women by the Pakistani army. The theme of dehumanisation is revisited briefly. The main focus, however, is on understanding the individual and social consequences of sexualised and reproductive violence and how, in this example, rape was used as a tool of genocide. A discussion of the regulation of the post-war maternal body concludes this case study analysis. A comparison of both iterations of the woman-as-nation thesis brings the chapter to a close.

Terminology

For both case studies, I will draw upon Halbmayr's (2010, p. 30) notion of sexualised violence:

> The term sexualized violence makes it clear that male violence against females is not about sexuality but is a show of power on the part of the perpetrator and includes many forms of violence with sexual connotations, including humiliation, intimidation,

and destruction… From this we can derive that violent acts can be understood as sexualized if they are directed at the most intimate part of a person and, as such, against that person's physical, emotional, and spiritual integrity.

I will also draw upon Grey's (2017, p. 906) notion of reproductive violence. Reproductive violence – violence that violates a person's reproductive autonomy or violence that is directed against an individual due to their reproductive capabilities – encompasses forced impregnation, forced miscarriage, forced sterilisation and forced abortion (Grey, 2017, p. 907).

Sexualised violence against Jewish women will refer to rape and other bodily sex-based violations that can be viewed as emotional expressions of violence (e.g. public nakedness and the shaving of hair from intimate parts of the body). All of these can be understood as sexualised violence as they are directed at the most intimate part of a person. Whilst perpetrator motivation may not always be rooted in sexual desire or gratification, the female victim may, nonetheless, experience the attack as a violation of her sexuality. In the case of the Holocaust, reproductive violence will refer to forced abortion and forced sterilisation. In Bangladesh, sexualised violence will refer to rape, while reproductive violence will be used to capture the assault and regulation of women's reproductive bodies during and following the 1971 Liberation War.

In this chapter, the differences between genocidal rape and rape used during the Holocaust are highlighted. At this point, it will be useful to outline the concept of genocide.

Genocide is defined in Article 2 of *The Convention on the Prevention and Punishment* of the *Crime of Genocide* (2014) as:

> [A]ny of the following acts committed with intent to destroy, in whole or in part, a national, ethnical, racial or religious group, as such: (a) killing members of the group; (b) causing serious bodily or mental harm to members of the group; (c) deliberately inflicting on the group conditions of life calculated to bring about its physical destruction in whole or in part; (d) imposing measures intended to prevent births within the group; (e) forcibly transferring children of the group to another group.

Based on this definition, rape can, and is, used as a tool of genocide. In this context, it is used intentionally and systematically as a weapon of war. Examples include the 1971 Liberation War, the former Yugoslavia and Rwanda. These will all be discussed in due course.

In the Introduction, I argued that this book engages in a qualitative analysis of gender and the violence(s) of war/armed conflict, tracing the distinct ways in which both genders suffer. To this end, I begin my analysis of the first case study (the Holocaust) by highlighting the unique ways in which women experienced sexualised and reproductive violence during this genocide. This forms part of a broader comment on the importance of a gendered analysis of the Holocaust.

I also promised that where possible I would draw upon victim and/or survivor testimonies. Throughout this chapter, I include testimonies of Holocaust survivors that have been archived by the USC Shoah Foundation – The Institute for Visual History and Education. Let us start with a gendered analysis of the Holocaust.

The Holocaust Through a Gendered Lens

Ringelheim (1958/1993, p. 375) was asking crucial questions about gender and the Holocaust as far back as 1985. Among them were:

> [I]f you were Jewish, in what ways did it matter whether you were a man or a woman ... Is there ... anything to be seen in statistics about the number of men killed compared to women?

On the subject of the function of sexism within Nazi racist ideology, Tec (2003, p. 8) advances a different argument to Ringelheim. She argues that there is no systematic data to suggest that women were more oppressed than men during the Holocaust. Furthermore, she is less interested in whether more women than men died, and more interested in how 'women and men fared in different Holocaust settings, and how they responded to their circumstances'.

More recently, in the edited collection by Hedgepeth and Saidel (2010), *Sexual Violence Against Jewish Women During the Holocaust,* the following questions were raised: 'what happened to women during the Holocaust?' and '...was there anything different in their experience because they were women?' (Reinharz, 2010, p. ix). Taking these as my point of departure, the questions I hope to answer are: why did soldiers of the Third Reich rape Jewish women if, firstly, sexual relationships with Jews were a criminal offence and, secondly, rape was not an explicit function of the genocidal campaign?

Whilst Jewish women were raped by non-German allies, collaborators, civilians and fellow prisoners (see Friedman, 2002 and the edited collection by Hedgepeth and Saidel, 2010), this chapter will focus on the rape of Jewish women by German men: soldiers, guards, members of the Third Reich and SS members. Coerced sexual activities (forced prostitution and sexual slavery) and sex for survival – 'entitlement rape' (Fogelman, 2012, p. 20) – also formed part of women's gendered experience of the Holocaust. They also formed part of women's experiences of the 1971 Liberation War. These will not be reviewed here (a more detailed analysis of coerced sexual activities, including sexual exploitation and abuse, are discussed in Chapters 3 and 4).

As we know, the Holocaust was a genocide that targeted all Jews as Jews (Banwell, 2016). It also targeted other non-Aryan groups that it deemed inferior and undesirable such as homosexuals, Roma, the mentally ill and disabled people, as well as a number of political and religious opponents (Fogelman, 2012). So, whilst a gendered analysis of the Holocaust may be a legitimate focus of investigation, it is still important to answer the questions: why women? Why gender? (Weitzman & Ofer, 1998). It is because the Holocaust – and the Final Solution in particular – was the first event that did not treat the female population as the inevitable spoils of war. Viewed as the carriers of the next generation of Jews, the Nazi eugenicist policy explicitly targeted pregnant women for death: women whose pregnancies were visible were killed immediately upon arrival at a concentration camp (Goldenberg, 1998, 2013; Horowitz, 1998; Katz, 2012; Patterson, 2013; Perl, 1984/1993; Weitzman & Ofer, 1998). As articulated by Yolan Frank: 'some women were taken away for men's pleasure and when they got pregnant ... they are sent back to the gas chamber'.[1]

It may seem illogical to focus on gender when Nazi ideology was premised on the status of Jews as Jews and their genocidal policy targeted them based on their 'race'. Yet, it is clear from women's testimonies that they experienced the Holocaust differently from men (Goldenberg, 1998; Horowitz, 1998; Weitzman & Ofer, 1998). Women were vulnerable to sexualised and reproductive violence in a number of ways: rape, forced abortion, forced sterilisation, sexual abuse, pregnancy, childbirth and the killing of their newborns. Most of these are uniquely female experiences and women suffered them as women and as Jews (Friedman, 2002).

By examining the genocidal violence women experienced during the Holocaust, it is not my intention to ignore or dismiss the violence(s) visited upon men, nor do I wish to reduce the Holocaust to an example of sexism (Rittner & Roth, 1993). We know that Jewish men were also targeted and attacked as Jews and as men. Indeed, as Tec (2003) argues, given the Nazi emphasis on patriarchal values – which depicted men as rational, aggressive and more powerful than women – Jewish men were regarded as a greater threat to the political system than women. Thus, the goal of annihilating the Jews began with the extermination of Jewish men. Men endured indignities and assaults on their biology, including sexual assault and rape (Friedman, 2002; Horowitz, 1998). According to Chalmers (2015), male rape occurred more often within the context of coerced homosexual interactions. Young boys would provide sexual favours, or act as sexual slaves, in order to receive food and better living conditions. This was mainly in the concentration camps. Overall, Chalmers (2015) argues that the sexual abuse of men was less prevalent. This may be the result of underreporting (Chalmers, 2015; this theme is addressed in more detail in Chapter 6).

An Overview of Wartime Rape and Genocidal Rape

Explanations of wartime rape and genocidal rape can be demarcated along macro-, meso- and micro-levels. Gender plays an integral part at every level. At the macro-level, rape is central to a regime or policy directive (Waller, 2012, p. 85). It is used as a political and social tool to achieve the goals of genocide and ethnic cleansing (Waller, 2012). The consequences of rape in this context are death, both literally and figuratively (social and psychological) (Card, 1996). It destroys communities and social bonds. It 'dilutes' – and in some instances eradicates – the next generation (Waller, 2012). Rape, in cases of ethnic cleansing

---

[1]Interview 35354, USC Shoah Foundation testimony.

and genocide, acts as a statement of hetero-nationality and serves as an ethno-marker (Lentin, 1999). It may also serve as an attack upon the nation's culture of women (Cohn, 2013). This is the weapon-of-war paradigm.

At the meso-level, patriarchy, phallocentrism, the military institution and hegemonic masculinity all socialise men to embody a violent and aggressive heterosexual masculinity, whereby rape is normalised and used to achieve and perform this type of masculinity. And at the micro-level, in stark contrast to the weapon-of-war thesis, wartime rape is considered an opportunistic crime (Davies & True, 2015). Enloe (2000) referred to this as 'recreational rape'. It can be related to the 'pressure-cooker' theory. This views wartime rape as a result of men's biological/innate sexual drive and/or the result of the chaos of war (Mullins, 2009a). Individual men, at the micro-level, use rape and sexual violence to feminise their victims and to subvert their marginal position within the gender hierarchy. Rape is used not out of lust, but out of aggression to enhance masculine identity (Banwell, 2014).

Generally speaking then, rape has political, social (genocide and ethnic cleansing) and gendered (phallocentrism, misogyny and hegemonic heterosexual masculinity) motivations. These operate at all three levels of analysis. More inclusive studies consider the victimisation of males as well as females during war/armed conflict and offer theoretical frameworks for understanding sexualised and genocidal violence against males (see Chapter 6 of this book). I acknowledge the multiple dimensions and motivations of conflict-related sexual violence and argue that in some cases rape is used as a weapon of war, while in others it is not (see Chapters 2, 4 and 6).

It is worth reiterating: what unites these traditional understandings of genocide and wartime sexual violence is the tendency to view dehumanisation as a precursor to this type of violence (see Fogelman, 2012; Friedman, 2002; Hagan & Rymond-Richmond, 2008; Waller, 2012). I offer a different interpretation. Based on the woman-as-nation thesis, I propose the following: during the Holocaust Jewish women were subjected to sexualised and reproductive violence precisely because of their essentialised Jewishness. Dehumanisation may have been what followed – it may have been implicated in the process of the violence, as a by-product – but it was not the condition under which this violence was performed in the first instance. Dehumanisation was not a precondition of this violence.

The use of rape against Jewish women – unlike rape used in Bangladesh, the former Yugoslavia, Rwanda, Darfur, and the DRC – was not an official component of the Final Solution (Goldenberg, 2013). However, in order to understand the sexualised and reproductive violence against Jewish women by German men, it will be useful to consider examples where rape *is* used as an official weapon. As I will be examining the DRC in the following chapter and Darfur in Chapter 6, I will limit my discussion in this chapter to genocidal rape in Rwanda and the former Yugoslavia, before comparing the use of rape during the Holocaust. A more detailed analysis of genocidal rape in Bangladesh forms the second part of this chapter. Space will not permit an in-depth analysis of the causes of the genocides in Rwanda or the former Yugoslavia, nor the conflicts that formed the backdrop to them. For my purposes here, I will be focusing on the issue of genocidal rape, starting with genocidal rape during the Rwandan genocide.

The Rwandan genocide began on April 6, 1994 when the plane of the Rwandan president, Habyarimana, was shot down (Buss, 2009; Mullins, 2009b). It lasted three months and it is estimated that 800,000 Rwandans, mainly Tutsi, were killed during this time (Buss, 2009). Between 250,000 and 500,000 Rwandan Tutsi women were raped during the 12 weeks of the genocide. Perpetrators were primarily Hutu men (Buss, 2009; Jones, 2002; Mullins, 2009a, 2009b; Sharlach, 1999, 2000). The rapes involved sexual mutilation and torture. As Sharlach (1999, pp. 395–396) notes: '[t]he mere extermination of Tutsi was insufficient; the Interahamwe inflicted upon the Tutsi every imaginable act of sadism, including rape, before killing them'. Women were gang raped and raped to death (Sharlach, 1999). There is also evidence to suggest that the deliberate transmission of HIV was a component of genocidal rape in Rwanda. Reports from survivors note that HIV positive Hutu men raped Tutsi women in order to transmit the disease (see Sharlach, 1999, 2000).

Genocidal rape was also used during the Bosnian genocide. The Yugoslav wars (the Croatian war of independence, 1991–1995 and the Bosnian war, 1992–1995) took place between 1991 and 1995 in the former Yugoslavia, resulting in the dismantling of the Socialist Federal Republic of Yugoslavia. Although these wars were fought over territory, nationalism and independence, for my purposes here, I will focus on the ethnic cleansing of Bosnians by Serbs and Bosnian-Serbs. A key element of this genocide was the systematic rape and the enforced impregnation of Muslim and Croatian women by Serbian men (Chinkin & Kaldor, 2013; Diken & Lausten, 2005; Sharlach, 2000; Takševa, 2015). It is estimated that between 25,000 and 40,000 Bosnian women were victims of rape and forced pregnancy (Takševa, 2015. Men were also victims of reproductive and genocidal violence; see Chapter 6).

The International Criminal Court (ICC) defines forced pregnancy as: 'the unlawful confinement of a woman forcibly made pregnant, with the intent of affecting the ethnic composition of any population or carrying out other grave violations of international law' (Rome Statue of the Criminal Court, 2011, p. 4). In the case of the conflict in the former Yugoslavia, women were assaulted in the streets and in their homes. This was mainly by ethnically Serbian soldiers (Sharlach, 2000; Takševa, 2015). Others were detained in 'rape camps' where they were repeatedly raped until they became pregnant and held captive until access to safe abortion was no longer possible (Takševa, 2015). As noted in the genocide convention, this prevents births within the group. This is because women's wombs are occupied with babies from a different ethnic group, which results in the birth of ethnically mixed children. These children serve as a symbolic reminder of the genocide (Mullins, 2009a). More than that, as Mullins (2009a, p. 18) and Takai (2011) point out, in societies where patrilineal parentage determines lineage membership, these children – who belonged to the father's ethnic group, rather than the mother's – altered the community's ethnic group membership. This amounts to 'transferring children of the group to another group' (Article 11(e) of the Genocide convention).

As well as forced pregnancy, women's inability and/or unwillingness to engage in sexual relations following rape (not least due to the physical injuries women sustain), also 'prevents births' and contributes to the elimination of the group. It is important to note that, in addition to their physical injuries, women also have to live with the psychological and social impact of rape. In both of the examples discussed above, it is those who are raped, not those who rape, who are stigmatised (Sharlach, 2000; this also applies to male victims, see Chapter 6). According to the logic of the woman-as-nation thesis, genocidal rape not only dishonours the woman, it also dishonours the ethnic group to which she belongs. Women may be ostracised or expelled in order to restore lost honour and men may refuse to engage in marriage and/or sexual relationships with 'spoiled' women which, again, serves to destroy the group (Takai, 2011).

The Limitations of a Macro-level Understanding

Unlike the examples of systematic and genocidal rape discussed above (Rwanda, the former Yugoslavia), rape was not carried out in this manner during the Nazi genocide (see also Wood, 2009 who discusses the absence of systematic rape during the civil war in Sri Lanka). The aim of the Final Solution was the elimination of all European Jews. In this context then, as Goldenberg (2013) points out, sexual violence is a redundant weapon of terror. Given this, trying to understand the individual motivations and the context/conditions under which rape took place during this genocide becomes slightly more complicated.

During the Holocaust, women became more undesirable given the various oppressions they were subjected to. Yet, this did not deter German men from raping them. For Fogelman (2012, p. 18) then, it is 'a myth that only pretty women were raped'. In the beginning, however, before women were subjected to various physical degradations, the motivation for rape may have been based on reinforcing masculine identity and used for sexual gratification. In the latter stages of their imprisonment – when their feminine attributes and attractiveness had been stripped away, through a series of degradations – the motivation to rape may have arisen from aggression, power and dominance (Fogelman, 2012). Indeed, testimonies from survivors and witnesses describe instances of brutal and sadistic violence (see Perl, 1984/1993). As illustrated by Sara Moses, this was also the case for instances of sexualised violence and abuse:

> [T]here were two men there and there were some other people in the room, I think. I was put on a table. From what I remember, [it was] a table or it could have been a high table. I was very little so it seemed like it was very high up from where I was and I was very violently sexually abused. And I remember being hit, I remember crying and I wanted to get out of there. And I was calling people

and screaming and I remember one thing that stands out in my mind that one of them told me that they would stand me on my head and cut me right in half. And they wanted me to stop screaming and I've had nightmares about that most of my life.[2]

Another survivor, Doris Roe, talks about being taken into a doctor's room where a female doctor strapped her to a bed. Three naked SS men entered the room. The female doctor instructed the men to rape her. She describes being gang raped by these men. She described her legs being tied to the bed so that she could not escape. After the first three men raped her, another three men entered the room. She describes being raped by 12 men in total. She believed that rape was used as a form of initiation for these men. She stated that the officer's bit off her nipples while she was in Birkenau so she could not breastfeed her child.[3] This viscerally reminds us of Halbmayr's argument that violence is sexualised if it is directed at the most intimate part of a person's body.

'Sadistic rape' (see Fogelman, 2012) allowed German soldiers omnipotent control over their victims, whist simultaneously reducing German soldiers' sense of impotence. Fogelman (2012) argues that soldiers, who may have felt as though they were powerless cogs in a machine, could use sadistic rape to reinstate power. Related to this motivation is ego-gratification (Fogelman, 2012). For ordinary men, seeking to subvert their marginal positions within German society, the Nazi regime offered them success, notoriety and a chance to advance their careers (Fogelman, 2012). Excessive violence, through rape and various acts of sexualised violence, boosted their self-esteem and 'add[ed] to the already-increased bravado of being an officer' and 'having power and privileges' (Fogelman, 2012, p. 23).

However, in order to appreciate the more specific meaning of rape during the Holocaust, we must, as Fogelman (2012) suggests, place this behaviour within the social, political and cultural context of the Third Reich. This moves us away from the limitations of the macro- towards a meso-level of understanding. Despite transgressing German policy, there was, paradoxically, as Katz (2012) points out, something 'political' about the sexualised violence committed against Jewish women. The political coding of woman-as-Jew relocates this sexualised violence from an individual attack, to an assault upon the collective Jewish body (particularly when we consider the various acts of reproductive violence that were carried out).

Sexualised, Genocidal and Reproductive Violence Against Jewish Women During the Holocaust

Lentin (1999) argues that the definition of genocide must be gendered in order to acknowledge that many of these political campaigns – aimed at the 'alteration or elimination of a future ethnic group', through sexual slavery, mass rape and

---

[2]Interview 29016, USC Shoah Foundation testimony.
[3]Interview 23687, USC Shoah Foundation testimony.

mass sterilisation – are transmitted through and upon women's bodies. Indeed, in the context of the Holocaust, the Nazi eugenic vision of German racial superiority specifically targeted Jewish women as child-bearers (Bock, 1984/1993). The reproductive body of the Jewish woman became a 'biological danger', as their wombs would 'bear future generations' of Jews (Levenkron, 2010, p. 15). To create a superior Aryan race, Nazi race-hygiene policies demanded the elimination of inferior races. Women's sexuality and their reproductive capabilities became integral components of this agenda. In order to better understand this assault on women's sexuality – in all its devastating forms – it will be useful to unpack Halbmayr's concept of 'sexualised violence' in more detail.

Halbmayr's definition also encompasses indirect, emotional expressions of violence in the form of (sexualised) humiliations. Here, they include: forced public nakedness, shaving of hair and invasive physical examinations. Male guards carried out these degrading public humiliations knowing that they would be experienced as grotesque sexual violations (Aoláin, 2000). By placing this sexualised violence within the historical–political context of the Holocaust, we can view this as part of a continuum of genocidal violence. At one of end of the spectrum, we have rape and other forms of direct physical, reproductive/genocidal violence (forced sterilisation and forced abortion), and at the other, we have these more indirect forms of sex-based violations.

Rape was committed by Germans and their Nazi collaborators, as well as by other Jews. This took place in the ghettos, in hiding and in the concentration camps. In the ghettos, Jewish women were also vulnerable to murder, including the murder of their children, as well as forced abortions and a number of other sex-based violations. Women were also sexually assaulted while they were being transported from the ghettos to the camps (Aoláin, 2000; Katz, 2012). Whilst some similarities may be drawn, the rape of Jewish women during the Holocaust involved factors that complicate a comparison with wartime rape in other contexts (Katz, 2012). Three distinctive features can be identified. First, we have the crime of Rassenschande. The law against Rassenschande (racial defilement) prohibited sexual relations between Aryans and non-Aryans. This involved all sexual relationships between Aryans and Jews, consensual or otherwise. Between 1935 and 1945, 2,000 cases were brought before the courts. Sentences for those found guilty of committing Rassenschande averaged between four and five years (Katz, 2012).[4] Second, if these sexual encounters resulted in pregnancy, these women and their foetuses would have to be murdered. Unlike rape in other contexts, where the genocidal aim is to contaminate the bloodline by reproducing an ethnically mixed cohort of children, contamination of the German bloodline was antithetical to Nazi ideology. And third, unlike other examples of wartime rape, where emphasis is placed on the violation of the woman's body, German men who raped Jewish women violated their own existence and jeopardised their membership in the future master race (Goldenberg, 2013). Below I will elaborate on the

---

[4]See Decision of the Nuremberg special court in the Katzenberger race defilement case.

first and second of these distinct characteristics: the crime of Rassenschande and the murder of forcibly impregnated Jewish women.

The requirement to kill Jewish women following the violation of Rassenschande – and its potential reproductive consequences – was particularly common in the Skarzysko-Kamienna concentration camp. In the words of survivor Milla Doktorczyk:

> My friend, she was working alongside me in Skarzysko. One beautiful girl, tall and slim, a beauty…Came one time, a German, he took her away from the machine. They raped her a couple of times, everybody, and then they killed her…They raped her in the middle, one after another one, and they killed her…[5]

Paula Neyman, another survivor, recounts the rape and murder of a pregnant Jewish women at the Bruss-Sophienwalde Concentration Camp:

> They dragged her out, four young Germans, each one had a leg or an arm and they threw her on the snow and…the commanders…they made everybody stand and watch…in full view of these young girls. Six or eight raped this pregnant girl. They picked her up like a sack of potatoes…and threw her on the truck. She was never heard of [again].[6]

Fogelman (2012) argues that some acts of rape were committed clandestinely, whereas others were done in public to humiliate and dehumanise the victim. During their interviews, a number of survivors talked about women being dragged to the forest to be raped in secret. They discussed the methods guards used to conceal their crime of race defilement. For them, it was clear that these guards were aware of the law of Rassenschande. This is clearly illustrated by Bronia Shlagbaum's account:

> A Jewish girl. You know. He want a Jewish girl. You know. To the forest. And he raped her. And it was Rassenschande. That means, how come a German should rape a Jewish girl? So they wanted to wipe up all the footsteps. They were ashamed.[7]

In a similar account, Ana Cymerman states:

> One day he comes over to me and says to me I should come with him in a room and he's going to show me what to do. So I did. You had to. He asked me. He would like to have sex with me.

---

[5]Interview 15012, USC Shoah Foundation testimony.
[6]Interview 4788, USC Shoah Foundation testimony.
[7]Interview 10747, USC Shoah Foundation testimony.

She explains that she was surprised that, as a German, he wanted to rape her. She was aware of the law of Rassenschande. She explains that at the time she was thinking to herself: '[h]ow can you say this to me? I'm a Jew. A dirty Jew. You shouldn't say that to me. Because I'm Jewish'.[8] Sonia Nightingale also references Rassenschande. She explains that sexual molestation happened a lot '…it was how they call it… Germans shouldn't touch a Jewish girl…Shouldn't even look at her'.[9] Sonia struggles to find the correct phrase and so the interviewer suggests Rassenschande. She then explains that they shot the women afterwards.

Based on the interpretations of survivors, we can argue that these acts (rape and murder), including the manner in which they were carried out, were perpetrated against 'woman-as-Jew': an essentialised group and bearers of the next generation.

Having reviewed these acts of sexualised violence, we will now consider acts of reproductive violence in the form of forced sterilisation and forced abortion.

Assault on Jewish Motherhood

Aoláin (2000, p. 61) argues that the separation of children from their mothers and the removal of their capacity to bear children count as explicit sexual harms. It is an assault upon a woman's bodily integrity 'both in its actual and symbolic manifestations.' As a symbolic function, this act communicates to the wider ethnic or cultural group that the destruction of mother and child denotes the achievement of broader military aims: the elimination of that particular group (Aoláin, 2000).

Forced sterilisation was carried out on thousands of women without the consent, or often the knowledge, of the female victims (see Halbmayr, 2010). These genocidal experiments (which largely took place at Auschwitz, Ravensbrück and other concentration camps) were conducted by means of X-ray, surgery and drugs (Aoláin 2000, p. 56). The topic of sterilisation was discussed by a number of survivors. Elizabeth Feldman de Jong states, '[t]hey tried to give big injections in your womb. The needles were very painful. They pulled pieces of the womb… so you could not get children'.[10] In response to questions about medical experiments, Sylvia Amir stated: '[h]e put two injections in [to the uterus] and closed the tubes. He closed the tubes and this was sterilisation'.[11] Magda Blau talks about the experiment centre in the camps. When asked about the experiments that were carried out, she states: '[f]irst of all they did sterilization…and they made different operations on woman … [T]aking out the woman's business'. Magda points to her abdomen. She explains that this was done to hundreds of Jewish women: '[a]ll Jewish women'.[12]

---

[8]Interview 8641, USC Shoah Foundation testimony.
[9]Interview 1832, USC Shoah Foundation testimony.
[10]Interview 543, USC Shoah Foundation testimony.
[11]Interview 6000, USC Shoah Foundation testimony.
[12]Interview 19441, USC Shoah Foundation testimony.

Forced abortions were also performed as part of the racist ideology. Indeed, abortions were forbidden for Aryan women who were considered to be the bearers of the future 'master race' (Halbmayr, 2010, p. 37). In many of the forced-labor camps and the concentration camps, abortion was not even an option: Jewish women were immediately condemned to death. A number of survivors also discuss the murder of newly born babies. Pearl Iroff explains: '[t]here was one girl that was pregnant...and then she gave birth to the baby...and the doctor killed the baby'.[13] Similarly, Ruth Foster explains:

> One baby was born ... the mother carried the full term of pregnancy ... the SS ... it came to our commandant ... it came to his ears that there was a child born in the ghetto ... the mother was brought with this little baby of a few days into the hospital ... the soft part of the baby's head had to be pressed in ... had to be killed. It wasn't shot, but it was killed that way.[14]

Describing the birth of a child in Auschwitz, Isabella Leitner states:

> Most of us are born to live – to die, but to live first. You, dear darling, you are being born only to die ...You belong to the gas chamber. Your mother has no rights... She is not a mother. She is just a dirty Jew who has soiled the Aryan landscape with another dirty Jew. (Leitner, 1978/1993, pp. 31–32)

Women were forced to kill infants in order to save the mother's life. This murder of a newborn requires mothers to '...kill something of themselves, part of their own souls, part of the essence of the feminine' (Patterson, 2013, p. 172). Furthermore, Patterson argues that the unique condition of the Holocaust caused '...the murder not only of human beings but of the very origin of human life and of human sanctity...the Jewish mother' (Patterson, 2013, p. 171). Doris Roe describes giving birth to a little girl. A few weeks after the baby was born she informed the nurse that her baby was hungry. She recalls the nurse telling her that the baby would not cry for much longer: '[s]he walked up to the bunk and picked up my baby and slammed her head against the bottom of the bunk. I passed out'.[15]

In a similar incident, Eva Lassman recalls:

> A woman was with me who was pregnant. They let her carry the baby to term. When she delivered, the Germans send in a Jewish man to take the baby away from her. And the baby was pinched by the nose. It was suffocated. She never saw her baby.[16]

---

[13]Interview 34942, USC Shoah Foundation testimony.
[14]Interview 9538, USC Shoah Foundation testimony.
[15]Interview 23687, USC Shoah Foundation testimony.
[16]Interview 51181, USC Shoah Foundation testimony.

Let us reflect upon these stories in relation to the concept of essentialisation:

> Essentializing the out-group means that there is something bad about all of them, every one of them ... Nazis knew perfectly well that Jews were not literally rats ... But they did believe that everyone in that category, old and young, strong and weak, threatening and helpless—all must be exterminated, just as all vermin must be exterminated. Essentializing turns the enemy into a single dangerous and irredeemable character. (Chirot & McCauley, 2006, pp. 84–85).

Chirot and McCauley (2006, p. 86) further argue:

> The very ideas of pollution and contamination require the idea of essence, an unseen spirit or nature that is endangered by contact or infection. The German volk had to be protected from the foreign and degrading Jewish essence.

Making a similar argument, Hagan and Rymond-Richmond (2008) argue that by definition, genocidal killing involves killing by category and by membership in a group rather than by individual guilt or criminality. Similarly, La Capra (1994, p. 104) refers to the Nazis' 'exorcism' of the Jews through racial essentialism/hypostatisation.

Based on these arguments, I argue that these assaults on motherhood were carried out on woman-as-Jew.

'He Used to Pick the Most Pretty Girls'.[17]

Sharon Marcus (391 as cited in Flaschka, 2010, p. 78) states:

> Masculine power and feminine powerlessness neither simply precede nor cause rape; rather, rape is one of culture's many modes of feminizing women. A rapist chooses his target because he recognizes her to be a woman, but a rapist also strives to imprint the gender identity of 'feminine victim' on his target.

To paraphrase Flaschka (2010): if we accept this position, then it makes theoretical sense to ask Jewish female survivors if they understood their rape as a reminder that they were female/feminine in an environment that had stripped them of their feminine qualities. This question forms the basis of Flaschka's argument. It supports my argument against the dehumanisation hypothesis. The testimonies of female survivors who were raped and witnessed other rapes believed they were raped because of their female attractiveness.

---

[17]Interview 450, USC Shoah Foundation testimony.

Here are two examples. Eve Gabori:

> [T]hey looked at me, and I was a beautiful girl...I was all sunburned, even my hair grew about half an inch. I looked healthy my face was red and brown, because the sun was beating down. This girl was tall, huge, huge beautiful grey eyes, very delicate... they told us to go into the barrack to wash the floor...and it was horrible. We went in. They locked the door, grabbed this girl and went into this other small room. I heard her screaming. I knew what they were doing to her. I never saw the girl again.[18]

Ester Gomo:

> He did not let me go. In his eyes I was very pretty. In his eyes. And he started to make me compliments. 'Beautiful breasts'...that I'm very young...he says he can't resist me. He took his right hand and twisted my breast.[19]

The concentration camps 'challenged women's identities as women' (Flaschka, 2010, p. 80). When women entered the camps their heads were shaven, and they were given formless clothing. Starvation meant loss of body weight, especially from their breasts and hips. This diminished their quintessentially feminine attributes (Flaschka, 2010). Perhaps the rape of these women served, paradoxically, to reinforce their gender identity that had hitherto been challenged by the camp environment. In this context, rape may have functioned to remind women that they were women in an environment that challenged their identities as women (Flaschka, 2010). In fact, the survivor accounts presented above – and many others – suggest that this was the case. This does not support the notion that victims were dehumanised before they were raped.

According to an anonymous female survivor, '[a]mong the many defeats at the end of this war is the defeat of the male sex' (Anonymous, 1954/2011, p. 64). Based on the laws of *The Protection of German Blood and German Honor* and Rassenschande, one way of interpreting the actions of soldiers of the Third Reich is to view them as the actions of weak men: their actions had an existential cost and undermined their German identity. This may have been the consequence of their actions, yet, what was their purpose? Mass rape in this instance did not occur. Its use was not explicitly genocidal. Impregnated women were killed so the aim of rape in this context, unlike genocidal rape in other contexts, was not to contaminate the bloodline or to reproduce an ethnically mixed cohort of children.

In terms of contextualising and interpreting the behaviour of German men, sexualised violence was not enacted upon a dehumanised body. It was carried

---

[18]Interview 1544, USC Shoah Foundation testimony.
[19]Interview 23436, USC Shoah Foundation testimony.

out on the reproductive bodies of Jewish women. It was, as Patterson (2013) has argued, an assault on Jewish motherhood, as the source of the Jewish people is the Jewish mother. The concentration camps were described as places that were the anti-thesis of the maternal. In the concentration camps, motherly love – pregnancy and maternity itself – were capital crimes, often resulting in women's immediate death.

Forced sterilisation and forced abortion are acts of reproductive genocidal violence. Unlike the use of rape, they did not contradict the Nazi eugenic vision of creating an Aryan race. Their devastating genocidal logic is apparent. Both examples, however, benefit from an analysis which views Jewish women as an essentialised group: woman-as-Jew. Moving beyond the dehumanisation thesis allows us to understand the political, racial and gendered dynamics (intersubjective) and meanings (degradation/humiliation) behind this sexualised and reproductive violence. In the context of the Holocaust, I would argue that Jewish women faced a double jeopardy: first as women (as socially, economically and politically subordinate to men) and second, as Jews (perceived to be racially inferior to Germans). From a gendered perspective, both the feminine/feminised (through rape) and maternal Jewish body were attacked.

Having considered sexualised and genocidal violence against Jewish women during the Holocaust, this chapter will now address both phenomena against Bengali women and girls during the 1971 Liberation War.

Rape and Genocidal Violence During the 1971 Liberation War in Bangladesh

Following the partition from India during the 1940s, Pakistan was divided into West (now Pakistan) and East Pakistan. Following three decades of tension – stemming from the economic, political and racial marginalisation of East Pakistan by the West – in March 1971, East Pakistan (now Bangladesh) declared its independence. This led to the 1971 Liberation War (Takai, 2011; see also Bose, 2007; Brownmiller, 1975; Mookherjee, 2006, 2007, 2015; Sharlach, 2000). It is estimated that 3 million people died during this nine-month war (Mookherjee, 2006, 2007, 2015; Sharlach, 2000).

There is a paucity of literature on the subject of the Liberation War in Bangladesh both generally and specifically on the use of rape and sexual violence during the war. As articulated by a survivor:

> There is an erasure of the 1971 history of genocide committed by Pakistan in Bangladesh in the world holocaust archives … It is important to record that this is one of the world's earliest and most heinous genocides, where perhaps the largest number of women were targeted by systematic rape, torture and subsequent execution. (Dr Rabbee, a survivor, as cited in Hossain, 2016)

Like with the other examples discussed, and as noted above, genocide was a feature of this war. This was a genocide committed by West Pakistanis against

East Pakistani Bengalis. West Pakistanis were an exclusively Muslin group, while East Pakistani Bengalis were an ethnic group comprised mainly of Hindus, as well as some Muslims. The former deemed the latter racially inferior (Sharlach, 2000; Takai, 2011). Responding to the genocide – and believing that non-Bengalis were supporting West Pakistan – the Bengalis attacked and murdered 150,000 non-Bengalis in East Pakistan (Sharlach, 2000). Over the course of the nine months, West Pakistani soldiers raided houses, killed men and raped Bengali women of all castes and religions (Brownmiller, 1975, Sharlach, 2000). And while it is important to acknowledge that this was a genocide committed against the Bengalis as an ethnic group (see Beachler, 2007 for a detailed review of this genocide), gender played a significant role during this war. Gender-based violence (GBV) was committed against males and females during this war. While men and boys were executed and expelled during this genocide, regrettably there is a dearth of in-depth information about their experiences. By no means do I wish to diminish the violence(s) inflicted upon men and boys during this nine-month war however, given the focus of this chapter, I will be addressing the unique sex-based violations women and girls suffered during and in the aftermath of this war.

It is estimated that between 200,000 and 400,000 women and girls were raped during the genocide (Mookherjee, 2007, 2015; Sharlach, 2000; Takai, 2011. Some have contested these figures. See Bose (2007) for a more detailed discussion). In the words of a reporter:

> A stream of victims and eyewitnesses tell how truckloads of Pakistani soldiers ... swooped down on villages in the night, rounding up women by force. Some were raped on the spot. Others were carried off to military compounds. (War correspondent Joseph Fired as cited in Brownmiller, 1975, p. 79)

This is corroborated by a survivor who – translating an excerpt from the book *Ami Birangona Bolchi* (*The War Heroine Speaks*) – states:

> [Women were] abducted, tortured and raped in concentration camps by the Pakistani army who set up rape camps in all towns and villages they went to. It was part of a systematic plan to disempower and destroy the vertebrae of Bengali society. (cited in Hossain, 2016)

The assaults against women were widespread and systematic: the Pakistani army raped hundreds and thousands of Bengali women and girls leading, in part, to the 'destruction of the Bengalis as a group' (Takai, 2011, p. 414). Rape, in this instance, was used as a weapon of war. According to *Newsweek* (1971), it was used as a '...calculated policy of terror amounting to genocide (as cited in Sharlach, 2000, p. 95). In a similar vein to the rape of Jewish women by German men, this violence was not carried out on a dehumanised group: it was carried out on an ethnic group deemed racially inferior. Before moving on to consider rape and sexualised violence against Bengali women and girls, it is worth pausing to outline the steps involved when dehumanising an ethnic group that has been identified as inferior.

This process of identifying certain groups as lesser is based on the logic of 'us-them' distinctions. This involves highlighting and exaggerating the differences between an in-group and an out-group. Closely related to this concept is moral disengagement. This involves a process of detachment, whereby certain 'individuals and groups are placed outside of the moral boundary' (Waller, 2012, p. 88). For Waller (2012, p. 89) '[m]oral disengagement is facilitated by the dehumanisation of the victims'. The argument goes like this: dehumanisation occurs when the target group is identified as a separate category of people belonging to a distinct racial, ethnic, religious or political group that perpetrators view as inferior and/or threatening. I disagree. Surely identifying 'them' as belonging to an identifiable 'group' contradicts the central premise of the dehumanisation argument? Furthermore, this 'Othering' of the victim does not always involve dehumanising the victim. Less dramatic processes to that of dehumanisation are that of 'difference' and 'distance'. The concept of 'difference', which is based on 'us-them' thinking or, 'Othering', creates a 'social context for cruelty' (Waller, 2012, p. 92). In this context, victims, in this case the Bengali ethnic group, are placed in binary opposition to the perpetrators. They become the vessel onto which perpetrators project all of their anxieties, insecurities and hostilities. The out-group are disparaged and treated as undesirable and unwanted elements of society (Lang, 2010).

Having outlined my opposition to the dehumanisation thesis, let us continue with our discussion of rape and sexualised violence committed against Bengali women and girls. The Women's Media Centre, specifically the Women Under Siege journalism project, is dedicated to researching how rape and other forms of sexualised violence are used as weapons during war/armed conflict. In their section on the war in Bangladesh, they outline how sexualised violence was used as a weapon during this war (see Women's Media Centre (WMC), n.d.). The rapes involved sexual torture and gang rape. Women were often murdered after they were raped. Some women died from their injuries and some killed themselves following the assault (Sharlach, 2000). According to a local newspaper, others '… fled to Pakistan with their Pakistani captors rather than face what awaited them in Bangladeshi society' (WMC, n.d.).

Here I would like to remind readers of Halbmayr's (2010) notion of sexualised violence discussed above. Specifically, the idea that sexual violence encompasses both indirect and direct forms of sex-based violations that include: humiliation, intimidation and destruction. Indeed, the impact of sexual violence committed against Bengali women and girls was not just physical. It was also social and psychological (as in the case of Rwanda and the former Yugoslavia discussed earlier). As established, the consequences of genocidal rape are death, both literally and figuratively (social and psychological). In terms of the latter, in Bangladesh, female victims were ostracised; and their families and their communities were 'spoiled' (Brownmiller, 1975; Mookherjee, 2006, 2015, Sharlach, 2000).

Becoming Abject: The Individual and Social Consequences of Rape

Here I will return to a point raised in the Introduction: pre-war gender arrange-ments and social divisions. In the context of Bangladesh, the importance of pre-war gender relations needs to be considered alongside religious and cultural traditions. Prior to the war, Bengali women lived in strict isolation from men, both in public and in the home. Modesty and chastity were key features of this Purdah-based culture and family honour was linked to a woman's status (Brown-miller, 1975; Takai, 2011). Regarded as men's private property, the rape of women in Bangladeshi society was treated as an insult to the husband (Mookherjee, 2006). Following the war, female victims of genocidal rape were expelled from these respectable communities. They were blamed for bringing dishonour on their families and many families shunned these women (Sharlach, 2000; Takai, 2011). The deliberate use of rape to achieve this humiliation and the destruction of the group amounts to genocide.

Diken and Lausten (2005) discuss these ideas of humiliation and shame in relation to abjection. In their article, *Becoming Abject: Rape as a Weapon of War*, they draw upon the concept of abjection in their discussion of the rape victim. Put simply, the abject is that which provokes disgust. It is that which is deemed perverse, dangerous and threatening (Kristeva, 1982). In her book, *Powers of Horror: An Essay on Abjection*, Kristeva (1982) provides a detailed analysis of abjection. Treating that which is abject as a form of pollution, she distinguishes between abjection from without (disease) and abjection from within (menstrual blood). Here, I am interested in applying her ideas about impurity, contamina-tion and defilement to the excluded bodies of women violated during war. To do so, I will draw on the work of Diken and Lausten (2005, p. 113). They argue that rape victims often view themselves as abject, 'dirty' and morally inferior; and regard their bodies as marked by a stigma that is hard to remove. Key to my pur-pose here is their assertion that abjection is communal as well as individual. This is because, according to the twisted logic of the coding of woman-as-nation, genocidal rape is not simply an attack upon an individual female, it is an attack upon the group to which she belongs. Diken and Lausten (2005) also discuss the pollution/contamination associated with rape and the impact this has on the purity of the victim.

On the subject of both the physical and the social-symbolic element of geno-cide, Card (2008, p. 180) argues that while 'physical destruction', as outlined in the genocide convention, can relate to mass murder or the 'interference with bio-logical reproduction' (as in the case of forced pregnancy resulting from genocidal rape), there are other ways to physically destroy a community. Here she proposed the idea of genocide as 'social death'; as the destruction of 'social vitality'. By social death, she means that victims are stripped of their group membership and their social identities, of attributes that give their lives meaning.

While Diken and Lausten's (2005) analysis is based on the Bosnian war. I want to apply their thinking, and Card's (2008) notion of social death, to the 1971 Liberation War in Bangladesh.

Birangonas (war heroines) was the term used by the Bengali government to refer to all of the female victims of rape during the Bangladesh war (see Mookherjee, 2015 for a more detailed discussion). They set up rehabilitation centres for the survivors and offered rewards to men who would marry the raped women (Mookherjee, 2006, 2007, 2015). Yet, their attempts were unsuccessful. Instead of being valorised as war heroines, they were treated with disrespect (Takai, 2011). Most Bengalis refused to issue marriage proposals or allow survivors to return to their families (Sharlach, 2000). As a result, many fled to West Pakistan or committed suicide (Takai, 2011). Paradoxically, alongside these public attempts to reintegrate female victims/survivors, attempts were also made to conceal the sexual violence that had occurred during the nine-month war.

Mookherjee (2006, p. 433) considers the silence and public secrecy surrounding the use of rape against Bengali women and girls. She highlights the contradictions between survivors' 'national position as icons of honor' and their treatment in their communities where villagers would subject them to various forms of *khota* (sarcastic and scornful comments). As one survivor recalls: 'I was branded a bad girl, a slut...by local people' (Das, 2011). Based on the lives of three women, Kajoli, Moyna, and Rohima, from Enayetpur, a village in western Bangladesh, Mookherjee (2006) traces the various subjectivities that were constructed in relation to the raped women (see also Mookherjee, 2015). As a result of khota, which affected both the women and their families, the women refrained from mixing and socialising with others for fear of being scorned. They also refrained from talking about what had happened, believing it was too shameful. Shame in this context is linked to family and community. In addition, sexuality, purity and honour are linked with shame. Indeed, as relayed by the women, *man ijjot* – 'meaning status and honor linked to sexual relationships' – is of the utmost importance (see Mookherjee, 2006, p. 438).

Understanding the Genocidal Rape in Bangladesh

Taking on board this work by Diken and Lausten (2005); Card (2008) and Mookherjee (2006), all discussed above, as well as evidence from survivors, reporters and eyewitnesses, I posit that the rape and sexualised violence committed against Bengali women and girls amounts to the crime of genocide. Here, physical destruction is not simply based on 'killing members of the group or, causing serious bodily harm', it is also caused through social death. The depiction of raped woman as abject, inferior, polluted and in need of expulsion, caused serious mental harm. This is included in the definition of genocide.

There is also evidence to suggest that forced impregnation (defined above) was the aim behind the mass rape of Bengali women and girls of reproductive age (Takai, 2011). In the words of a Pakistani soldier: '[w]e are going. But we are leaving our seed behind' (as cited by Sharlach, 2000, p. 95). However, the claim of forced impregnation is hard to prove. Debates have emerged within the literature on the subject of genocidal rape. For some, forced impregnation is what constitutes genocide, not the rape itself. For others, proving intent is problematic (see Card, 2008; Cudd, 2008; Sharlach, 1999, 2000). Indeed, I use these deliberations to inform discussions with my students during seminars. A common response from these students is: 'if the consequences of an act are genocidal does it matter if there was no intent...?' The answer is yes. An act is defined as genocidal based on its intent to destroy. Herein lies the conundrum. Even if the consequences of rape *appear* to be genocidal – that is they destroy in whole or in part members of a group – this is redundant if genocidal intent was absent. Regardless then, if, in some instances, the consequences of rape may speak to some of the elements listed under the genocide convention: pregnancy following rape by members of a different ethnic group, expulsion of the group and so on, this will not count as genocide, unless enacted with the explicit intent of destroying members of the group. A prime example of this is the case of Bangladesh.

With regards to rape, as outlined above, there is sufficient evidence to suggest that this was used as a genocidal tool. There is less support, however, for the case of forced impregnation. Forced pregnancy, like rape, can constitute the crime of genocide. Article 11(d) of the Genocide Convention involves 'imposing measures intended to prevent births within the group' (The Convention on the Prevention and Punishment of the Crime of Genocide, 2014). As mentioned earlier, forced pregnancy prevents women from carrying babies from their own ethnic group. And:

> By preventing births within the target group, perpetrators of forced pregnancy are 'deliberately inflicting' on the target group conditions of life that will cause the destruction (i.e., weakening by de-population) of the target group. (Takai, 2011, p. 404)

According to numerous sources, 25,000 babies were born as a result of the widespread use of rape during the 1971 war (Brownmiller, 2011; Takai, 2011). Viewed as a constant reminder of the assault on Bengali society, as well as its cultural identity, these war-babies were rejected by the Bangladeshi government. Female survivors were either forced to have abortions or give their babies up for adoption oversees (Brownmiller, 1975, Mookherjee, 2007). I will discuss both of these issues in more detail below.

Despite the number of babies born as a result of the systematic rape of Bengali women, there are, Takai (2011) argues, problems in prosecuting forced pregnancy as a crime of genocide. In a very detailed article, Takai (2011) outlines the reasons for this. First, the perpetrators must be of a different ethnic group to the victims in order for it to contaminate the bloodline or to involve the 'transferring of children' from one group to the other. Therefore, to paraphrase Takai (2011), as the Bangladeshi government can only prosecute Bengali nationals with this crime (where perpetrator and victim are of the same 'bloodline'), forced pregnancy cannot be tried and charged in this case. Second, within international criminal law (as outlined above), forced pregnancy requires the detention of the victim for the full length of the pregnancy (this is a theme I will return to in chapter 4). Despite evidence that rape camps did exist (Brownmiller, 1975, WMC, n.d.), there is insufficient evidence to prove that victims were detained until they gave birth (see Takai, 2011 for more details). The legal requirements regarding forced pregnancy notwithstanding, I would argue that these acts of sexualised violence are also examples of reproductive violence: pregnancies resulting from rape are a violation of women's reproductive autonomy.

The Regulation of Women's Post-war Reproductive Bodies

Even if forced pregnancy, as an act of genocide, cannot be proven in the case of the 1971 war, it is still important to unpack the impact and implications these pregnancies had for female victims/survivors. In her research on raped Bengali women, and their 'war-babies', Mookherjee (2007) considers how the State attempted to rehabilitate these women and, in the process, regulate their reproductive bodies. This speaks to Grey's (2017) notion of reproductive violence.

Following the war, the new government set up rehabilitation centres offering women abortions or adoption for those too far along in their pregnancies to undergo an abortion (Mookherjee, 2007, see also Brownmiller, 1975). During this time, the State lifted the ban on both of these practices to facilitate the removal of these 'war-babies', who brought with them painful memories of war (Mookherjee, 2007). Motherhood, in the immediate aftermath of the war in Bangladesh, was premised on protecting raped women from 'the emotions of motherhood' through the use of these State policies (Mookherjee, 2007, p. 339). Furthermore, this construction of motherhood draws a distinction between legitimate and illegitimate motherhood '…and emphasizes a nationalist project that seeks to contain illegitimate motherhoods so that these same women might become available to nation-building programmes as legitimate mothers' (Mookherjee, 2007, p. 350).

It can be argued that this removal of 'war-babies' (Mookherjee, 2007) was part of a cleansing ritual, designed to purify the abject, polluted woman. In the words of one survivor: 'Bangladesh became a free nation and I a fallen woman' (Das, 2011). But more than that – and here we return to Cohn's woman-as-nation thesis – these State policies restored national honour through the control/regulation of women's sexual and reproductive bodies. In the context of the Indian subcontinent, we might think of Cohn's phrase along these lines: nation-as-mother and woman as mothers of the nation.

This regulation of motherhood can be contrasted to the assault on Jewish motherhood (discussed above) in the following ways. In the context of the Holocaust, the separation of children from their mothers and the removal of their capacity to reproduce children from their own ethnic group (through forced abortion and forced sterilisation) formed part of the Nazi genocidal campaign. In the case of Bangladesh, while the removal of 'war-babies' was not done through explicit use of force, this was, nevertheless, a State-wide policy. A policy carried out in response to genocide, rather than a component of it. It was the antidote, rather than the annihilation.

Concluding Comments

Both of the cases discussed in detail in this chapter are illustrations of the woman-as-nation thesis. In the first example, rape by German soldiers against

Jewish women was not an official strategy of the war. In the second example, rape was used as a tool of genocide. Yet in both examples, sexualised violence was genocidal. It was used as an attack upon the nation's culture of women. Context-specific analyses reformulate the coding of woman-as-nation to: woman-as-Jew, in the case of the Holocaust, and mother-as-nation, in the case of Bangladesh. It can be argued that less is known and/or has been written about the use of rape and sexualised violence during these genocides. Only recently has research been carried out on the subject of sexualised violence against Jewish women during the Holocaust (see Banwell, 2016 for a more detailed review). Unfortunately, research into rape and sexualised violence during the 1971 Bangladesh War remains limited. It is hoped that this chapter, which has also included the concept of reproductive violence, has enriched the reader's knowledge and understanding of the gender-specific and the unique ways in which women were targeted during these genocides. Moving on to more recent examples of gender and the violence(s) of armed conflict, the next chapter focuses on rape and sexual violence in the DRC.

Chapter 2

Conflict-related Sexual Violence in the DRC

Introduction

The book, *A Thousand Sisters: My Journey into the Worst Place on Earth to Be a Woman*, was written by Lisa Shannon. It is based on her 'work' in the DRC. Lisa first learned about rape and the crimes being committed in the Congo after watching an episode of *Oprah*. After conducting more research into the atrocities being committed in the DRC, she asked herself: 'what if I had tried to help?' (Shannon, 2011, p. 37). This question would lead Lisa to abandon her career, her fiancé and her comfortable life in the US to raise money and dedicate herself to the plight of raped women in the DRC.

In the foreword to the book, Zainab Salbi (as cited in Shannon, 2011, p.12 emphasis in the original) explains that for survivors, theirs is a story of 'triumph over evil, the sheer force of *will* to survive and stand tall'. Shannon's, on the other hand:

> […] is a heroine's journey of a woman…who was not afraid to confront the conflict in the Congo, who did not worry about how much it would cost her personally to engage.

Zainab continues:

> Lisa Shannon is one of those individuals who has decided to take a stand against an evil that does not oppress her directly but offends her with its very existence.

Shannon herself admits that, despite living a good life before going to the DRC, she was not very happy. Her journey to the Congo, and her work with raped

Gender and the Violence(s) of War and Armed Conflict:
More Dangerous to be a Woman?, 43–63
Copyright © 2020 by Stacy Banwell. Published by Emerald Publishing Limited.
doi:10.1108/978-1-78769-115-520201004

women, gave her sense of meaning. These women inspired her, she explains, and she tried to restructure her life to emulate theirs. It is hard to separate Shannon's own personal reasons for going to the DRC (her belief that it would fill a void in her own life) from her genuine desire to address the atrocities being committed there. To clarify: I am not criticising Shannon *per se*. It is clear from survivor testimonies that they have benefited (perhaps only on a superficial level) from her fundraising activities and grassroots activism in the DRC. My concern is that this speaks to the broader pattern of the securitisation (Hirschauer, 2014) and fetishisation (Meger, 2016a, 2016b) of wartime rape and sexual violence outlined in the Introduction.

Baaz and Stern (2013) voice similar reservations regarding Lisa Shannon's story. For them, Lisa Shannon's journey to the Congo, and her work with victims, is an example of a gendered civilising mission. Lisa's mission, according to their analysis of the postcolonial feminist critique, is an example of the 'white savior narrative', where marginalised women of colour in the Global South are 'rescued' by their more emancipated western sisters (recall my discussion in the Introduction of the visuality/master narrative of the GET CROSS! campaign). Let us unpack this postcolonial feminist critique in more detail. Postcolonial feminists challenge essentialist claims of 'woman' as a universal and homogenous category, recognising women's diverse identities, locations and experiences (Agathangelou & Turcotte, 2015; Mohanty, 1988; Steans, 2013). Postcolonial feminists acknowledge '…the impact and ongoing legacies of colonialism and imperialism [and] forms of neo-colonial and neo-imperialist domination' (Steans, 2013, p. 124). This scholarship draws attention to inequalities and divisions between the Global North and the Global South, both past and present (Agathangelou & Turcotte, 2015; McKinnon, 2016; Mohanty, 1988; Olivius, 2016a, 2016b; Spivak, 1988; Steans, 2013). It criticises hegemonic (read as western) discourses for orientalist and ethnocentric depictions of individuals in colonised lands. Within these narratives, men are often depicted as other, inferior and savage (Steans, 2013), while the 'average third-world' woman is regarded as '…ignorant, poor, uneducated, tradition-bound, religious, domesticated, family-oriented, victimized…' (Mohanty, 1988, p. 65). And finally, postcolonial feminists problematise gender mainstreaming policy and practice (Agathangelou & Turcotte, 2015) by questioning the actions of privileged western women who claim to be speaking for, and working on behalf of, their non-liberated, non-western, oppressed counterparts (Mohanty, 1988; Spivak, 1988).

Of particular note within the postcolonial feminist critique is Spivak's pivotal essay, *Can the subaltern speak?* In this piece, Spivak (1988, p. 76) critiques western (postcolonial) academic writing – specifically Foucault and Deleuze's conversations about power, desire and subjectivity – for the ways in which it/they speak for and re-present the subaltern. On the subject of epistemic violence, she states: '[t]he clearest available example of such epistemic violence is the remotely orchestrated, far-flung, and heterogenous project to constitute the colonial subject as Other'. Epistemic violence refers to the harm that is done through knowledge and discourse when certain voices/experiences are obscured (Teo, 2014). The example that Spivak (1988, p. 76) uses to illustrate this is 'the epistemic violence of the codification of Hindu Law', specifically widow sacrifice in India. In a bid to 'save' and protect Indian women from this ritual, the British abolished widow sacrifice in 1829. As Spivak (1988, p. 94 emphasis in the original) explains:

> [...] what interests me is that the protection of woman (today the 'third-world woman') becomes a signifier for the establishment of a *good* society...In this particular case, the process also allowed the redefinition as a crime of what had been tolerated, known, or adulated as ritual...

Through this example, we see how western imperial powers make decisions on behalf of women they deem as *objects in need of protection*; individuals who cannot speak or make decisions for themselves.

Departing from this scholarship on the securitisation and fetishisation of rape and sexual violence in the Congo – as well as the gendered civilising missions that accompany these processes – I examine the feminist political economy of violence against women and girls in the DRC. Following on from the previous chapter, this facilitates an understanding of how gender informs the experiences of victims/survivors *and* perpetrators of conflict-related sexual violence (CRSV). It does so across three levels of analysis: macro- meso- and micro.

The feminist political economy approach addresses the relationship between the economic, the social and the political (see Alsaba & Kapilashrami, 2016; Davies & True, 2015; Meger, 2016a; True, 2010, 2012). It also addresses the macro- (global), meso- and micro- (local) contexts within which gender-based violence (GBV) occurs. It demonstrates how GBV is both produced and reproduced within and beyond the conflict zone. Existing research on the political economy of violence against women and girls in the DRC analyses the links between economic globalisation, neoliberalism (as it relates to the World Bank and the International Monetary Fund) and the violence(s) of armed conflict (see Leatherman, 2011; Meger, 2015; Mullins & Rothe, 2008; Turshen, 2016). I use this work as a springboard to provide a feminist analysis of rape and sexual violence in the DRC. I do so by drawing on the concept of globalisation masculinities. These include masculinities of conquest and settlement, masculinities of empire and masculinities of postcolonialism and neoliberalism (Connell, 1998, 2005). In this chapter, I will consider masculinities of postcolonialism and neoliberalism, focusing mainly on the latter and how it interacts with economic globalisation and hyper-capitalism vis-à-vis the conflict in the DRC (more on this shortly).

As noted in the previous chapter, there are two main schools of thought within the literature on wartime rape and sexual violence. The first views sexual violence as a by-product of war/armed conflict: an inevitable part of conflict (for a more detailed discussion, see Baaz & Stern, 2013; Banwell, 2016; Cohen, Green, & Wood, 2013; Davies & True, 2015; Fogelman, 2012; Meger, 2016a; Schneider, Banholzer, & Albarracin, 2015; Wood, 2014). The second – the weapon-of-war paradigm – emphasises the strategic purposes of this violence (Askin, 2003; Buss, 2009; Card, 1996; Leatherman, 2011; Mackenzie, 2010). In the context of this chapter, and its analysis of the DRC, I will be arguing that rape falls under this second category. Its use is widespread, and it is being used as a tactic by actors within and beyond the conflict zone.

When I first started writing about the Congo, back in 2011, rape was being used as a weapon of war at an alarming rate (Africa Research Bulletin, 2011; Holmes, 2007; Meger, 2010; Ohambe, Muhigwa, & Wa Mamba, 2005). When I wrote this chapter over the course of 2018–2019, fighting had resumed in the Congo and there was a resurgence in the use of rape as a terror tactic against civilians. While improvements have been made with regards to international trade regulations, as well as Congolese rape laws, that armed groups and security forces still engage in the illegal exploitation of minerals contained within the DRC – using rape to gain access to such sites – speaks to the persistence of CRSV in the Congo. What follows is an analysis that draws upon both of these periods in order to best illustrate the conflict-related crimes being committed in the DRC.

Outline of the Chapter

This chapter argues that the rape and sexual violence committed in the DRC is being perpetrated and/or facilitated at the macro-, meso- and micro- levels. Beginning with an outline of the terminology used, the chapter then provides an overview of the origins and current status of the conflict in the DRC. This is followed with a review of the use of rape and sexual violence within the Congo. Drawing on the feminist political economy approach, the chapter then traces how GBV operates at all three levels in the DRC. It starts with an examination of the macro-level. Here I tease out the economic dimension of the conflict, drawing on globalisation masculinities to unpack the relationship between neoliberalism, business masculinity, hyper-capitalism and the State-corporate crimes being committed in the DRC. The chapter then moves on to examine the meso-level, exploring heterosexual militarised masculinity; pre-existing gender inequalities within Congolese society, concluding with a review of rape laws in the Congo. These sections comprise the main body of this chapter. They are followed by an analysis of the micro-level. This section includes an exploration of how individual men use rape and sexual violence to subvert their marginal positions within the gender hierarchy. While this section is shorter than the previous sections, nevertheless, it conveys how individual men contribute to, and gain from, the political economy of this conflict. As a result of these economic (hyper-capitalist), political and gendered (hegemonic heterosexual masculinity) aspirations – which operate at all three levels – rape is used as a weapon of war against women and girls in the Congo. Not only does this breach international rape laws, it also implicates transnational companies in State-corporate crimes.

The chapter closes with some suggestions on how we should respond to the war crimes and crimes against humanity being committed in the DRC. Here, the merits of using a gendered lens to tackle GBV at the macro-, meso- and micro-levels is explored.

Terminology

This chapter draws on the following definition of State crimes, as outlined by Mullins and Rothe (2008, p. 83):

> Any action that violates international public law, and/or a [S]tates' own domestic law when these actions are committed by individual actors acting on behalf of, or in the name of the [S]tate even when such acts are motivated by their personal economical, political and ideological interests.

The term hyper-capitalism is used to convey the speed and intensity of the global market where business interests seem to dominate all elements of life (Gurashi, 2017; Vujnovic, 2017). '[C]ritical scholars believe that this new type of capitalist system has moved towards an extreme laissez-faire capitalism that is marked by greed, selfishness, destruction, wars, and exploitation' (Ritzer, 2011 as cited in Gurashi, 2017, pp. 184–185). In this chapter, I examine how hyper-capitalism '…places the interests and demands of capital and its controllers above the interests and needs of…nations' (Mullins & Rothe, 2008, p. 83) and creates criminogenic environments within the political economy of war.

The types of GBV being committed in the Congo include, but are not limited to: rape and sexual violence (both are linked to and separate from the conflict); sexual exploitation; forced and early marriage, as well as forced recruitment of child soldiers (both boys and girls); domestic violence; female genital mutilation (Home Office, 2018); and labour trafficking and trafficking for sexual purposes (Jenkins, 2012). CRSV refers to:

> [R]ape, sexual slavery, forced prostitution, forced pregnancy, forced abortion, enforced sterilisation, forced marriage and any other form of sexual violence of comparable gravity perpetrated against women, men, girls or boys that is directly or indirectly linked to a conflict. (United Nations (UN), 2018b, p. 3)

This chapter focuses on rape and sexual violence against women and girls in the DRC. In this context then, GBV and CRSV are limited to rape and sexual violence. I will use the term CRSV when referring to rape and sexual violence to acknowledge that this violence is linked to the conflict.

Before we begin unpacking the use of rape and sexual violence in the DRC, it will be useful to review the origins of this conflict.

The Conflict in the DRC: Past and Present

Space will not permit a detailed analysis of the origins of the conflict in the DRC (for a more detailed discussion of this history, see Human Rights Watch [HRW], 2005, 2008; Meger, 2010). Rather, what follows is a brief overview of this complex armed conflict. The armed conflict in the DRC dates back to 1998. Officially, the conflict ended in 2002 following a peace agreement. However, the fighting did not cease and new rebel groups, to the time of writing, remain active in the eastern part of the Congo.

Often described as 'Africa's World War' – as it involved at least nine African nations – this conflict is best understood in the wider context of other regional conflicts: the civil wars in Angola, Sudan and Uganda and the Rwandan genocide (Meger, 2010, p. 124; see also Leatherman, 2011; Mantz, 2008, p. 35). Government forces of the aforementioned countries, along with foreign groups, have formed alliances with internal armed groups in the DRC creating both an internal and an international dimension to the conflict (HRW, 2005).

In 1996, Laurent Kabila overthrew President Mobutu, Zaire's longstanding dictator. He was supported by both the Ugandan 'People's Defense Force' and the Rwandan 'Patriotic Army' (Meger, 2010, p. 125). Once installed as president, Kabila renamed the country 'The Democratic Republic of the Congo' (HRW, 2006). Despite their support, once in power, Kabila began removing Rwandans from senior positions within his government (HRW, 2002; Meger, 2010). This was met with hostility from Rwandan and Ugandan government forces who attempted a coup in 1998 (HRW, 2006; Meger, 2010). Their attempts to remove Kabila from power were unsuccessful. Due, in large part, to the support of Zimbabwe and Angola, Kabila retained his position (HRW, 2002). The support provided by Zimbabwe and Angola was purely strategic: both countries had failing economies; access to Congolese minerals would alleviate their diminishing economies (Meger, 2010). After their unsuccessful attempt to overthrow Kabila, the governments of Rwanda and Uganda began supporting the various rebel groups who were fighting against Laurent Kabila's government in the eastern provinces of the DRC. These rebel groups included: the Congolese Rally for Democracy, the Movement for the Liberation of the Congo, as well as the community-based rebel group, the Mai Mai (HRW, 1999; Meger, 2010, p. 125).

Following the assassination of Laurent Kabila in 2001, fighting continued against the government led by Joseph Kabila, Laurent's son. Instability characterised the Congolese government during this period. Anti-government rebel groups, backed by Rwanda and Uganda, used this to their advantage to control access to the mineral-rich regions of the Congo (Meger, 2010). To complicate matters further, a number of extra-national militia groups subsequently joined the conflict, most notably the Democratic Forces for the Liberation of Rwanda (FDLR). This group is mainly formed of Rwandan Interahamwe génocidaires, who were involved in the killings in Rwanda, but had fled into the region following the end of the genocide in 1994 (The New Humanitarian, 2013). The FDLR resumed their violent campaign against Tutsis in the Congo. With a lack of support from the Congolese government, various Tutsi militia groups – most notably the National Congress for the Defense of the People headed by Laurent Nkunda – began fighting against both the Congolese army (Forces Armées de la République Démocratique du Congo – FARDC) and the FDLR (Meger, 2010; see also The New Humanitarian, 2013). Violence persisted in the eastern DRC, perpetrated by a complex network of armed groups. These included the Congolese army (FARDC), the FDLR, Mai Mai groups and various other rebel groups (see The New Humanitarian, 2013 for a more detailed breakdown of these groups; see also HRW, 2006).

At the time of writing (2018), there had been renewed violence and political unrest in the DRC following President Joseph Kabila's refusal to step down when his term ended in December 2016. Opposition groups were quickly repressed. Government security forces and various armed groups attacked civilians, shooting and killing a number of protestors (Burke, 2018; Council on Foreign Relations, 2018; HRW, 2018b). In addition to the political turmoil, violence between armed groups continues in the eastern part of the country. According to HRW (2018b), more than 100 armed groups remain active in North Kivu and South Kivu in the eastern part of the country. These groups, which include the FDLR and allied Nyatura groups, the Allied Democratic Forces, the Nduma Defense of Congo-Renové, Mai Mai groups and armed groups from Burundi, continue to attack and terrorise civilians. Indeed, many of the commanders of these groups are implicated in war crimes, including ethnic massacres, forced recruitment of children, and rape and pillage (HRW, 2018b, pp. 3–4). These groups continue to fund their activities through mineral exploitation (Burke, 2018; Council on Foreign Relations, 2018).

Following the resurgence in fighting in the eastern part of the Congo, the humanitarian situation worsened, with, according to HRW (2018b, p. 4), 'the country facing Africa's largest displacement crisis in 2017.' It is believed that more than 4.5 million people have been displaced, 2.7 million have been internally displaced, 'famine is expected to affect 7.7 million Congolese and a national cholera epidemic is spreading across the country' (HRW, 2018b, p. 4; see also Burke, 2018; Council on Foreign Relations, 2018). Added to this, there has been a drop in international humanitarian funding (HRW, 2018b). Finally, exacerbating the situation, in June 2019 the DRC suffered an outbreak of Ebola.

Rape and Sexual Violence in the DRC

Referred to as 'the rape capital of the world' (Africa Research Bulletin, 2011), the eastern Congo has witnessed the rape of women and girls '...on a scale never seen before' (Nolen, 2005, p. 56 cited by Meger, 2010, p. 126). The International Rescue Committee registered 40,000 cases of GBV in the DRC between 2003 and 2006 (Dallman, 2009, p. 6). During this period, hundreds of thousands of women and girls were raped (Shannon, 2011). More than 32,000 cases of CRSV were registered in South Kivu between 2005 and 2007 (Holmes, 2007). It is believed that the actual number is more than double this (Turshen, 2016). Research by Ohambe et al. (2005, p. 33), based on interviews with victims and perpetrators, and an analysis of 3,000 files relating to cases of rape and sexual violence in the South Kivu region, identified four types of rape. These include: individual rape, gang rape, rape where victims are forced to rape one another, and rape where objects are inserted into women's vaginas. The researchers also found that 70% of the rapes were planned in advance with a specific aim in mind: 'to terrorize, loot, rape and then leave' (Ohambe et al., 2005, p. 35). The perpetrators of CRSV are not limited to armed groups, civilians are also guilty of this type of violence (Mertens & Pardy, 2017). Women and girls have also been subjected to sexual exploitation and abuse (SEA) by armed groups and UN peacekeepers (Lynch, 2004 as cited in Meger, 2010). While this phenomenon (SEA by UN peacekeepers and humanitarian workers) will not be explored in the context of this chapter, it is an issue that I will address in subsequent chapters.

Despite the signing of a peace agreement in 2002, the installation of a transitional government in 2003, followed by general elections in 2006, CRSV continued to be a major problem in the DRC (Baaz & Stern, 2009; Shannon, 2011). During 2006, in the South Kivu province, 27,000 sexual assaults were reported (Onsrud, Sjøveian, Luhiriri, & Mukwege, 2008, p. 265). Due to the persistent use of rape and sexual violence in the DRC, in 2008 another peace agreement was drafted. At this time, 22 armed groups signed a cease-fire agreement organised by the European Union, the US, the African Union and the UN (HRW, 2008, p. 1). This peace programme contained instructions for the Congolese government 'to protect civilians and respect international humanitarian and human rights law' (HRW, 2008, p. 1). Yet, according to a report by HRW (2008), CRSV against females continued at its previous rate since the peace agreement was put in place. Fighting and violence continued in the eastern part of the country in 2011: men, women and children continued to be targeted for crimes of sexual violence. According to the UN, in 2010, 300 civilians were raped between July 30, 2010 and August 2, 2010, and, on New Year's Day 2011, over 30 women were raped in the town of Fizi in South Kivu (see Africa Research Bulletin, 2011).

Renewed fighting in the DRC has led to a surge in CRSV (Burke, 2018; United Nations DRC, 2019). During 2018 *The United Nations Organization Stabilization Mission in the Democratic Republic of the Congo* (MONUSCO) recorded 1,049 cases of CRSV. This figure is higher than the previous year (see United Nations DRC, 2019). Further evidence of the increase in rape and sexual violence is provided by a Médecins Sans Frontières (MSF) health worker who reported that 60 women were raped by one armed group when it captured a village market in January 2018 (see Burke, 2018). The organisation found that incidents of CRSV had doubled each month in 2018 compared to 2017 (see Burke, 2018). There is a concern that, with the growing hostilities between the various ethnic groups who are competing over land in the Kivu region, as well as the competition over minerals contained in the mines, violence, including CRSV, will increase (Burke, 2018; United Nations DRC, 2019).

In this preceding section I have provided various figures on rape and sexual violence in the Congo. Before we proceed, two points of clarification are required. First, caution must be taken when reviewing this data. To avoid engaging in the securitisation and fetishisation of rape and sexual violence in the Congo, we must remain cognizant of the various types of violence being committed there, as well as the fact that both genders are impacted. I am focusing on women and girls in this chapter as it relates to the discussion at hand. The experiences of men and boys will be addressed later in the book. Second, by providing this information, my intention is not to quantify or reduce victims' experiences to numbers, my aim is to illustrate that rape in the DRC is widespread and systematic, employed as a tactic and a weapon of terror in the political economy of this armed conflict.

As noted at the beginning of this chapter, the feminist political economy approach traces the relationship between the economic, the social and the political. It facilitates an understanding of how GBV – which affects individuals at the local/micro-level – is informed by institutions and global policies and practices that take place at the meso- and macro-levels, respectively. In the words of Leatherman (2011, p. 147): '[t]he global economy of sexual violence [in the DRC] operates at multiple levels of power and depravation'. The remainder of this chapter will unpack each stage of this process, beginning at the macro-level.

The Macro-level: Economic Globalisation and CRSV in the Congo

There is an obvious economic dimension to the sexual violence that is occurring in the eastern provinces of the DRC. As noted in the Introduction, new war economies are decentralised and are open to the global economy (Chinkin & Kaldor 2013; Turshen, 2016). These wars are financed by violent and criminal activities. Relevant to my discussion of the DRC are the following activities: looting, pillaging, and the extraction, sale and illegal transport of minerals to transnational corporations through regional and international criminal networks.

Transnational corporations from various nations all compete for access and control over the extraction, sale and illegal transport of minerals contained in the eastern provinces of the DRC. Those involved include: government officials, foreign militia, foreign governments who back the militias, the Congolese army, the Mai Mai and other home-grown militia and the Interahamwe (Leatherman, 2011; Mantz, 2008, 2010; Mullins & Rothe, 2008). According to the *UN Report of the Panel of Experts on the Illegal Exploitation of Natural Resources and Other Forms of Wealth of the DRC*, 125 companies are involved in this global market, many of which are African-based companies, but a significant number of transnational corporations were also named. These included ones from UK and the US as well as Canada, Belgium, Germany, Israel, Switzerland and the Netherlands (see Mullins & Rothe, 2008, p. 92).

Combatants on the ground use rape as a tactic to terrorise the civilian population. Using rape as a weapon allows them to maintain control over the mines that contain these minerals, as many of the villagers will flee their homes to escape the violence, thus leaving the land open to economic exploitation (Meger, 2010). Indeed, the DRC is believed to contain an estimated $24 trillion of untapped mineral resources (Council on Foreign Relations, 2018). Thus, there is an economic incentive for all involved to maintain the chaos of the conflict to sustain access to these minerals (Meger, 2010). In particular demand are gold, tin and coltan (Meger, 2010). The latter is a mineral used for the making of mobile phones and electronics, of which the DRC holds an estimated 80% of the world's deposits (Leatherman, 2011; Mantz, 2008; Mullins & Rothe, 2008). Coltan, for example, is distributed through elaborate international channels. Whilst the government has attempted to issue authorised mineral extraction, official permissions are redundant when, as Mullins and Rothe (2008, p. 81) note, transnationals will 'enter the Congolese jungles to negotiate with warlords to gain access to minerals'. The local militias who control access to these minerals will sell them to high-level middlemen who in turn sell to South Africa, Rwanda, Belgium and others. These intermediaries then sell these minerals to customers in Europe, the US and Japan (Mantz, 2008). Hundreds of millions of dollars of illegally mined minerals continue to end up on the global market each year (see Global Witness, 2016). Gold, for example, passes through transit countries like Uganda, the United Arab Emirates (UAE) and Switzerland; ending up in jewellery and electronic circuit boards (Global Witness, 2016, p. 2).

This illegal exploitation of conflict minerals in the DRC is not simply about the economic greed of particular groups within the Congo, but rather, it is an example of hypercapitalism and economic globalisation more broadly. Put simply, the chaos of the conflict in the DRC benefits those higher up the gender order who utilise the carnage of the conflict zone to obfuscate their illegal transactions. To draw on findings published by the '*Panel of Experts on the Illegal Exploitation of Natural Resources and Other Forms of Wealth of the [DRC]*' (UN Security Council [UNSCR], 2002, p. 32): companies involved in the illegal exportation of DRC minerals contribute 'directly or indirectly...to the ongoing conflict and to human rights abuses'. These internal and external actors, who rely on the chaos of the conflict to engage in these illegal transactions, are therefore complicit in committing war crimes and crimes against humanity.

In a recent study (2015), the *Organization for Economic Cooperation and Development* (OECD) carried out a review of mining sites in the DRC to ensure that they were not contributing to the conflict through their resource procurement policies (OECD, 2015; see also the United States Agency for International Development [USAID] Responsible Minerals Trade Program). Standards set by the OECD (2015) require that companies do not obtain resources from sites where there is a risk of direct or indirect support from non-State armed groups or security forces. Data gathered from these artisanal mining sites found improvements in some areas, while others either stagnated or worse, witnessed an increase in the presence of armed groups. Data on conflict financing for 2013/2014 found that interference from criminal networks at mining sites involved the following: illegal taxation of resources; illegal trading; digging for minerals; and forced labour (OECD, 2015; see also the letter of the UN 2018a Group of Experts on the DRC). Therefore, companies trading with these militarised mining sites (that are being exploited illegally) are not only in violation of the OECD *Due Diligence Guidance*, they are also guilty of contributing directly and indirectly to the conflict. And while trading has improved – the US for example, complies with supply chain checks that meet the OECD standard – transnational companies still fail to meet the minimal legal standards and therefore continue to engage in the illegal exploitation of minerals in the Congo (Global Witness, 2016; Institute for Security Studies Africa, 2016; Pickles, 2016). Indeed, according to a recent survey, of the 275 US companies that took part, only 51% had revised how they monitor their supply chains following concerns about human rights abuses. Across the globe, very few organisations actively monitor the supply chain risk (Pickles,

2016). In terms of the Congo, companies involved in the gold sector have been required by law, since 2002, to adhere to the OECD guidance. Many companies operating in the DRC have failed to meet these due diligence standards (Global Witness, 2016).

In order to understand the gendered nature of this enterprise, it is useful to draw on Connell's gender hierarchy and her concept of globalisation masculinities. For the purposes of this chapter, a brief overview of the former will suffice. Connell (2005) identifies four types of masculinity: hegemonic, complicit, marginalised and subordinate. Hegemonic masculinity – as the most dominant form of masculinity – is positioned above the others. This is the idealised type of masculinity. Complicit masculinity is available to men who enjoy the benefits of patriarchy without displaying the dominance associated with hegemonic masculinity (Connell & Messerchmidt, 2005). Marginalised masculinity refers to men who are unable to meet the requirements of complicit or hegemonic masculinity, while subordinated masculinities are prevented from achieving hegemonic masculinity. Regardless of the historical period, hegemonic masculinity sits at the top of the world gender order, subordinating other masculinities and femininities. For men in receipt of the benefits of patriarchy and capitalism (complicit masculinity), hegemony does not require physical and/or sexual violence (although it may use force and competitive aggression); rather, as Connell and Messerschmidt (2005, p. 832) argue, it involves 'ascendancy achieved through culture, institutions and persuasion'. For marginal masculinities, hegemony often relies on ascendancy through violence. In different contexts – across local and global planes – different methods of achieving hegemonic masculinity are employed.

Earlier I pointed to the emergence of globalisation masculinities within this world gender order. With regards to masculinities of postcolonialism and neoliberalism, to draw on Connell (1998, p. 15): the neoliberal world is a gendered world. It has 'implicit gender politics and is based, in general, on the attributes and interests of the male entrepreneur'. It involves 'the increasingly unregulated power of transnational corporations [which] places strategic power in the hands of particular groups of men'. In this context of a gender world order, and within the global arena of gender relations and global markets, 'the hegemonic form of masculinity...is the masculinity associated with those who control its dominant institutions: the business executives who operate in global markets...' (Connell, 1998, p. 16). Connell refers to this as transnational business masculinity and, to return to the point I made above, this form of masculinity does not require physical force: 'the patriarchal dividend on which it rests is accumulated by impersonal, institutional means' (Connell, 1998, p. 16). Indeed, as Connell and Wood note: '...[i]n discussions of contemporary capitalism, it is widely acknowledged that the most powerful institutions, excepting only major [S]tates, are transnational corporations operating in global markets' (Connell & Wood, 2005, p. 347).

Others have also argued that international trade and global markets are inherently arenas of gender politics and gender hierarchies (Acker, 2004; Beasley, 2008; Hooper, 2001). Furthermore, they suggest that there is an implicit masculinisation that underpins these macro-structural systems in a world gender order (Freeman, 2001 as cited by Acker, 2004, p. 19). Hegemonic masculinity – or more appropriately in this context, business masculinity – is described as 'aggressive, ruthless and competitive' and '...is supported and reinforced by the ethos of the free market, competition, and a "win or die" environment' (Acker, 2004, p. 29).

Let us apply this to the CRSV taking place in the DRC. At the macro-level, we see how international government bodies and transnational companies exploit economic opportunities in marginalised parts of the world; taking advantage of the chaos and disorder of war zones to serve their economic ambitions (Leatherman, 2011). Business masculinity, which serves as a proxy for hegemonic masculinity in this context, is deployed by elites working within these global institutions who take advantage of and exploit the subordinate position of allied masculinities (the Congolese government and other local groups working on the ground). These are positioned lower down the hierarchy (Leatherman, 2011) As noted earlier, as well as committing State-corporate crimes, the actions of these men – who are striving to achieve business masculinity within a neoliberal, gendered world - implicates them in war crimes and crimes against humanity.

The Meso-level: Heterosexual Masculinity and the Military

'The militarized groups of the DRC are, like all militaries, a place where men learn to associate violence with masculinity' (Meger, 2010, p. 128).

Indeed, to draw on Canning (2010, p. 854), an important aspect of rape in conflict is the construction of heterosexual masculinity through external social institutions and the socialisation process that takes place in the military. To paraphrase Baaz and Stern (2009, p. 499): the institution of the military socialises men and boys to be masculine and aggressive through methods that are designed to produce soldiers who are able (and willing) to fight and kill (see also Canning, 2010; Hooper, 2001; Leatherman, 2011; Meger, 2010, 2016b; Trenholm, Olsson, Blomqvst & Ahlberg, 2013; Zubriggen, 2010). This work stresses that this militarised heterosexual masculinity must be understood as an institutionalised and globalised phenomenon. With regards to the situation in the Congo, as Meger (2010, p. 128) argues, understanding why individual soldiers actively choose to engage in rape and sexual violence '...requires an understanding of the social constructions of masculinity both within Congolese society and, most importantly, within the military institution'. I will deal with these in reverse order when placing them at the meso- and micro-levels.

According to Ohambe et al. (2005, p. 46), the armies and militias, which consist mostly of young men, are made up of individuals with very little education, some of whom are illiterate. The army offers these young men, whose lives are characterised by 'extreme poverty and a lack of alternative employment opportunities', a means of gaining an income and of acquiring 'social promotion and power' (Ohambe et al, 2005). Baaz and Stern (2009) explore the narratives of soldiers guilty of committing mass rape in the DRC. Their article focuses primarily on the explanations the soldiers provide and argues that their explanations of rape must be understood in relation to notions of different masculinities. The authors interview one of the main perpetrators of CRSV in the DRC: the

FARDC (Baaz & Stern, 2009). The discourses of the soldiers interviewed by Baaz and Stern (2009) relied heavily on constructions of masculinity (and femininity), which were formed and reinforced within the military institution. They state: '[t]he main ideal of masculinity which the soldiers drew upon to explain sexual violence was that of the (hetero) sexually potent male fighter' (Baaz & Stern, 2009, p. 505). Under this line of thinking, the soldier's sexual needs are treated as a 'natural driving force which required "satisfaction" from women whose role it is to satisfy these needs' (p. 505). This depiction of masculinity, Baaz and Stern (2009) argue, is reproduced in many other military institutions across the globe. These ideas about satisfying sexual desires and the performance of militarised masculinity are reproduced in the accounts of child soldiers interviewed by Trenholm et al. (2013) in the DRC.

The Meso-level: Pre-existing Gender Inequalities and CRSV in the DRC

As alluded to in the Introduction, women and girls in countries with high levels of gender-based discrimination and inequality are at a much higher risk of sexual victimisation during armed conflict (Leatherman, 2011). In the words of Freedman (2011, p. 171):

> Sexual and gender-based violence in the DRC cannot be viewed merely as a product of conflict, but must also be considered in relation to persistent gender inequalities that characterize Congolese societies.

As in the case of Iraq and Syria, these inequalities are exacerbated during conflict where women – who find themselves in the role of the head of household (in the absence of their husbands, who are missing or have been killed) – become responsible for the survival of themselves and their children.

Historically, women have been victims of domestic slavery, forced and unpaid labour in the Congo (I only touch upon these issues briefly here, for a more detailed account see Robertson & Klein's, 1997, *Women & Slavery in Africa*). Domestic slavery was widespread throughout pre-colonial Africa. Slavery reduced women's status from wife and mother to that of commoditised property (Turshen, 2016, p. 45). Indeed, slave labour impacted gender relations more broadly. Even following abolition, women were still treated as the property of men and restrictions were placed upon their freedom (Turshen, 2016). Gender inequality remained a feature of Congolese life post-slavery and during the colonial period. Women continued to face barriers in matters relating to land ownership, inheritance rights, access to meaningful education and access to divorce. These constraints would continue following independence in 1960 (Mbambi & Faray-Kele, 2010; OECD, 2017). Within current Congolese society, women remain disadvantaged socially, culturally and economically. For my purposes here, I will focus on women's socio-cultural status. For a discussion of women's economic position, see Turshen (2016).

In terms of the socio-cultural landscape, Congolese customs place women at a lower status to men. Even though literacy and education rates for men are low, they are even lower for women, and it is uncommon for a woman to hold a position of power or authority in Congolese society (Banwell, 2014; Meger, 2010; Ohambe et al., 2005). Access to education and healthcare, including reproductive healthcare, is severely diminished for women and girls in the DRC. With regards to the latter (see Emmanuel, 2016; Freedman, 2011; Luneghe, 2017), the scale of rape and sexual violence in the country increases the burden on an already deficient healthcare system (MSF, 2016). In terms of education, families make the decision to keep girls at home so they can assist with household tasks and provide additional income for the family (Freedman, 2011, p. 172) Indeed, many girls do not complete their primary school education (Freedman, 2011; see also Mbambi & Faray-Kele, 2010; OECD, 2017).

These inequalities are reflected in Congolese customary laws, which impact heavily on the lives of rural women. As will be discussed below, these customary laws at once reflect/reproduce women's inferior status within Congolese society, while at the same time, they identify them as the core of the community (this is reminiscent of the woman-as-nation thesis and the notion of women as centres of gravity discussed previously).

The Family Code, a legal instrument which contains rules concerning the structure and organisation of the family, requires a woman to obtain her husband's consent before gaining employment or engaging in legal transactions (Home Office, 2018; Mbambi & Faray-Kele, 2010; OECD, 2019; Ohambe et al., 2005). In Congolese society, women are responsible for childcare and all domestic responsibilities (OECD, 2019). They are, as Meger (2010) argues, considered the core of society. Thus (as demonstrated in the previous chapter), when a woman is raped, this is seen as an attack upon the entire community. It is also an attack upon men and (heterosexual) masculinity. A husband's role, as outlined in Congolese Family Law, is to protect his wife. When a woman is raped or sexually assaulted, this sends a clear message to the husband that he has been unable to protect his wife and carry out his masculine duty (Meger, 2010). This, according to various writers, is why rape is such an effective weapon as it strikes at the heart of men's masculine identities (Baaz & Stern, 2009; Meger, 2010). This further subordinates an already non-hegemonic masculinity.

The Meso-level: Rape Laws of the Congo

Before addressing how wartime rape and sexual violence are dealt with at the local level in the DRC, I will begin by tracing developments at the international level. Rape has been present in war/armed conflict throughout history. In new wars, its use is widespread and systematic (the weapon-of-war paradigm) (Baaz & Stern, 2009; Meger, 2010). Up until the 1990s, this crime remained largely invisible (Dallman, 2009) or, at best, marginalised (Baaz & Stern, 2009) and was, as Canning (2010, p. 851) points out, 'sidelined legally, academically, and politically'. During the last decade of the twentieth century, however, rape and sexual violence during armed conflict started to receive widespread media, political and academic attention (Canning, 2010; Dallman, 2009, Dixon, 2002; Leatherman, 2011; Mertus, 2004).

Following the genocides in Rwanda in 1994 and the former Yugoslavia between 1992 and 1995, CRSV was treated as a human rights violation (Skjels-bæk, 2001). The International Criminal Tribunal for the former Yugoslavia (ICTY) in 1993 and the International Criminal Tribunal for Rwanda (ICTR) in 1994 were the first war tribunals to include rape and sexual violence as war crimes (Skjelsbaek, 2001). The ICTR was the first to treat rape as a crime against humanity and as an act of genocide (see previous chapter). Prior to this, wartime rape and sexual violence were prohibited under the Geneva Conventions of 1949 and their Additional Protocols of 1977. Since the ICTY and the ICTR, the UN Security Council has passed a number of resolutions to address rape and sexual violence during war/armed conflict: UNSCR 1325 (2000) which focuses on the impacts of war/armed conflict on women and girls and UNSCR 1820 (2008) which treats wartime rape and sexual violence as war crimes (Canning, 2010, p. 849; see also UNSCR 1888 (2009a); UNSCR 1889 (2009b); UNSCR 1960 (2010); and, UNSCR 2106 (2013a).

The creation of the International Criminal Court (ICC) in 1998 was another important development for international humanitarian law and human rights (Canning, 2010; Dallman, 2009). This was the 'first mechanism for holding leaders of States accountable for genocide and other serious international crimes', including wartime rape and sexual violence (Dallman, 2009, p. 1). Under Articles 7 and 8 of the Rome Statute of the ICC, combatants guilty of committing widespread systematic sexual violence against any civilian population are charged with war crimes and crimes against humanity (Rome Statute of the International Criminal Court, 1998).

In addition to the provisions listed above, Just War Theory outlines the various principles relating to the moral legitimacy of war. It is based on two elements: *jus ad bellum* – just war-making and *jus in bello* – just war-fighting. The first is based on the moral reasoning that justifies the resort to war. The second is based on the permissibility of the means used to wage war (Orend, 2000; Sjoberg, 2006b). Just war-fighting contains the non-combatant immunity principle. This 'protects' civilians during war, offering them 'immunity' from the violence(s) of war/armed conflict. Under this principle, '[no] intrinsically heinous means' – such as mass rape campaigns – are to be employed (Orend, 2000, p. 121, emphasis in the original).

Prior to these developments in international law, rape and sexual violence were simply considered as the inevitable and unfortunate side-effects of war/armed conflict (Meger, 2010, p. 120; see also Canning, 2010). However, as is demonstrated in this chapter, the use of rape and sexual violence during war/armed conflict can be far more complex, widespread and systematic (Meger, 2010; Skjelsbæk, 2001). Indeed, as established so far: wartime rape and sexual violence do not happen in a vacuum. They are informed by gender politics and the pre-existing socio-economic and cultural landscape (Baaz & Stern, 2009, 2013; Banwell, 2014, 2018; Davies & True, 2015; Freedman, 2011; Leatherman, 2011; Meger, 2010, 2016a; Ohambe et al., 2005; Skjelsbæk, 2001).

Having addressed how rape and sexual violence are dealt with by international law and war crime tribunals, I will now review how these crimes are addressed at the meso-level in the DRC.

Rape and other types of sexual violence are dealt with in Congolese legislation. However, compared with the scale of CRSV in the Congo, the number of those who have been convicted is relatively low. The Congo has ratified a number of Human Rights legislation; which includes regulations relating to the protection of women and girls during peacetime and armed conflict. These include rape, forced prostitution and sex-based discrimination. All armed forces in the Congo have been under increasing pressure to adhere to these rules (Dallman, 2009; HRW, 2005).

The ICC has held jurisdiction over crimes included in the Rome Statute and committed in the DRC from 2002. In the same year, the DRC ratified the Rome Statute. The court has been investigating war crimes and crimes against humanity in the DRC since the 1990s.This includes rape and sexual violence. However, of the two men who have been convicted – Thomas Lubanga Dyilo and Germain Katanga – rape is not included in the list of convictions (The ICC DRC n.d.) Furthermore, despite this work by the ICC, most trials involving rape are carried out by the FARDC's military courts. Where, in the majority of cases, the accused are members of the FARDC (Stokes, 2014). Indeed, these courts, and the 2002 Military Code more broadly, remain incompatible with international law (AfriMap & The Open Society Initiative for Southern Africa, 2009).

Despite improvements to local laws prohibiting the widespread use of rape and sexual violence (Home Office, 2018), and the involvement of the ICC, most perpetrators go unpunished (Goetze, 2008, Meger, 2010). The reasons for this include: women's desire to remain silent (Ohambe et al., 2005; Stokes, 2014); difficulties in obtaining evidence (Stokes, 2014); high fees demanded by prosecutors and judges; the difficulty victims face when trying to pay for their travel costs from the countryside to get to court (Goetze, 2008); the prohibitive cost of mobile courts (Maya, 2012); commanding officers arranging for the accused to be transferred elsewhere; and, widespread corruption and the use of bribes by judges to influence the result of an investigation or trial (HRW, 2005, p. 42). However, the main obstacle continues to be the lack of rape charges filed in the first instance. Survivors fail to file charges for a number of reasons. In many instances, the women are unable to identify the perpetrator or are unable to locate them; in the majority of the cases, the women fear retribution or have been bullied and threatened into remaining silent, or they are not aware that prosecution is even an option (HRW, 2005). Perhaps the main reasons for women's silence are shame, guilt and fear of being stigmatised by members of their community (HRW, 2005, pp. 36–37).

There have been some steps in the right direction. Most notably is the conviction and imprisonment of Lt. Col. Kibibi Mutware of the DR Congolese army (FARDC) for the mass rapes committed on New Year's Day in 2011. Mutware was found guilty of committing crimes against humanity for ordering his troops to rape, beat and loot from the population of Fizi. Three officers serving under Mutware were also sentenced (Africa Research Bulletin, 2011; Smith, 2011).

There was also a landmark case in 2014 where 39 members of the FARCD stood trial for committing rape. However, only two of the soldiers were convicted of rape and sentenced to life imprisonment (Stokes, 2014; Stokes & Muyali, 2014). The number of soldiers acquitted was 13 while 24 were found guilty of pillaging (Stokes & Muyali, 2014). Two years later, 12 members of a Congolese militia group were convicted of raping 37 toddlers and young girls (Maclean, 2017). Of these, 10 were also convicted of crimes against humanity (Maclean, 2017). And more recently, in 2019, Bosco Ntaganda was convicted by the ICC for war crimes committed in the DRC (see Burke, 2019).

The Micro-level: Rape and Hegemonic Masculinity in the DRC

Within the civil zone in the DRC, marginalised males try to live up to hegemonic constructions of masculinity. The particular version of hegemonic masculinity that these men aspire to is constructed as heterosexual and operates in contra-distinction to homosexuality (Hooper, 2001). 'Hegemonic masculinity', Hooper (2001, p. 59) argues, 'is tied to phallocentrism'. She continues:

> [...] both the image of the penis as [a] weapon and the conven-tional construction of heterosexual relations revolve around phal-locentric discourse. Hegemonic masculinity, then, can be seen to be largely, but not exclusively, phallocentric.... (Hooper, 2001, pp. 59 60; see also Clark, 2017)

Men in Congolese society, according to these localised discourses of hegem-onic heterosexual masculinity are supposed '...to have a high sex drive, to obtain multiple partners, to bestow gifts in exchange for sex, [and] to be financially capa-ble of purchasing one or multiple wives'. In sum, they are expected to have '... the physical, economic, and social power to protect their wives from other men' (Mechanic, 2004, p. 15 as cited in Meger, 2010, p. 129). Various ethnic, cultural and socio-economic constraints prevent them from achieving this ideal. Subordi-nate masculinity turns into hypermasculinity within the conflict zone to resolve this tension.

This enactment of hypermasculinity – which involves aggression, excessive toughness and violence – offers these marginalised men the opportunity to take advantage of the chaos of the conflict to challenge their marginal position within the gender hierarchy. Baaz and Stern (2009) discovered that for the soldiers of the FARDC it was their failure to live up to the expectations of 'the provider' (the cou-pling of manhood with money and material wealth) and 'the sexually potent fighter' (Baaz & Stern, 2009, p. 511), alongside 'negative and sexualized images of women', that led them to rape (Baaz & Stern, 2009, p. 507; see also Trenholm et al., 2013).

At the meso-level, I discussed the socio-cultural (violence against women and girls) and socio-economic (poverty) climate in the DRC. I also discussed the insti-tution of the military as a place where an aggressive hegemonic heterosexual mas-culinity is reinforced. Both of these coalesce with the construction of hegemonic violent heterosexual masculinity at the micro-level – where individual men use rape and sexual violence to achieve this type of masculinity – to create a situation where such violence(s) are expected and accepted.

Responding to War Crimes and Crimes Against Humanity in the DRC Through a Gendered Lens

The United Nations office on Genocide Prevention and the Responsibility to Protect provides detailed information regarding the history, nature and current meaning of the terms crimes against humanity and war crimes. What follows is a summary of this information. Crimes against humanity have been dealt with under international law through international courts such as the ICC, the ICTY and the ICTR. The 1998 Rome Statute of the ICC contains the most comprehensive and up-to-date definition. Article 7 of the statute includes a list of acts that are 'committed as part of a widespread or systematic attack directed against any civilian population, with knowledge of the attack'. Of relevance to this chapter are the following acts: 'rape...or any other form of sexual violence of comparable gravity'; and '[o]ther inhumane acts of a similar character intentionally causing great suffering, or serious injury to body or to mental or physical health' (United Nations Office on Genocide Prevention and the Responsibility to Protect: crimes against humanity). All those guilty of committing acts of rape and sexual violence in the DRC are guilty of committing crimes against humanity. I would also argue that transnational corporations involved in the illegal exportation of minerals contained within the DRC, who rely on the use of CRSV to engage in these activities, are also guilty of committing crimes against humanity.

War crimes are listed in 'international criminal law treaties', 'international humanitarian law' and 'international customary law' (United Nations Office on Genocide Prevention and the Responsibility to Protect: War crimes). Acts relating to my discussion here are those that wilfully cause 'great suffering, or serious injury to body or health'. This includes: '[c]ommitting rape...or any other form of sexual violence'; '[i]ntentionally directing attacks against the civilian population as such or against individual civilians not taking direct part in hostilities' and '[p]illaging a town or place, even when taken by assault'. Furthermore, war crimes contain two main elements: a contextual and a mental element. The former means that 'the conduct took place in the context of and was associated with an international/non-international armed conflict' while the latter, refers to 'intent and knowledge both with regards to the individual act and the contextual element' (United Nations Office on Genocide Prevention and the Responsibility to Protect: war crimes). I argue that combatants on the ground, who use rape and sexual violence as a tactic to terrorise the local population to gain access to the minerals contained in the DRC, are guilty of committing war crimes. Based on the contextual and mental element, transnational corporations involved in these illegal transactions are also complicit in committing war crimes.

At the macro-level then, companies and transnational corporations directly involved in the illegal exportation of the Congo's minerals should be prosecuted for committing State-corporate crimes. They should also be found guilty of committing war crimes and crimes against humanity either 'directly or indirectly' (UNSCR, 2002, p. 32). Government forces, militia groups and civilians involved in the conflict in the DRC, specifically the use of rape and sexual violence, are also guilty of committing war crimes and crimes against humanity.

Gender relationships, the construction of hegemonic masculinity, and ideas about women and femininity need to be tackled at the meso- and micro-levels, both within and outside the conflict zone. Firstly, at the meso-level, attention must be paid to the military and the issue of militarisation: 'after all, it is militaristic culture that legitimates violence as a way of solving conflict' (Farwell, 2004, p. 394; see also Baaz & Stern 2009; Canning, 2010; Meger, 2010; Zubriggen, 2010). Within the context of the armed conflict in the Congo, empirical research demonstrates that constructions of masculinity, along with soldiers' engagement with the discourse of the 'heterosexual potent male fighter' (Baaz & Stern, 2009) are reinforced by the military institution which normalises rape and sexual violence. This culture of militarised heterosexual masculinity needs to be reformulated and negative and sexualised images of women removed from the vocabulary of motive/justification.

Secondly, at the meso- and micro-levels, gender discrimination needs to be eliminated and replaced with an emphasis on equality between the sexes. This must be extended to men and boys who are not part of the military or quasi-military groups, as an increasing amount of rape is committed by civilians and militias (Mertens & Pardy, 2017). Women also need to be given equal rights to men, and outdated laws that restrict women's autonomy need to be abolished. Expansion upon existing education programmes to teach women about their human rights, the law, and other rights awareness-raising issues (Ohambe et al., 2005) is also needed.

With regard to the *jus in bello* principle of Just War Theory it is clear from the mass rape committed in the DRC that this has been violated, and women (as well as men) have not been protected under the non-combatant immunity principle. What is needed is a gendered analysis of CRSV, an approach that unpacks the root causes of such violence and introduces tools to prohibit it. Feminists should reformulate the discussion by connecting it to real people's lives. Sjoberg (2006b, p. 102) labels this reformulation 'empathetic war-fighting' which considers '...the impacts of *in bello* decision-making on real people's lives – both in the short and in the long term'. According to this feminist revision, the lives of civilians are of paramount concern. Here, it is worth quoting Sjoberg (2013, p. 298) at length:

> [A] feminist ethic generally moves away from abstracting human suffering in war...and toward assigning culpability for all of the effects of war-fighting – immediate or long-term....It therefore pays attention to the impacts of strategic and tactical decision-making on 'real' people's lives particularly at the margins of global politics, making a special effort to take note of those impacts least likely to be taken into account in traditional war theorizing...

This commitment to addressing the lives of civilian women and girls is evident in the work being carried out by the UN and various NGOs in the region as well as various projects carried out by feminist charities (see Baaz & Stern, 2013; Meger, 2016b, Mertens & Pardy, 2017 for a critical review of this type of work). Although I have only focused on one example of the CRSV that is being perpetrated in the Congo (rape and sexual violence), it is vital that advocacy groups, alongside UN policies, address the *range* of conflict violence committed against both genders in the DRC. An inclusive approach, that includes the participation of all those affected by the conflict, is critical for securing peace and stability in the DRC

According to Orend (2000), Just War Theory as it stands is incomplete. If we are to provide a comprehensive and compelling account of the ethics of war and peace, Just War Theory needs to incorporate a new category: *jus post bellum* – just peace. For Bass (2004, p. 404), a central element for achieving *jus post bellum* will be the use of war crimes trials. We have witnessed some arrests and convictions of those guilty of committing rape and crimes against humanity in the DRC, however, we need a more thorough and robust investigation into these violations of international law. As a minimum, rape laws in the Congo must be enforced and *all* allegations of CRSV must be fully investigated.

It is worth repeating: rape and sexual violence during armed conflict are linked to pre-established gendered relationships (Leatherman, 2011; Meger, 2010; Ohambe et al., 2005). In the context of the Congo, this means revising the current socio-structural, cultural and economic landscape. If we are to change the belief that the 'Congo is the worst place on earth to be a woman', then the post-conflict responsibility lies in establishing a more gender-just society at both the meso- and micro-levels in the manners suggested above.

Conclusion

Hooper (2001) argues that hegemonic masculinity is in a constant state of production and reproduction '…in the micropolitics of everyday life in local situations' (p. 230). To this, I would like to add the macro-politics of globalisation, specifically economic globalisation and masculinities of postcolonialism and neoliberalism. Viewing the CRSV that is being committed in the Congo within a context of globalisation is key to understanding this aspect of the armed conflict. It is also key to ending this type of violence against civilian women and girls.

State-corporate crimes are being committed through global markets and global trade that are both directly and indirectly related to the CRSV that is being committed in the Congo. Given that these two things cannot be separated, transnational corporations, and companies involved in the illegal exploitation of the Congo's natural minerals and resources, need to be brought to justice and prosecuted for committing State-corporate crimes.

Returning to Hooper's (2001, p. 230) 'micro-politics of everyday life', in the Congo, hegemonic masculinity is enacted within the military institution which promotes sexual violence. Individual men are also relying on constructions of hegemonic masculinity or, rather, hypermasculinity (alongside the use of rape) to restore lost hegemony. In all three instances, gender plays a central part in explaining CRSV in the Congo. In line with Sjoberg's (2006b) notion of a feminist ethics of war, Leatherman (2011, p. 173) argues that '[g]endered advocacy must be both moral advocacy and policy advocacy'. In the case of the former, this needs to identify and raise awareness of the structural forms of injustice and the network of power relations that enable sexual violence as a weapon of war. An ethics of care places emphasis on sensitivity, empathy, responsiveness and taking responsibility. It requires:

> [...] that we care about each other as fellow members of a community and also of the global community. In contrast to the individualism that underlies rationality and masculinist thinking in hegemonic approaches to international relations, an ethics of care emphasizes persons as 'relational and interdependent'. (Leatherman, 2011, p. 175)

Together, a feminist ethics of war (Sjoberg, 2006b) and an ethics of care (Leatherman, 2011) can reformulate the non-combatant immunity principle to ensure that it protects women and girls (as well as men and boys) from the violence(s) of war/armed conflict. (Sjoberg, 2006a, 2006b). Ultimately what is needed is the ending of impunity for all perpetrators and accomplices of CRSV in the Congo.

This chapter has illustrated the ways in which gender informs the experiences of both those who *experience* the violence(s) of armed conflict, as well as those who *perpetrate* such acts. Furthermore, in the case study reviewed here, we see how constructions of femininity, in conjunction with constructions of transnational business masculinity (at the macro-level) and hegemonic heterosexual masculinity (at the meso- and micro-levels), have deleterious effects on victims, survivors and actors within and beyond the conflict zone. The feminist political economy approach facilitated my analysis of these three levels of analysis. At the macro-level, I explored the global gender hierarchy, within which globalisation masculinities are situated. Focusing on masculinities of postcolonialism and neoliberalism, I examined the relationship between business masculinity (a ruthless and competitive masculinity enacted by men within transnational organisations), economic globalisation and new war economies. I then traced how all of these phenomena interact to implicate these transnational companies (and the men within them) in State-corporate crimes, war crimes and crimes against humanity.

At the meso- and micro-levels, criminal activities within these new war economies – which rely upon rape and sexual violence – are carried out against the backdrop of institutional and individual enactments of hegemonic (heterosexual) masculinity. Here, I examined how rape is employed as a tactic to secure access to the mineral wealth in the DRC. Both internal and external actors, involved in the political economy of this conflict, benefit from this strategic use of rape. All of these actions have devastating effects on women and girls at the local level. The next two chapters continue with the theme of the political economy of violence against women and girls in Iraq and Syria, respectively.

Chapter 3

Empire-building and Coerced Sexual Activities in Post-invasion/occupation Iraq

Introduction

In an interview with Nicola Pratt (2011, p. 613), discussing United Nations Security Council Resolution (UNSCR) 1325, Susan Abbas, director of the Iraqi women's leadership, stated:

> I do not believe that there are any women that faced the challenges of lack of security and peace more than women in Iraq. For a very long time, women in Iraq have been living with wars, conflicts, and occupation.

Before the First Gulf War, Iraqi women enjoyed relatively good socio-economic, cultural and political conditions. However, both the 1991 and the 2003 US-led invasions had a detrimental effect on the Iraqi economy. With regards to sexual gender-based violence (SGBV), while this may have been an issue prior to these invasions, the 2003 Anglo-American military intervention contributed to an increase in SGBV and a decline in women's rights. It is useful to unpack this in a bit more detail. During the 1970s, women's status and rights were formally encoded within the new Iraqi Provisional Constitution. This granted women equal rights before the law. Changes were also made to labour, employment and Personal Status Laws. These granted women enhanced education and workplace opportunities and greater equality in marriage, divorce and inheritance (Human Rights Watch [HRW], 2011). However, after over three decades of conflict, Iraq's political and economic landscape had weakened dramatically. This can be attributed to the 1980 attack on Iraq, the 1990 invasion and occupation of Kuwait – followed by the coalition military response in 1991 – and the subsequent economic sanctions endorsed by the Security Council (see Kamp, 2009, p. 197). Following Iraq's defeat during the First Gulf War, in order to consolidate power, Saddam Hussein turned to religious fundamentalists and conservatives for support. This had a detrimental effect on women. Restrictions on their freedom of movement were reinstated and their protections under the law were removed (HRW, 2011). Following the most recent US-led intervention in Iraq (2003–2011), insecurity and sectarian violence increased exponentially. Social and economic instability, as well as looting and violent attacks, characterised the post-invasion period in Iraq. Iraqi women and girls became victims of domestic violence, abduction, honour killings and rape (Al-Ali, 2018; HRW, 2003, 2011, 2014a, 2014b; Oxfam International, 2009).

Islamic State of Iraq and Syria (ISIS) have committed serious human rights violations, crimes against humanity and war crimes, including genocidal violence, in both Iraq and Syria. As ISIS will be revisited in the following chapter, it is worth taking a moment to trace the origins of this extremist group. The roots of ISIS can be traced back to 2004 and Musab al-Zarqawi. Al-Zarqawi, a Jordanian, formed al-Qaeda (AQI) in Iraq, pledging his allegiance to Osama Bin Laden (The Week, 2019). Zarqawi was killed by a US drone strike in 2006. Following his death, AQI was merged with other insurgent groups to form Islamic State in Iraq (ISI) (Muir, 2017). After a series of interventions by the US-led coalition in Iraq, resulting in the death of the new ISI and al-Qaeda leader, Ibrahim Awad al-Badri (also known as Abu Bakr al-Baghdadi) became leader. In 2013, he consolidated forces in Iraq and Syria to create ISI and Syria Levant (The Week, 2019).

In 2014, the group announced the creation of a caliphate in Iraq, renaming themselves Islamic State (Muir, 2017, The Week, 2019). As Muir (2017) notes, the group has undergone a series of name changes throughout the course of its history. This, he argues, reflects the ever-changing nature of its members and their manifestos. ISIS came into use when the group began taking over large parts of northern and eastern Syria in 2014. ISIS is the name I will be using in this and in the following chapter. While it is generally agreed that the caliphate in Iraq and Syria has collapsed (Chulov, 2019), at the time of writing (July 2019), the group itself has not been defeated (The Week, 2019).

In Iraq, ISIS have used suicide bombings and improvised explosive devices, as well as car bombings, to kill civilians. This is in addition to launching chemical attacks against civilian infrastructure and populated areas. They have engaged in unlawful killings and executions, including public beheadings and other acts of torture. Rape and sexual slavery, as well as other acts of sexual violence have also been committed by the group.[1] Other crimes perpetrated by ISIS include: forced marriage, trafficking and the recruitment of child soldiers (HRW, 2017, 2018a).

---

[1]Al-Ali (2018) provides a critique of the selective focus on rape and sexual violence at the expense of other forms of SGBV perpetrated by ISIS in Iraq. See also Foster and Minwalla (2018) for a critique of the media's reporting of these crimes.

They have also imposed severe restrictions on women's freedom of movement (HRW, 2017, 2018a). As noted above, a more detailed analysis of ISIS is provided in the following chapter with reference to the atrocities committed in Syria. Given the aim of this chapter – to examine the gendered impact of the US invasion on civilian women – the focus of analysis is limited to the period up to, and including, the formal withdrawal of western forces in December 2011. Here is a brief overview of this time period. In March 2003, the US-led invasion of Iraq was launched, and formal occupation commenced in May 2003 (Hagan, Kaiser, Rothenberg, Hanson, & Parker, 2012). Saddam Hussein was captured in December 2003 and coalition forces withdrew from Iraq in 2011. My reason for focusing on this period is to illustrate the cause-and-effect relationship between the invasion and occupation, and women and girls' involvement in coerced sexual activities within and beyond the conflict zone.

In terms of the post-invasion period, and the removal of Saddam Hussein, a key focus of this chapter is UNSCR 1483 (2003, p. 4). Of relevance to this chapter is section 14, which states:

> [T]he Development Fund for Iraq shall be used...to meet the humanitarian needs of the Iraqi people, for the economic reconstruction and repair of Iraq's infrastructure, for the continued disarmament of Iraq, and for the costs of Iraqi civilian administration, and for other purposes benefiting the people of Iraq.

We will examine the impact of the US economic regime in more detail in due course. Briefly, according to Whyte (2007), this economic 'shock therapy' experiment was based upon the profit-seeking activities of US companies. This was a western capitalist agenda that did not benefit the Iraqi people (Whyte, 2007; see Hagan et al., 2012 for a detailed review of the economic cost of the conflict). Throughout the course of this chapter, I examine its impact on women and girls.

Outline of the Chapter

This chapter addresses both the direct and indirect consequences of the 2003 Iraq invasion and occupation. Criminologists have described this offensive action in Iraq as a State crime, a crime of aggression and an illegal intervention under international law (Kramer & Michalowski, 2005, 2011; see also Whyte, 2007 who describes this economic agenda as a war crime that violates the Hague and Geneva treaties). What follows is a gendered analysis of this criminal invasion and occupation. Pre-war security and gender relations in Iraq will be compared with the situation post-invasion/occupation. Using the example of forced prostitution – and drawing on women's and men's differential involvement in informal economies – I will argue that economic policies, specifically the privatisation agenda of the west and its illegal occupation, resulted in women either being forced into the illicit economy as a means of survival or, trafficked for sexual slavery by profit-seeking (male) criminal networks who exploited the informal economy in post-invasion/occupation Iraq.

By focusing on the experiences of women and girls, I am not suggesting that men and boys have not suffered in the aftermath of this invasion/occupation. Indeed, we know that men and boys have been victims of the following: abductions, executions, beheadings and religiously motivated attacks, sexualised violence and torture in detention (this is unpacked in detail in Chapter 6), as well as forced disappearance and forced recruitment. They also make up the majority of casualties and fatalities (Inter-agency Information and Analysis Unit [IAU], 2008). However, my reasoning for focusing on women is threefold. First and foremost, I want to move beyond the immediate impact of the invasion and occupation to draw attention to structural as well as interpersonal forms of violence (distinction provided below). Second, by focusing on women's situation pre- and post-invasion/occupation, I am able to scrutinise the gendered justificatory narratives used in the lead up to the military intervention. Briefly, the war on terror narrative – created by the Bush administration – used the long-term oppression of women as a justification for invading Iraq (Nayak, 2006; Shepherd, 2006; Stabile & Kumar, 2005; Steans, 2008). However, in the context of Iraq, as will be demonstrated, this was not the real motivation for the invasion (more on this shortly). And third, focusing on women and girls underscores how SGBV is part of a continuum of violence that is both produced and reproduced during armed conflict.

As with the previous chapters, I will examine how gender and the violence(s) of war/armed conflict are connected at the macro-, meso- and micro-levels. While certain forms of SGBV existed prior to the invasion/occupation, this chapter demonstrates how they were exacerbated as a result of US and UK economic policies linked to the invasion. While it is possible to attribute the rise of ISIS to the power vacuum that was left behind following the withdrawal of coalition forces in 2011, this is not the focus of this chapter.

The chapter begins with a discussion of the terminology and analytical frameworks that are used. This is a followed by a critical reading of the lead up to the invasion and the justificatory narratives surrounding it. To underscore the fallacy of this narrative, pre-war gender arrangements and forms of GBV are compared with the situation post-invasion/occupation. Before exploring the informal economy in post-invasion/occupation Iraq – specifically Iraqi women's involvement in forced prostitution – we will examine women's involvement in coerced sexual activities in both old and new wars. In this section, I will also review the various feminist positions on this. Up to this point in the book, we have considered two examples of the deliberate targeting of women during war/armed conflict. In the first case, we explored the woman-as-nation thesis and how women and their reproductive bodies became victims of genocidal violence. In the second case, we examined the tactical use of rape within new war economies. In this and the following chapter, we will advance our discussion by considering examples of women who are victims, survivors and agents. We do so by unpacking their victimisation vis-à-vis coerced sexual activities, as well their participation in such (forced) acts.

Drawing on the political economy approach, the latter part of the chapter will demonstrate how GBV, in the form of forced prostitution, can be linked to top-down macro-level economic policies and practices such as global capitalism and neoliberalism. In simple terms, and for the purposes of this chapter, neoliberalism, to borrow from Isenberg (2011), involves transferring the control of the economy form the public to the private sector. The goal is to create a more efficient and effective government, while at the same time strengthening the economy of the country (Isenberg, 2011). Returning to Connell's (1998, 2005) globalisation masculinities (discussed in the previous chapter), this chapter argues that the invasion of Iraq was a pre-emptive strike based on masculinities of empire, postcolonialism and neoliberalism.

Terminology

Article one of *The Declaration on the Elimination of Violence against Women* [DEVAW] (United Nations General Assembly, 1993, p. 2) defines violence against women as:

> [A]ny act of gender-based violence that results in, or is likely to result in, physical, sexual or psychological harm or suffering to women, including threats of such acts, coercion or arbitrary deprivation of liberty, whether occurring in public or in private life.

The definition of violence against women contained within the DEVAW also includes trafficking and forced prostitution.

GBV refers to two broad categories of violence against women: interpersonal and institutional/structural (see the report of the Special Rapporteur on violence against women, United Nations General Assembly, 2013a). The former includes physical, sexual, economic, emotional and psychological forms of violence and abuse. The latter refers to any form of structural inequality or discrimination that maintains women's subordinate position (United Nations General Assembly, 2013a). Structural violence is particularly gendered. It refers to women's lack of access to employment, education, welfare, healthcare and social, economic and political infrastructure. Women are vulnerable to this type of violence during war/armed conflict. They are also vulnerable to it in peacetime societies, particularly ones that are deeply patriarchal, where material inequalities between men and women are high and women's status as equal citizens is undermined. In this chapter, forced prostitution is considered a form of structural GBV. As will be demonstrated in due course, on an architectural and systemic level, women were denied access to the formal labour market as a result of the invasion/occupation. As such, their involvement in forced prostitution – resulting from a lack of employment opportunities – constitutes a form of structural violence.

This chapter will also consider cases where women and girls were trafficked for sexual purposes and forced into prostitution. Both trafficking (for sexual purposes) and forced prostitution (as a form of structural GBV) are included in the DEVAW and increases in both can be traced back to the US-led invasion/occupation. Distinctions between these two will be addressed in the latter part of this chapter however, for now, and for ease, forced prostitution will be used to refer to both practices.[2]

Analytical Framework

This chapter draws on the feminist political economy approach (outlined in the previous chapter) to examine coerced sexual activities in post-invasion/occupation Iraq. True (2010, pp. 44–45) identifies three elements within the feminist political economy model: the first is the division of labour within the gendered public–private sphere; the second is the 'contemporary global, macro-economic environment'; and the third is the 'gendered dimensions of war and peace'. This chapter will draw on the second and third elements, demonstrating how they are interconnected in the case of Iraq. In my example of forced prostitution in post-invasion/occupation Iraq, a political economy approach enables an analysis that links macro-level economic and political foreign policy agendas, such as neoliberalism, with GBV (forced prostitution) taking place at the local level within and beyond the conflict zone.

Empire-building in Iraq

Now that I have outlined the terminology and the analytical framework, I will examine the motivations for the invasion and occupation of Iraq. For certain criminologists, 'economic interests, geopolitical concerns, military power projection, and imperial domination were the primary motives for invading Iraq' (Kramer & Michalowski, 2011, p. 106). This argument made by Kramer and Michalowski (2011) is one that I share. In my own work, however, I unpack the gendered impact of this imperial geopolitical endeavour. I will do so here in relation to the public face (i.e. the justificatory narrative) of the Bush administration's war on terror. Following the 9/11 attacks, the US began its war on terror. Since then it has attempted to overthrow regimes in Afghanistan and Iraq. The US reoriented its security strategy to create the right of pre-emptive self-defence. As Kramer and Michalowski (2005, 2011, p. 101) note, according to the principles of international relations, as reflected in the UN Charter, the fact that a US-led coalition invaded 'a sovereign nation without provocation or legal authorization' makes this act illegal and a State crime. Official narratives used by the Bush administration in the run-up to the invasion used the plight of Iraqi women to justify its political and economic interests in Iraq. Indeed, during this time, the US State Department publicised the abuses (e.g. rape, torture and beheadings) women had suffered under the Iraqi regime (Al-Ali, 2018). Likewise, in the UK, under the direction of Tony Blair, the then Prime Minister, the Foreign and Commonwealth Office were vocal about human rights abuses against women in

---

[2]Although referred to as 'the war in Iraq', this invasion and occupation and, perhaps, more importantly, the consequences of this offensive action, are best aligned with the new war doctrine (see Introduction).

Iraq (Al-Ali, 2018). Many have criticised the timing of this sudden interest in the human rights abuses taking place under Saddam Hussein. For years, activists had been trying to draw attention to these crimes, and yet, by and large, their voices went unheard (Al-Ali, 2018).

Jabbra (2006) provides a detailed analysis of representations of American and middle eastern men and women following the 9/11 terrorist attacks. These, she argues, were used as part of the campaign to promote military intervention in Iraq, as well as Afghanistan. These gendered and racialised images in newspapers, news-magazines, advertisements and internet sites, played a crucial role in the justificatory war narrative (Jabbra, 2006). As Jabbra (2006, p.252) argues, colonial and imperial histories were drawn upon 'to sell a war agenda'. Readers will recall my discussion of the postcolonial feminist critique in the previous chapter. Framing our analysis within masculinities of empire and post-colonialism, we can use this critical feminist postcolonial lens to reveal how the ostensible rescue narrative of 'white men saving brown women from brown men' (Spivak, 1988, p. 92) was, in reality, a hyper-masculine, orientalist pursuit to 're-masculinise' the US empire following the 9/11 attacks (Al-Ali & Pratt, 2009b; Nayak, 2006; Richter-Montpetit, 2007; see also Foster & Minwalla, 2018). As succinctly put by Riley (2013, p. 51) and Cockburn (2012, p. 29) respectively: 'the U.S does "do women", but only when it suits the goals of empire-building' and 'wars are not fought "for" gender issues in the way that they are some-times fought "for" oil resources or "for" national autonomy'. Indeed, we see this reflected in US foreign policy spending. According to the US State Depart-ment, during 2003–2004, the US committed $21 billion to the reconstruction project in Iraq (Caprioli & Douglass, 2008). Yet only a fraction ($500 million) was allocated to supporting the social and political needs of Iraqi women (Caprioli & Douglass, 2008).

GBV Before and After the 2003 'Humanitarian' Intervention in Iraq

Examining 'society's hierarchy of gender, ethnicity, political and civil rights' (Davies & True, 2015, p. 7) in pre-conflict situations will facilitate a better under-standing of how and why GBV is used during war/armed conflict (see Alsaba & Kapilashrami, 2016; Leatherman, 2011). Furthermore, if we want to unpack the gendered dimensions of war/armed conflict we need to pay attention to 'local histories and prewar gender relations', as well as to the 'global processes…within which they are embedded' (Cohn, 2013, p. 27). To this end, the chapter will now consider pre-war gender relations in Iraq, comparing them with the situation post-invasion/occupation. I will also consider the impact of macro-level eco-nomic policies on local gender relations, specifically women's and men's differen-tial involvement in the informal economy.

Even under Saddam Hussein's regime of religious conservatism, women still enjoyed certain freedoms. These included freedom of movement, access to educa-tion and access to employment opportunities (Al-Ali, 2005, 2018). However, as Al-Ali (2018) points out, when we consider the 35-year (1968–2003) history of the Ba'th regime,[3] it is important to acknowledge the contradictory and changing policies towards women and gender. This, as she notes, challenges any generalised or indeed simplistic assessments of this period. For example, women living in urban parts of the country, who were not engaged in opposition politics, fared better than those based in rural areas or those affiliated with opposition groups (Al-Ali, 2018; see also Sjoberg, 2006b, 2007). However, this changed significantly following the US-led invasion.

In the words of Susan Abbas - interviewed by Nicola Pratt (2011, p. 614):

> The presence of the occupying international troops in Iraq has contributed to the increase in violence against women and girls, because the occupation has caused the collapse of [S]tate institutions, the disintegration of social control mechanisms, and the spread of extremist groups that target and use women. Extremist groups deliver their messages by targeting women, either by killing them or kidnapping them, or even threatening them, leading to forced migration.

Let us unpack this in more detail.

Increases in violence, fear of rape and sexual violence, as well as the military presence, excluded women and girls from participating in public life and from attending school, going to work and accessing health care, or simply leaving their homes (HRW, 2003). Professional women and female political activists were killed, and armed groups attacked women's organisations and family-planning clinics (Lee-Koo, 2011; Peterson, 2009). To reiterate: even before the 2003 invasion and occupation, the 1990 economic sanctions had a considerable impact on the basic infrastructure of Iraq. This led to major social and economic strain for ordinary Iraqi families. Limited electricity, restricted access to healthcare and a shortage of food and water made women's domestic responsibilities even more demanding and labour-intensive post-2003 (Peterson, 2009). Al-Ali (2005, p. 744) lists child mortality, malnutrition, increased rates of cancer, 'epidemic diseases and birth defects' as some of 'the most obvious "side-effects" of the sanctions regime'. High unemployment and the breakdown of the economy also had a huge impact on the day-to-day lives of Iraqi women (Al-Ali, 2005).

In addition, the level of everyday violence in Iraq increased throughout the invasion/occupation. Despite the promises, freedom and democracy did not prevail following 2003. Instead, Iraq was plagued by waves of violence as well as social, economic and political chaos. As a result of the invasion/occupation, there was an increase in women's victimisation of random 'street' violence; domestic violence; violence perpetrated by militias and armed groups; targeted abuse and abduction; rape and sexual abuse; and violence committed by the multi-national

---

[3]This was a totalitarian Arab-socialist regime that governed life in a one-party State under the dictatorship of Saddam Hussein. This party ruled over every aspect of public and private life (see Faust, 2015).

forces in Iraq (Oxfam International, 2009, p. 5; see also HRW, 2003, 2011, 2014b; Lee-Koo, 2011; Peterson, 2009). Accurate data on SGBV in Iraq during this period (2003–2011) is hard to come by. However, the IAU (2008) provides a detailed review of 113 reports documenting GBV in Iraq between 2003 and 2008. They recorded 21,000 cases of GBV between March 2003 and May 2008. These included murder, abduction and the ill treatment and torture of male detainees; honour-related violence; religiously motivated attacks; the killing of male and female professionals; trafficking and forced prostitution; as well as rape and sexual violence. According to one report, between April 2004 and September 2005, 400 women and 35 men were raped in Baghdad alone, and 60 females were raped between February and June 2006, while 80 were sexually assaulted. In the conclusion of their report, the IAU (2008, p. 22) noted: '[i]t appears that the situation, rather than improving, has worsened especially in the context…of the ongoing war in Iraq'.

Given the stigma attached to victims of rape, it is plausible that the actual number of victims and survivors is much higher than the figures provided above. What seems to be clear is that there was an increase in rape against women during this period (2003–2011). This rise in sexual violence accounts for the dramatic increase in honour killings during this time. Honour killings were used to remove the shame attached to raped women and restore lost family honour (Lee-Koo, 2011). The Kurdistan Regional Government's (KRG) Ministry for Human Rights reported 166 honour killings in 2007 and 163 in 2008 (see United Nations Assistance Mission for Iraq, 2008). The KRG passed the Family Violence Law in 2011 with the aim of criminalising domestic violence and honour killings. However, officials did not enforce this law, and HRW (2014b) reported that male family members continued to attack and kill female relatives following the implementation of the law.

A Feminist Analysis of Informal Economies in Iraq

To reiterate: a political economy approach looks at the relationship between GBV and macro-level processes of political and economic power. When the formal economy collapses, people are forced into illicit economies (Sjoberg, 2013). '[A] key feature of illicit economies is the re-commoditization of women and children as "resources" to be trafficked and exploited' (Raven-Roberts, 2013, p. 45). Following military intervention and the collapse of the formal economy in Iraq, women were pushed into prostitution as a means of survival (see Dakkak, 2007; Enloe, 2010; Peterson, 2009; Riley, 2013; Sjoberg, 2013; Zoepf, 2007). Alternatively, they were trafficked for sexual slavery by profit-seeking criminal networks who exploited the informal economy. In both examples, female bodies were reduced to commodities and used as currency within the informal economy in post-invasion/occupation Iraq.

Informal economies in post-conflict situations consist of coping, combat and criminal (Peterson, 2009). To paraphrase Peterson (2009, pp. 42–43), coping economies are aimed at survival and the social reproduction of families and households. Strategies may include trading organs, selling infants for adoption, entering children into sexual slavery and/or selling daughters into early marriage. Combat economies are motivated by military goals. They directly supply and support fighters and insurgents. Finally, criminal economies are concerned with profit making. They directly or indirectly supply and fund conflict-related activities.

Informal economies are gendered in the case of Iraq (Banwell, 2015b; Peterson, 2009). Despite unemployment levels rising for both men and women in post-invasion Iraq, men were much more likely to resort to combat and criminal activities. Conversely, women were much more likely to engage in coping economies, involving informal activities which included, but were not limited to, forced prostitution. Feminists have suggested that, as a result of their perceived impotence and emasculation – caused by unemployment, an inability to provide for and support their families and the presence of foreign forces – men engaged in aggressive behaviours (Lee-Koo, 2011; True, 2012) Indeed, as Lee-Koo (2011, p. 1629) notes, the decision by the Coalition Provisional Army to remove the Iraqi Army left 300,000 Iraqi men unemployed. As argued in the previous chapter, marginalised masculinities resort to aggressive behaviours to reconstitute subordinated masculine identities. In this case, these behaviours manifested both directly, through physical violence, and indirectly, through engaging in combat and criminal economies. Involvement in the latter included, but was not limited to, trafficking, looting and/or kidnapping to support financial and political endeavours (Peterson, 2009).

As discussed above, decades of conflict had devastating consequences on the economy of Iraq. Another effect of over three decades of conflict was (and is) the large number of widows and female-headed households in Iraq. Margaret Owen provides a sobering account of the plight and needs of conflict widows and wives of the disappeared in her article *Widowhood Issues in the Context of United Nations Security Council Resolution 1325*. Referring to the *UN Division for the Advancement of Women* (UNDAW) 2001 report, she states: '[w]idowhood is one of the most neglected of all gender and human rights issues' (Owen, 2011, p. 616). At the time her article was published, it was estimated that there were between one and five million widows and wives of the missing in Iraq. Describing widowhood as a 'social death', Owen (2011, p. 618) argues that, because of discriminatory practices in matters relating to 'inheritance, land and property rights', generally speaking, these women are among the 'poorest of the poor' (see previous chapter for a discussion of this in the DRC). As a 'survival' strategy, children of widows were removed from school to help support the household. Daughters were more at risk of having their education revoked and were at a higher risk of underage marriage or trafficking (Owen, 2011). The following section of this chapter will address coerced sexual activities (and others) in more detail.

Sexual Slavery and Coerced Sexual Activities During Old and New Wars

The distinction between old and new wars was established in the Introduction. Despite the differences, coerced sexual activities have existed across both types. Indeed, throughout history, women have been enslaved for sexual purposes and, as Kempadoo (2001, p. 30) notes, prostitution around military bases has been well documented in 'India, Hawaii, Vietnam, the Philippines, Japan and Korea'. She states:

> [T]he operation of foreign...troops at various times in history has produced particular forms of prostitution where the military, often in collusion with the local [S]tate or government, tolerated, regulated, or encouraged the provision of sexual services by local women to the troops.

It is interesting that Kempadoo (2001) uses the term prostitution rather than forced prostitution as I would argue that women, in these situations, have been coerced into providing sexual services. In this book, coerced sexual activities will refer to forced prostitution, sexual slavery and survival sex (also referred to as transactional sex). I will define each of these before considering their prevalence across old and new wars and the feminist contribution to this subject.

Forced Prostitution

In the document, *Elements of Crimes* (International Criminal Court (ICC), 2011, p. 9) enforced prostitution is defined as:

> The perpetrator caused one or more persons to engage in one or more acts of a sexual nature by force, or by threat of force or coercion, such as that caused by fear of violence, duress, detention, psychological oppression or abuse of power, against such person or persons or another person, or by taking advantage of a coercive environment or such person's or persons' incapacity to give genuine consent.

It is also acknowledged that 'force' does not necessarily involve 'coercion from a third party'. It can also reflect a lack of alternative means of survival (End Violence Against Women, 2014, p. 3). Article 6 of the UN General Recommendation on VAW acknowledges that poverty and unemployment can 'force' females into prostitution (as cited in End Violence Against Women, 2014). Furthermore, understanding force or coercion as a feature of women and girls' poverty and unemployment, means treating gender inequality as a form of force (End Violence Against Women, 2014). In this sense, forced prostitution is a form of structural GBV. In my discussion below, I will consider forced prostitution as a form of structural violence as per the definition of force outlined above. I will also address instances where women and girls are trafficked for sexual purposes and are forced into prostitution. Human trafficking, as defined by Article 3 of the *Protocol to Prevent, Suppress and Punish Trafficking in Persons*, can be demarcated along three lines: the act (recruitment, transportation and transfer); the means (threat or use of force, coercion, abduction, fraud and deception); and finally, the purpose (sexual exploitation, forced labour and slavery (see United Nations Human Rights Office of the High Commissioner, 2010).

Sexual Slavery

Sexual slavery is listed as a crime under the Rome Statute of the ICC. It is defined in *Elements of Crime* (ICC, 2011, p. 8) as:

> The perpetrator exercised any or all of the powers attaching to the right of ownership over one or more persons, such as by purchasing, selling, lending or bartering such a person or persons, or by imposing on them a similar deprivation of liberty.[4]

The perpetrator must also have 'caused such person or persons to engage in one or more acts of a sexual nature'.

Survival Sex

This refers to situations where individuals provide sex in exchange for food, shelter, accommodation or any other means of survival (Chalmers, 2015; Levenkron, 2010).

Coerced sexual activities vis-à-vis war/armed conflict are both historical and contemporary. As established in Chapter 1, Bengali women were forced into prostitution during the 1971 Liberation War; and across Europe, the Nazis created a system of '[S]tate-controlled brothels' during the Second World War (Chalmers, 2015, p. 186; Levenkron, 2010; Sommer, 2010; see also Person, 2015 for a discussion of forced prostitution in the Warsaw Ghetto). Reports note that both sexes engaged in survival sex during the Holocaust (for a more detailed discussion, see Chalmers, 2015; Fogelman, 2012; Levenkron, 2010). However, as Collins (2017) argues, the most prominent example of sexual slavery during this time took place in Asia. Thousands of women from Korea, China, Japan and the Philippines were forced into sexual slavery by the Japanese army (Heit, 2009; O'Brien, 2016). As many as 200,000 women, mainly Korean, were forced into prostitution during this time (Heit, 2009). Referred to as 'comfort women', their role was to provide sexual services to soldiers located at 'comfort stations'[5] (Argibay, 2003;

---

[4]*Elements of Crime* is a document that contains more information regarding articles 6, 7 and 8 of the Rome Statute.

[5]It was believed that the institutionalisation of prostitution would prevent further incidents of rape and sexual violence against local women. Prior to the establishment of the comfort stations, members of the imperial army had raped and mutilated Chinese women in 1937 in the city of Nanking (Argibay, 2003; Collins, 2017; Heit, 2009). Referred to as the 'Rape of Nanking,' estimates suggest that between 20,000 and 80,000 Chinese women were assaulted (Collins, 2017). The Rape of Nanking was part of a larger targeted attack against civilians by the Japanese army

Collins, 2017; Motoyama, 2018; O'Brien, 2016). These stations were situated in Japan, the Philippines, China, Indonesia, Hong Kong and Thailand. For most of the comfort women, recruitment involved deception, coercion and force, and once recruited they were beaten and raped. The stories of the comfort women remained untold until the 1980s and 1990s. In 1992, the UN identified the comfort women system as a crime against humanity, and as a system of sexual slavery contrary to international law. Then finally in 1993, following a long period of denial, Japan finally accepted responsibility for the comfort stations (see Motoyama, 2018 for more details). As noted above, more recently ISIS abducted and enslaved Yazidi women and forced them into sexual slavery (more on this in the following chapter).

The subject of coerced sexual activities in the context of war/armed conflict is a contentious one. Feminists disagree on where female victimisation ends, and agency, if exhibited at all, begins. Let us explore this in more detail.

Feminist Debates About Coerced Sexual Activities

We begin with Fogelman (2012). Fogelman (2012, p. 22) prefers to use the term 'entitlement rape', rather than survival sex. For her, terms such as 'sex in exchange for food' facilitate victim precipitation. According to her analysis of 'survival sex' during the Holocaust, this was an act of rape, where, in this example, the male perpetrator feels entitled to rape the female victim because he believes he has done her a favour. In line with Fogelman's analysis, more recently scholars have described coerced sexual activities, particularly when children are involved, as sexual exploitation and abuse (SEA) (Ferris, 2007, Freccero, Biswas, Whiting, Alrabe, & Seelinger, 2017; Highgate, 2007; Karim & Beardsley, 2016; Mudgway, 2017; Nduka-Agwu, 2009; O'Brien, 2011; Olivius, 2016a, 2016b).

Since the 1990s, there have been reports of this violence against local women and children by aid workers, peacekeepers, humanitarian workers and community leaders in post-conflict, crisis and emergency settings. In 2003, the Secretary General produced a Bulletin entitled *Special Measures for Protection from Sexual Exploitation and Sexual Abuse*. In it, sexual exploitation is defined as:

> [A]ny actual or attempted abuse of a position of vulnerability, differential power, or trust, for sexual purposes including but not limited to profiting monetarily, socially or politically from the sexual exploitation of another.

(Heit, 2009). According to estimates, between 260,000 and 350,000 civilians were shot, stabbed and burned alive during the massacre (Collins, 2017). Based on the 'pressure cooker theory', discussed in Chapter 1, it was believed that these 'comfort stations', by offering sex on demand, would satisfy men's innate sexual appetites. This would then curtail their desire for/need to rape.

While sexual abuse is defined as: 'the actual or threatened physical intrusion of a sexual nature, whether by force or under unequal coercive conditions' (United Nations Secretary General's Bulletin, 2003). This type of survival/transactional sex has been documented in peacekeeping missions in Kosovo, the DRC, West Africa, Haiti, East Timor and Cambodia (Karim & Beardsley, 2016; O'Brien, 2011). In this context, local women and children provide sex in exchange for food or other aid.

Many of the allegations of SEA by peacekeepers emerged prior to 2000. It was only in 2003 that the then UN Secretary General, Kofi Annan, prohibited SEA by UN forces (Mudgway, 2017; see Ferris, 2007 for more details of the responses by the UN High Commissioner for Refugees and the UN more generally). Since this time, the UN has adopted a zero-tolerance approach to SEA, banning peacekeepers from exchanging sex for money or for food. Despite this, transactional sex between peacekeepers and local women persists (Karim & Beardsley, 2016). In the last few years, research has uncovered SEA against young male refugees (Freccero et al. 2017; I will return to this in Chapter 6).

Feminists have criticised the UN zero-tolerance approach for the lack of agency women are afforded and for failing to consider the legitimacy of survival/transactional sex (Mudgway, 2017). Feminists such as Diane Otto (2007 as cited in Mudgway, 2017; Nduka-Agwu, 2009) believe that 'survival sex' – even when entered into as a result of poverty/unemployment – does involve consent and therefore should be treated differently from sexual offences such as rape, forced prostitution or sexual slavery. However, as Mudgway (2017, pp. 1456–1457) states:

> The assumption that these women are exercising agency in their 'choice' to engage in survival sex oversimplifies the reality of such relationships. It is not about agency…it is about survival.

And yet, Otto is not alone. Other feminists have raised concerns about reductive explanations of women's involvement in survival/transactional sex and the global sex trade more broadly (see Kempadoo, 2001; Kimm & Sauer, 2010; Sjoberg, 2013; Sullivan, 2003). In particular, concerns are raised around either/or binary positions that frame actions as either free or forced; voluntary or involuntary (O'Connor, 2017, p. 9). These writers encourage us to adopt a more nuanced approach, one that appreciates the complex nature of the choices women make in conflict and post-conflict settings.

These debates can be mapped onto larger debates about sex work and prostitution. Briefly, these fall into two main categories: abolitionists/radical feminists and sex radicals (Carline, 2011). The former view prostitution as a form of violence against women. They believe violence is intrinsic to prostitution and 'the distinction between "forced" and "voluntary" prostitution is… a myth' (Weitzer, 2005, p. 935). For these feminists, some type of coercion, exploitation and domination is always present (Weitzer, 2005). At the other end of the spectrum are the sex radicals who adopt a more progressive outlook. They reject the notion that prostitution or sex work more generally, '…is always already exploitative and victimizing…' (Carline, 2011, p. 316). They prefer to use the term sex worker and argue that sex work can and should be regarded as a legitimate from of labour.

While I recognise the merits (and indeed the shortcomings) of both view-points, I believe that, in the context of coerced sexual activities during war/armed conflict, we should adopt Liz Kelly's (1988) notion of a continuum of sexual violence, where at one end of the spectrum we have rape and aggressive acts of sexual violence, and at the other end, we have a range of consensual acts that are submitted to under duress and coercion. For my discussion of forced prostitution and survival/transactional sex in Iraq and Syria, respectively, I will employ Sjoberg and Gentry's (2008, p. 18) 'relational autonomy approach'. This approach views individual choices as '…neither completely independent of context (reactively autonomous) nor entirely involuntary (dependence), but somewhere in between, where they maintain identity independence but decide in a socially constrained world'. Put simply, '…no choice is completely independent either of its chooser or its context' (see also Sjoberg, 2007).

In cases where women have been trafficked for sexual purposes (Iraq) or have been enslaved for sexual purposes (Syria), I lean more towards the radical femi-nist viewpoint and regard these as acts of violence against women, where coer-cion, exploitation and domination are clearly present.

Having outlined the various types of coerced sexual activities relative to war/armed conflict, as well as the debates that arise when we try to understand women and girls' relationship to these behaviours (victims or agents), we will now con-sider such activities in post-invasion/occupation Iraq.

Trafficking, Sexual Slavery and Forced Prostitution in Post-invasion/occupation Iraq

The Forced Migration Review reports that almost 3,500 Iraqi women went miss-ing between 2003 and 2007. The likelihood is that many were trafficked for the purposes of sexual slavery and forced prostitution (Dakkak, 2007; HRW, 2011; Marcovich, 2010). In a more recent report for *Reuters*, Emma Batha reports that at least 10,000 women and girls were abducted or trafficked for sexual exploita-tion since the start of the war in 2003 (Batha, 2015). Iraq is the country of origin. Key destinations include Syria, the United Arab Emirates and other countries in the Gulf (HRW, 2011).

In a report for BBC news, Lina Sinjab (2007) investigated the experiences of Iraqi female refugees in Syria. She shares the story of Rafif, a 14-year-old Iraqi girl who, banned from earning money in the formal economy, was forced into the illicit economy in order to survive. She worked in clubs making $30 dollars a night but could earn $100 dollars if she agreed to go with men to their private villas. She says:

> A woman came and spoke to my mother, who agreed to send me to these places. We needed the money. I have already been arrested for prostitution and sent back to Iraq, but I came back with a false passport.

As Sinjab reports, not all women 'chose' to enter the industry. Nada, a 16-year-old Iraqi girl, was left by her father at the Iraq–Syria border where five men kidnapped her and took her to Damascus. She was raped, sold and forced to provide sexual services. Hassan (2007), reporting for *The Independent* in Damascus, came across a similar story of female Iraqi refugees forced into the illicit economy in order to survive. She states: 'no one knows how many end up as prostitutes, but Hana Ibrahim, founder of the Iraqi women's group Women's Will, puts the figure at 50,000' (Hassan, 2007). Hassan (2007) interviewed Fatima, an Iraqi refugee and mother of two, who went to Syria after her husband was killed. Like Rafif, she was denied access to formal employment and had to resort to selling sex in order to survive. These are three examples, but they represent a larger problem. As a UN refugee worker noted at this time: '[w]e are coming across increasing numbers of women who do not manage to make ends [meet] and are therefore more vulnerable to exploitative situations such as prostitution' (as cited in Sinjab 2007).

In their 2010 report, *Prostitution and Trafficking of Women and Girls in Iraq,* the Organization of Women's Freedom in Iraq (OWFI) documented over 70 cases of trafficking and forced prostitution in 2008. They estimated that at least 200 women and girls were sold into sexual slavery each year. The report is based on a police investigation into a criminal ring responsible for trafficking 128 women from the province of Diyala in 2007 (HRW, 2011; OWFI, 2010). Many of these women and girls, some of whom were as young as 12, had been displaced and had either been tricked into prostitution as part of the criminal economy or sold sex as a survival mechanism (coping economy) (Zoepf, 2007). In addition, prostitution exposed these women to sexual violence and abuse, which can lead to sexually transmitted diseases and exposure to HIV/AIDS (Sjoberg, 2013).

Arranged and forced marriages were also used as a means for traffickers to transport women internally and internationally. In some cases, the families were responsible for forcing the girl into marriage in order to alleviate dire economic circumstances (HRW, 2011; U.S. Department of State, 2012). Here, we can draw on Cohn's (2013) observation that women's unequal status and vulnerability leave women and girls open to sexually exploitative relationships. The activities of traffickers can be placed in Peterson's criminal economy. As HRW (2011) note, these are sophisticated and complex criminal networks. Younger girls, especially those under the age of 16, were the most lucrative. Girls as young as 11 and 12 were sold for up to $30,000, while older women were sold for around $2,000 (HRW, 2011).

In terms of forced prostitution, as a form of structural GBV, OWFI (2010) report a substantial rise in the number of women who engaged in forced prostitution following the 2003 invasion/occupation (see also Marcovich, 2010; Micha, About-Atta, Macaud, & Barnes, 2011).

Jamjoom (2009) shares the story of Wedad, who recounts her experience of becoming a prostitute:

> It was extremely difficult to make the decision to do this, because nobody goes into this wanting to do it. My situation forced me into it because I couldn't find a job and the government didn't have a job for me.

Yanar Mohammed, who works for OWFI, estimates that there were thousands more women like Wedad, who were forced into prostitution. Speaking in 2009, she states: '[i]n many of the cases, this is what happens. She is either a widow or an orphan of this war, and she has no alternatives' (see Jamjoom, 2009). Similarly, in 2007, in an interview with Zoepf (2007) in *The New York Times*, Sister Marie-Claude Naddaf – a nun from the Good Shepherd convent located in Damascus – stated: 'so many of the Iraqi women arriving now are living on their own with their children because the men in their families were killed or kidnapped'. She continues: 'I met three sisters-in-law recently who were living together and all prostituting themselves. They would go out on alternate nights…and then divide the money to feed all the children'.

According to a report by HRW, in 2011, female victims of trafficking, and those who engaged in forced prostitution, were subjected to harsh and unfair treatment by the Criminal Justice System. Many of the women and girls caught up in the illicit economy found themselves in prison. The Iraqi government prosecuted and convicted female victims for illegal acts committed while they were being trafficked, for example, for using false documents and engaging in prostitution (HRW, 2011). At the time of their report, HRW (2011) accused the Iraqi government of doing little to tackle the trafficking of women and girls. They highlighted the lack of criminal prosecutions brought against those engaged in human trafficking and the negligible support for victims. Furthermore, despite the implementation of counter-trafficking laws in 2010, enforcing this law was not a priority for authorities (HRW, 2011).

At this point, it will be useful to return to our discussion of coping, combat and criminal economies. For Peterson, prostitution is a reflection of how these economies intersect (Peterson, 2009, p. 56). She states:

> […] an upsurge in prostitution subjects increasing numbers of women and girls to adverse conditions that impede their role in social reproduction, while it simultaneously 'satisfies' male desires for access to women's bodies in the combat economy (occupying forces as well as Iraqis), and provides illicit profits for pimps and traffickers in the criminal economy.

Employing a gendered lens allows us to appreciate that forced prostitution – either as a coping strategy or through trafficking – is not a natural or necessary part of war/armed conflict. As argued earlier, it is linked to macro-level, structural exploitative economic systems.

Masculinities of Empire, Postcolonialism and Neoliberalism

Forced prostitution (as a means of survival) and the trafficking of females for sexual purposes are examples of the physical and structural GBV that was perpetrated against women and girls in and out of Iraq. True (2010, p. 40) argues that, when trying to address global violence against women, many approaches fail to make connections between the impact of the '…financial crises, macroeconomic policies and trade liberalisation' and the occurrence of GBV. What is missing is a political economy approach that provides a thorough gendered analysis of the socio-economic (and political) conditions that facilitate GBV. Attention needs to be paid to the relationship between global economic processes, such as neoliberalism, which operate at the macro-level, and forced prostitution (both as a means of survival and as a result of trafficking), which operates at local level.

Jacobson (2013, p. 228) argues that the neoliberal model has had a profound global impact across the 'industrialized North and the developing South'. She traces the implementation of this model to the International Monetary Fund and the World Bank (this was also discussed in the previous chapter; see also Kempadoo, 2001 who discusses this in the context of the global sex trade). As a result of war/armed conflict, and the economic crises of the 1980s, national governments in developing regions borrowed from these two western institutions. Their loans were approved on condition that these countries adopted the neoliberal model (Jacobson, 2013). As Isenberg notes, military subcontracting and privatisation are just some elements of neoliberalism (Isenberg, 2011). In the context of Iraq, and under the leadership of the Bush administration, to paraphrase Looney (2004, p. 1):

> Globalization, free markets, and reduced government involvement in the marketplace were regarded as the necessary components for rapid economic recovery in Iraq. For Iraqis, however, neoliberalism, particularly in its 'shock therapy' form, is just another example of an imprudent [w]estern experiment imposed upon a fragile state.

The key political justification for the imposition of this neoliberal regime was the argument that it was the only way to eradicate corruption from within Iraq's public sector (see Whyte, 2007 for a more detailed discussion). Yet, neoliberal reform in Iraq has come under widespread criticism from both within and outside the country (Duncanson, 2013; Looney, 2004). Herring and Rangwala (2005, p. 668), for example, argue that the economy of Iraq has been reconstituted from the top and from the bottom, reflecting a range of globalising agendas. Furthermore, they argue that, in order to understand how Iraq was reconstituted, we need to consider 'national, international and transnational' currency and investments; 'institutions of global neoliberalism' and US empire-building (Herring & Rangwala, 2005). Put simply, the Iraqi State, contrary to section 14 of UNSCR 1483 (2003), was locked into a neoliberal economic model. This is a constituent element of 'imperial globalization', a term coined by Herring and Rangwala (2005, p. 668). As such, we can apply Connell's masculinities of empire, postcolonialism and neoliberalism (Connell, 1998).

Space will not permit an in-depth review of the various Executive Orders (aimed at privatising the Iraqi economy) that were issued by the Coalition Provisional Army (see Whyte, 2007). Suffice to say, in addition to the 'profound and perhaps irreversible structural consequences for the Iraqi economy', under the Anglo-American privitisation agenda, 'national and international laws were… subordinated to neoliberal principles of economic organization' (Whyte, 2007, pp. 182, 186). In other words, this top-down socio-economic model, endorsed by the Coalition Provisional Army, involved western corporations and elites (those at the top), taking control over Iraqi oil revenue (those at the bottom) (Whyte, 2007; see also Duncanson, 2013).

Jacobson (2013, p. 229) argues that the neoliberal agenda – clearly a violation of UNSCR 1483 (2003), specifically the section concerning the development fund for Iraq – had gendered impacts. Speaking specifically about the gendered impact on war-shattered economies, she notes that neoliberalism involves 'shrinking the [S]tate', which leads to cuts in welfare and public spending. This monetary reduction, Jacobson argues, has an impact in precisely the areas that could be most enabling and empowering for women and girls affected by conflict. As demonstrated in this chapter, the privatisation of the economy in Iraq had a detrimental effect on females, particularly widows and female-headed households, where women and girls were forced into prostitution as a survival mechanism or, were trafficked for sexual slavery by profit-seeking criminal networks who exploited the informal economy in post-invasion/occupation Iraq.

Conclusion

A feminist ethics of war (discussed in the previous chapter) pays attention to interpersonal *and* structural forms of GBV during war/armed conflict. In the context of Iraq, this means acknowledging, as I have done in this chapter, the gendered consequences of this invasion and occupation, particularly for civilian women and girls, but for civilians more broadly.

The goal of this chapter was to unpack how neoliberal policies inform the violence(s) (both interpersonal and structural) of armed conflict. This chapter has demonstrated how the privatisation agenda of the west triggered the collapse of the formal economy in Iraq. This was replaced by an illicit economy which resulted in interpersonal and structural violence against women and girls. The detrimental impact of globalisation masculinities in Iraq forced women *and* men into the illicit economy. This chapter provides another example of how gender informs the experiences of victims, survivors and perpetrators, revealing the ways in which armed conflict impacts males and females in qualitatively different and differential ways.

Although the time period referred to in this piece is between 2003 and 2011, we can observe more recent examples of men's and women's engagement in informal economies within and beyond the conflict zone. This will be done in the following chapter with reference to Syria. Departing from the analysis provided here, in my discussion of survival sex in Syria and beyond, I unpack the relationship between extreme weather events, such as droughts, and coerced sexual activities.

Chapter 4

Structural Violence Against Conflict-affected Females in Syria

Introduction

> Wars are being fought on the bodies of women and children. Leymah Gbowee from the Women, Peace and Security Network (Taken from a video clip from the Stop Rape Now Website, n.d.)

> Sexual violence is the monstrosity of our century. Dr Denis Mukwege Director of Panzi Hospital (Stop Rape Now Website, n.d.)

> Sexual violence in conflict represents a great moral issue of our time and it merits the concerted focus of the Security Council. [It] casts a long shadow over our collective humanity. Statement made by Zainab Hawa Bangura, Special Representative of the Secretary-General on Sexual Violence in Conflict (United Nations Office for the Special Representative of the Secretary-General on Sexual Violence in Conflict [UN SRSG-SVC], 2015).

The statements above, made by an activist, a doctor and Zainab Hawa Bangura, respectively, reveal two things: (1) wartime rape and sexual violence are prioritised and indeed politicised within international security and (2) women (and children) are regarded as particularly at risk of such violence (Banwell, 2018; see also Aoláin, 2016; George & Shepherd, 2016; Puechguirbal, 2010; Shepherd, 2011; United Nations Security Council Resolutions [UNSCR], *1820*, 2008; *1888*, 2009a; *1960, 2010; 2106*, 2013a). As I argued elsewhere (see Banwell, 2018), this two-part message is reproduced within news media, policy and advocacy.[1] It is

---

[1]This chapter draws on my previous work on the securitisation of wartime rape and sexual violence in Syria. See Banwell (2018).

Gender and the Violence(s) of War and Armed Conflict:
More Dangerous to be a Woman?, 85–106
Copyright © 2020 by Stacy Banwell. Published by Emerald Publishing Limited.
This work is published under the Creative Commons Attribution (CC BY 4.0) licence.
Anyone may reproduce, distribute, translate and create derivative works of this work
(for both commercial and non-commercial purposes), subject to full attribution to the original
publication and authors. The full terms of this licence may be seen at http://creativecommons.org/
licences/by/4.0/legalcode" Knowledge Unlatched Open Access
doi:10.1108/978-1-78769-115-520201006

the securitisation narrative discussed in the Introduction. Here, as promised, I unpack it in more detail.

Writers from a variety of disciplines have drawn attention to the securitisation of wartime rape and sexual violence against women and girls (Baaz & Stern, 2013; Banwell, 2018; Crawford, Green, & Parkinson, 2014; Henry, 2014; Hirschauer, 2014; Kirby, 2015b; Mackenzie, 2010; Meger, 2016a, 2016b; Mertens & Pardy, 2017; True, 2010). Meger (2016a, 2016b), in her analysis of the securitisation of rape and sexual violence, draws upon Marx's (1867) concept of the commodity fetish to fully explain the processes at work. The commodity fetish, explains Meger (2016b), is where a material object, when it is exchanged for money, gains value that is independent from, and goes beyond, its obvious worth. As Meger (2016b, p. 151) states: '[t]he direct social relations that went into the production of the object become obscured behind the monetary value ascribed to it'. She believes that 'securitization similarly takes the securitized object as an independent material reality, and thereby obscures the underlying social relations that produce and give value to the object'.

There are, as Meger (2016a, 2016b) notes, three stages to the fetishisation of rape and sexual violence. First, sexual violence is homogenised as a discrete thing. It is identified as the most dangerous form of conflict violence. This removes it from the continuum of GBV that takes place during war/armed conflict (Meger, 2016b). It is also '...*generalized* across conflict-affected situations' (Meger, 2016a, p. 23 emphasis in the original; see also Meger, 2016b). Second, it becomes reified within media, policy and advocacy discourses. These influence international security agendas and practices. The third stage is about persuading donors that exceptional measures are required to address rape and sexual violence (Meger, 2016a; see also Baaz & Stern, 2013; Henry, 2014; Kirby, 2015b).

With reference to the securitisation of wartime rape in Syria, and following on from the previous chapter, this chapter examines structural forms of GBV in Syria: denial of reproductive healthcare (specifically a lack of access to safe abortion) resulting in unwanted pregnancy; denial of education, exacerbated by the use of early and forced marriage; and denial of employment opportunities, which leads to coerced sexual activities. Given that coerced sexual activities were discussed in the previous chapter, more time will be spent discussing the first two examples of structural GBV.

Fig. 1 (see page 87) is a perfect illustration of the securitisation of wartime rape. This figure and the press release that accompanied it (provided below) is another example of the visuality of master narratives discussed in the Introduction. The figure also exemplifies the rape-as-a-weapon of war narrative discussed in Chapters 1 and 2. In this figure, the penis and bullet are elided. It, and its ability to penetrate through rape, is presented as a weapon: one that is more effective than a gun. The poster was used by Amnesty International in 2009 as part of their 14-day London Underground poster campaign to draw attention to the use of rape as a weapon of war. The accompanying website stated that: '[t]he objective of the campaign is to highlight the effects of war on women and girls' (Amnesty International, 2009a). This focus on women and girls was reiterated in the Amnesty International press release by Kate Allen (Amnesty International, 2009b) who stated:

Fig. 1.   Amnesty – Rape Is Cheaper Than Bullets.[2]

> In previous and current conflicts, such as in Darfur and eastern
> Democratic Republic of Congo, hundreds of thousands of Wom-
> en's rights [are curtailed] and girls…are subjected to horrific acts
> of rape and sexual violence by armed forces and their perpetrators
> regularly go unpunished.

As established, women and girls are often depicted as wartime victims. This equation is often presented – both implicitly and explicitly – in visual form (this idea, and its visual representation, will be challenged in the following chapter when we consider images of women engaging in acts of sexualised violence). At first glance, the poster appears gender-neutral: men and boys can also be victims of wartime rape. However, for many of us – particularly those familiar with the securitisation of wartime rape and sexual violence – the gender of the perpetrator and victim is implied. For those in doubt, see the press statements cited above where women and girls are clearly marked as victims. I will return to the power of the visual within War Studies and International Relations more broadly shortly. First, I will outline the content and main arguments of the chapter.

Outline of the Chapter

The chapter begins with an outline of the terminology used and the analytical frameworks that are drawn upon to examine structural GBV in Syria. This is followed by an overview of the Syrian conflict. In order to redress the security agenda that prioritises rape and sexual violence against women and girls in Syria, I examine three examples of structural GBV. I start by examining women's access to safe abortion in conflict and/or crisis situations, arguing that the denial of reproductive healthcare services violates a number of international instruments that address GBV. Denial of reproductive healthcare will be discussed in relation to the Trump administration's foreign policy on abortion, specifically the defunding of

---

[2] This image was designed for Amnesty International UK by Different Kettle (2009a).

the United Nations Population Fund (UNFPA) in Syria.[3] The chapter then moves on to consider the importance of girls' access to education and how this is being curtailed by practices of early marriage that have increased since the onset of the conflict in Syria. Here, I demonstrate how fathers' use of early marriage forms part of the landscape of violence against women and girls in Syria. In my final example of structural violence, I examine how women resort to selling sex and/or providing sexual services as a means of survival within the informal economy in Syria and beyond. This is in response to increases in poverty and unemployment levels. I argue that both of these phenomena (poverty and unemployment) were exacerbated by the drought in Syria.[4] While a number of academics and experts alike have attributed the unrest in Syria, which led to the conflict, to the long-term drought (see Femia & Werrell, 2012; Gleick, 2014; Kelley, Mohtadi, Cane, Seager, & Kushnir, 2015), this is not my focus here. In Chapter 6, drawing on my concept of glocalisation masculinities, I explore the causal link between climate variability, extreme weather events (such as droughts) and armed conflict. My interest in this chapter is in exploring how these weather events – and the impact they have on the formal labour market – lead to coping, combat and criminal informal economies in Syria and beyond. While it is not possible to discern a simple cause-and-effect relationship between climate variability and the drought in Syria, research suggests that there is a correlation between these phenomena (Al-Riffai, Breisinger, Verner & Zhu, 2012; De Châtel, 2014; Gleick, 2014; Kelley et al., 2015). It is this research that I will draw upon when examining these issues.

This chapter offers a snapshot of three examples of structural GBV within and beyond the Syrian conflict zone. A chapter alone cannot do justice to each of these topics. Elsewhere I, and others, have written more extensively about these subjects (Banwell, 2018, 2019; Bartels et al., 2018; Foster, 2016; Foster, Arnott, & Hobstetter, 2017; Foster et al., 2016; Freedman, 2016; Mourtada, Schlecht, & DeJong, 2017). My purpose here is threefold: (1) to highlight the implications of the securitisation of rape and sexual violence (2) to broaden what is meant by GBV during armed conflict and (3) to link these examples of structural GBV to broader macro- and meso-level economic, environmental, political and institutional policies, practices and events.

Terminology and Analytical Frameworks

Structural violence, as defined in the previous chapter, refers to women's lack of access to healthcare, education and formal employment. As noted in Chapter 1,

---

[3]Elsewhere I have written about Trump's foreign policy on abortion in relation to gender essentialism and structural inequalities between the Global North and the Global South. See Banwell (2019).

[4]While Syria has experienced a number of droughts, the latest, which lasted two seasons, starting in 2006 and lasting until 2011, is considered to be the worst in the country's history (Gleick, 2014). This had a devastating effect, particularly in rural areas, on the country's agriculture, its livestock and its workforce (see Richani, 2016).

the definition of forced pregnancy, as outlined by the International Criminal Court, necessitates that a woman be forcibly made *and* kept pregnant, commonly through confinement. This then, '...excludes situations where the victim becomes pregnant by force but is not subsequently confined' (Grey, 2017, p. 921). I will adopt the term unwanted pregnancy when referring to Syrian women and girls who are raped and impregnated then subsequently denied access to safe abortion. It is my argument that this lack of access to safe abortion – which also denies women decision-making powers – is a form of structural violence that maintains women and girls' subordinate position (Banwell, 2019, p. 4). In this chapter, I reveal how the Trump administration's foreign policy on abortion, not only exacerbates females' experiences of interpersonal violence (wartime rape and forcible impregnation), it is also responsible for their experiences of structural violence (denial of access to safe abortion) (Banwell, 2019).

The feminist political economy approach demonstrates how females' social, political and economic marginalisation can be linked to macro-level systems and practices. In the context of this discussion, these will include economic globalisation and neoliberalism. The impact of these macro-level policies and practices, as well as State-level cultural and political policies and practices in Syria – patriarchy and neoliberalism – will be discussed in relation to all three examples of structural GBV. Whilst Syrian men and boys are victims of GBV within and beyond the conflict zone – indeed, their stories will be told in Chapter 6 – the fetishisation of rape and sexual violence in Syria occurs in relation to female victims. As such, women and girls' experiences of structural violence will form the basis of the discussion here.

Before we proceed, I want to return to a concern raised earlier in the book (see Chapter 2 for a discussion of the feminist postcolonial critique). Selective and sensationalist accounts of wartime rape and sexual violence are only part of the securitisation/fetishisation problem. A related issue is the tendency to speak for, or on behalf of victims/survivors. This often forms part of the broader western civilising mission. To redress this, this chapter will draw, as far as possible, on the words and statements of victims/survivors. For each of the examples of structural GBV, in addition to drawing on academic materials, I reference empirical research (in the form of published reports) carried out by NGOs and humanitarian organisations working on the ground in crisis settings. And for my discussion of unwanted pregnancies in Syria, I draw on data gathered by the Women's Media Centre (discussed in Chapter 1), which includes testimonies from witnesses and survivors.

The Conflict in Syria[5]

What follows, for the purposes of this chapter, is a brief overview of the conflict. According to the UN Office for the Coordination of Humanitarian Affairs,

---

[5]A comprehensive analysis of the origins, nature and current status of the conflict in Syria can be found in the United Nations (UN) General Assembly reports: *The Independent International Commission of Inquiry on the Syrian Arab Republic.*

11.7 million people in Syria require humanitarian assistance. Their 2019 report notes that extreme poverty and displacement continue to be key concerns, further stating: '[t]he widespread destruction of civilian infrastructure, depleted savings and limited economic opportunities have forced many to resort to harmful coping strategies. The result is extreme vulnerability' (United Nations Office for the Coordination of Humanitarian Affairs, n.d.). The latest figures (for the period March 2011–March 2019) published by *The Syrian Network for Human Rights*, places the civilian death toll at 224,948 (Syrian Network for Human Rights, n.d.).

At the time of writing, 2019, the crisis in Syria had reached its eighth year. It is likely that the conflict in Syria will be ongoing at the time this book is published and that the dynamics and actors involved will have changed considerably. The details provided below are based upon the period from when the conflict started, 2011, to the time of writing, July 2019.

The origins of the conflict can be traced to the Arab Spring pro-democracy demonstrations that took place in the southern city of Deraa in 2011 (BBC, 2019b). These started as peaceful protests against the government, but soon escalated into violent confrontations between government forces and armed rebels (BBC, 2019b). The conflict in Syria is complex. This is mainly due to the sheer number of actors involved. The US Defense Intelligence Agency has recorded as many as 1,200 different rebel groups involved in the fighting (see Schmitt & Mazzetti, 2013).

The situation is further compounded by regional and international support, for both sides of the conflict, in the form of military, financial, material and political assistance. Qatar, Saudi Arabia, Kuwait and Turkey provide financial support to oppositional forces in Syria (Gupta, 2016; Richani, 2016). Turkey, for example, provides assistance to Islamic groups (ISIS and the Al Nusra Front) who are competing for control of the border-crossing points between Syria and Turkey (Richani, 2016). The trading of stolen goods, money laundering and arms sales take place within these cross-border points (Richani, 2016, p. 57). Recruitment and rearmament have also taken place in Turkey. For Abboud (2017), the war economy in Syria is facilitated by the rise of this conflict elite. So, although these actors do not have direct control over these oppositional groups, their financial involvement – in the form of transactions and payments that secure the flow of goods and materials into regime areas – has contributed to the continuation of the conflict (Abboud, 2017; Banwell, 2018).

In terms of international support, the UK, France and the US assist groups opposing President Assad. Shia militias, including Hezbollah as well as Iraqi and Iranian militias, provide regional support for the Syrian government, while Russia provides international support (Banwell, 2018; Gupta, 2016; see Richani, 2016, for a more detailed breakdown of how these various actors have funded opposition groups in Syria). Russia was directly involved in the conflict from September 2015. It carried out airstrikes against opposition groups and provided support to soldiers on the ground (Beauchamp, 2017).

In 2014, Islamic State seized large parts of Iraq. Taking advantage of the chaos of the conflict in Syria, they secured land and power in the eastern part of the country. This meant that Assad and his army, as well as the numerous rebel groups, were then fighting a separate conflict against IS (BBC, 2019a). The latter – who changed their name to Islamic State of Iraq and Syria (ISIS) – faced resistance from government forces, rebel groups and Kurdish groups. This weakened their stronghold in northern and eastern parts of Syria (BBC, 2019a). In addition, Russia and a US-led multinational coalition conducted airstrikes against ISIS during this time. While ISIS were defeated in Raqqa, a city situated in the northeast of the country, in 2017 they were replaced by the extremist Al-Qaeda-linked group, Hayat Tahrir al-Sham (HTS) (Cockburn, 2017). The latter gained full control of Idlib province and began using 're-radicalisation' propaganda to recruit fighters from rival extremist groups to engage in further 'jihadist attacks' (Browne, 2018). Air strikes by the US, UK and France continued in 2018 and in 2019 Kurdish groups seized Baghouz in the eastern part of Syria (CNN, 2019). Despite numerous 'UN-mediated peace talks' (BBC, 2019b), confrontations between the different factions continue to this day, with opposing groups refusing to negotiate and agree a ceasefire (BBC, 2019a).

The Securitisation of Rape and Sexual Violence in Syria: What About Other Types of GBV?

Conflict-related sexual violence (CRSV) (as defined in Chapter 2) encompasses a whole range of behaviours, and yet:

> [...] both media and policy reports tend to either focus on rape at the expense of other forms of CRSV or, CRSV at the expense of other forms of conflict violence. This creates a hierarchy of victimization, placing rape and sexual violence above all other types of violence. (Banwell, 2018, p. 20)

The two main paradigms within the literature on wartime rape and sexual violence – rape as a by-product versus rape as-a-weapon of war – have already been discussed (see Chapters 1 and 2). Despite numerous critiques of the weapon-of-war paradigm (see Crawford, 2013; Kirby, 2012; Skjelsbæk, 2001), it is reproduced within media and policy documents, resulting in diverse behaviours being dealt with under the same security measure (Meger, 2016a). Here, the homogenising of sexual violence, as part of the securitisation process, leads to its fetishisation (Meger, 2016a).

This securitisation of rape and sexual violence can be applied to Syria. This has marginalised other forms of GBV (Alsaba & Kapilashrami, 2016; Crawford et al., 2014; Freedman, 2016; Meger, 2016a, 2016b). It is important at this point to review the violence(s) committed against women and girls in Syria. This includes: abduction and kidnapping to extract information (FIDH, 2012; The International Rescue Committee [IRC], 2013; UNFPA, 2017b; Women's International League for Peace and Freedom [WILPF], 2016); forced detention (FIDH, 2012; United Nations General Assembly, 2015; UNFPA, 2017b); forced recruitment (WILPF, 2016); and restrictions on females' freedom of

Fig. 2.   President Donald Trump Signing the Anti-abortion Executive Order, 2017 (Wikimedia.org, 2017).

movement (UNFPA, 2017b). Female political activists, and females who are related to male activists, have been subjected to forced detention and forced disappearance (Alsaba & Kapilashrami, 2016; HRW, 2014c; WILPF, 2016). Women have also been detained by the Syrian government for the purposes of weapons trading (WILPF, 2016). In addition, they have '…been executed, tortured and enslaved; denied access to fair trials; and denied access to health-care' (Banwell, 2018, p.17). To this spectrum of violence against women and girls in Syria, I add my three examples of structural violence. I will begin with the denial of reproductive health care that leads to unwanted pregnancies.

Fig. 2 shows the image of President Donald Trump signing the anti-abortion Executive Order. This reinstates the Global Gag Rule that was introduced by Ronald Reagan in 1984. While this is a partisan issue within US politics – every Democratic president has revoked the policy since its implementation, while every Republican president has reinstated it – the order signed on the 23 January 2017, goes further than any previous Republican-endorsed reinstatement. In brief, this Global Gag Rule withdraws US funding to international NGOs that either perform abortions as part of their family planning services or, 'provide abortion-related services' [6] (see Banwell, 2019, p. 1).

---

[6]As I write this chapter, the US has been criticised for threatening to veto a UNSCR on wartime rape because it offered sexual and reproductive healthcare to survivors. Concerned that this language was in fact referring to abortions, the US only agreed to sign the document once the language had been removed (see Ford, 2019 for more details).

For Rhiannon Cosslett, writing in *The Guardian* (2017), 'this photograph is what patriarchy looks like – a system of society or government in which men hold the power and women are largely excluded'. For me, the image was a reminder of Schweickart's essay, entitled *Reading Ourselves: Toward a Feminist Theory of Reading*. In this essay, Schweickart (1986) describes 'androcentric reading strategies'. This approach identifies texts that reproduce gender hierarchies, ascribing agency and universality to the 'male', while objectifying and immascualting [*sic*.] the 'female'. Here, we have both the text and the image of men authorising that text. Together they signify women's powerlessness and inferiority within a patriarchal political system. Here, it is useful to draw on the work of Christine Sylvester who uses art metaphors to understand the landscape of international relations. In her chapter, *Feminist Arts of International Relations* (2002), Sylvester (2002) outlines two feminist methods through which theories of the visual arts can be used to understand visual representations within international relations. The first is outlining. This involves 'inserting women…into the architects of war' (p. 276). The second is inlining. This recognises the difficulty of adding women into the existing landscape. The task, as identified by Sylvester (2002) and Managhan (2012), is to sight and cite what is marginalised, distorted and excluded from view. In Fig. 2., 'woman' is absent yet present. She is *cited*: The Anti-abortion Executive Order is based on women and their reproductive bodies. Yet, she is not *sighted*. She is figuratively and literally absent from the picture. Figuratively, she has no decision-making power in this situation.

In the same year as President Trump reinstated the Global Gag Rule, the US defunded UNFPA. While both are key elements of US foreign policy on abortion under the Trump administration, as UNFPA provides reproductive healthcare to women and girls affected by war/armed conflict, this will form the basis of the discussion here (for a detailed analysis of President Trump's revised Global Gag Rule, see Banwell, 2019). I included the image of President Trump as yet another example of the visuality of master narratives (see Introduction). Before we unpack the defunding of UNFPA, I will review the various instruments that have been put in place to address sexual GBV.

International Treaties that Address Sexual GBV Against Women and Girls

There are a number of international instruments that set out provisions for tackling sexual GBV. These are *The Convention on the Elimination of all Forms of Discrimination against Women* 1981 (CEDAW) (United Nations General Assembly, 1981); *The United Nations Declaration on the Elimination of Violence against Women* 1993 (DEVAW) (United Nations General Assembly, 1993); and *The Beijing Declaration and Platform for Action* 1995. The Beijing Declaration and Platform for Action (1995, p. 34) states that 'women have the right to the enjoyment of the highest attainable standard of physical and mental health'. This right, which is regarded as 'vital to their life and well-being', includes access to safe abortion.

Article three of the DEVAW declares that: '[w]omen are entitled to the equal enjoyment and protection of all human rights and fundamental freedoms in the political, economic, social, cultural, civil or any other field'. Among other things these include, '...[t]he right to be free from all forms of discrimination' and '[t]he right not to be subjected to torture, or other cruel, inhuman or degrading treatment or punishment' (United Nations General Assembly, 1993, p. 2). As noted in the previous chapter, violence against women and girls, as defined by the DEVAW, is any type of GBV that results in 'physical, sexual or psychological harm or suffering' (United Nations General Assembly, 1993). This is inclusive of physical, sexual and psychological violence *committed or condoned by the State*. These definitions encompass both interpersonal and structural violence.

In terms of UN Security Council Resolutions (UNSCR), UNSCR 2122 (2013b, p. 2) acknowledges women's right to 'access...the full range of sexual and reproductive health services, including...pregnancies resulting from rape, without discrimination.' While UNSCR 1889 (2009b, p. 4) addresses women's reproductive rights, their mental health and their 'access to justice, as well as enhancing [their] capacity to engage in public decision-making at all levels'. In addition, '[t]he Geneva conventions guarantee the rights to non-discriminatory medical care, humane treatment and freedom from torture, cruel, inhuman and degrading treatment' (Global Justice Centre, 2011, p. 22). Put simply, these conventions pledge comprehensive medical care for all individuals 'wounded and sick' in armed conflict (Global Justice Centre, 2011, p.1). Denial of access to safe abortion for women and girls impregnated through wartime rape violates their right to access the full and necessary medical care as guaranteed by Article 3 of the Geneva Conventions (Global Justice Centre, 2011).

To reiterate, US foreign policy on abortion has (1) banned new funding to NGOs that either perform abortions or, provide abortion-related services and (2) defunded UNFPA. As this policy marginalises women by denying them full decision-making power, it counts as a form of structural violence. In addition, this denial of access to safe abortion – which violates the international treaties and conventions listed above – is considered a form of torture. To place the defunding of UNFPA in context, let us review existing reproductive healthcare services for conflict-affected populations.

Reproductive Healthcare Provisions for Female Conflict-affected Populations

As the empirical research highlights, reproductive healthcare services for survivors of CRSV (see Onyango et al., 2016; Rouhani et al., 2016), particularly rape, are inadequate (Hakamies, Geissler, & Borchert, 2008; Krause et al., 2015; Masterson, Usta, Gupta, & Ettinger, 2014; Tappis, Freeman, Glass & Doocy, 2016; West, Isotta-Day, Ba-Break, & Morgan, 2016). Indeed, in cases of sexual violence-related pregnancies, there is a link between rape used in conflict and/or crisis situations and high rates of abortion (House of Lords, 2016). In countries that have restrictive abortion laws, the rate of unsafe abortion is high (Foster, 2016). This is also the case in crisis and conflict settings. As Foster (2016) notes, in such contexts, this has the greatest impact on young, poor, displaced and refugee women. It is estimated that unsafe abortions account for 25% of maternal deaths in crisis settings (Foster, 2016), while globally, every year, 50,000 deaths are caused by unsafe abortions (Foster, 2016; see also Bouvier, 2014; Shah, 2016). According to estimates provided by the World Health Organisation (WHO), 22 million unsafe abortions are performed annually (WHO, 2011 cited by Bouvier, 2014, p. 579). Unsafe abortions are defined as: '[p]rocedures for terminating an unintended pregnancy, carried out either by persons lacking the necessary skills or in an environment that does not conform to minimal medical standards, or both' (WHO, 2011 cited by Bouvier, 2014, p. 579; see also Foster et al., 2016; Schulte-Hillen, Staderini, & Saint-Sauveur, 2016).

Access to emergency contraception and/or safe abortion are vital resources for those forcibly impregnated as a result of rape (Bouvier, 2014; see also Duroch & Schulte-Hillen, 2015). Unfortunately, in conflict/crisis and post-conflict/crisis settings, where such resources are limited, our knowledge of sexual violence-related pregnancies is compromised (Onyango et al., 2016; Rouhani et al. 2016). While researchers have addressed the issue of women's access to safe abortion in humanitarian settings (Duroch & Schulte-Hillen, 2015; Foster et al., 2016; Foster et al., 2017; Schulte-Hillen et al., 2016; Tousaw et al., 2017), only research by Onyango et al. (2016) and Rouhani et al. (2016) specifically addresses the experiences of raped women seeking abortions in conflict/crisis settings (see Banwell, 2019, for a more detailed review).

For NGOs working with survivors of rape, aside from the chapter on abortion care in the revised Inter-agency Working Group (IAWG) *Field Manual on Reproductive Health in Crises 2010*, and some reference to abortion in the *Clinical Management of Rape Survivors* (WHO, 2004), there are very few guidelines on safe abortion and post-abortion care for survivors. This is also the case for the Minimum Initial Service Package for reproductive health. This package – which outlines the set of priority activities to be implemented at the onset of an emergency – aims to 'prevent and manage the consequences of sexual violence' (see Inter-agency Working Group on Reproductive Health in Crises, 2011). And yet, access to safe abortion following rape is afforded very little attention. It is against this backdrop that I review President Trump's foreign policy on abortion.

As noted earlier, the political economy approach attributes women's social, political and economic marginalisation to macro-level systems and practices. In this example of structural GBV, I consider economic globalisation. To paraphrase Shangquan (2000), economic globalisation, at its simplest, refers to the interdependence of world economics and increases in the international trade of commodities and services (Shangquan, 2000). It is a system that can create barriers for the provision of universal reproductive healthcare. For illustration, I will review the impact of the defunding of UNFPA.

The Defunding of UNFPA and its Impact in Syria

According to their website, UNFPA is responsible for the reproductive healthcare of women and youth in over 150 countries. To put it another way, this translates to over 80% of the world's population. This provision extends to women and girls in crisis situations (UNFPA, n.d., About Us). Although UNFPA does not promote abortion, it promotes 'universal access to voluntary family planning'. In contexts where abortion is illegal, UNFPA believes women should have access to post-abortion care, particularly when it is needed to save their lives. In countries where abortion is legal, UNFPA advocates for women's access to safe abortion (UNFPA, n.d., FAQ). UNFPA receives approximately $75m in financial support from the U.S. (Sampathkumar, 2017). During 2016, UNFPA (with this financial support from the US) prevented 2,340 maternal deaths, '[prevented] 947,000 unintended pregnancies' and '[prevented] 295,000 unsafe abortions' (UNFPA, 2017a).

The US is one of UNFPA's largest donors (Banwell, 2019). During 2017 and 2018, the Trump administration implemented the 'Kemp-Kasten amendment' thereby withholding funding from UNFPA. Dating back to 1985, this policy is based on the conviction that UNFPA supports coercive abortion in China. Despite the lack of evidence to support this claim (see Kaiser Family Foundation, 2019), the US State Department still withheld $32.5m from the 2017 budget (Kaiser Family Foundation, 2019; Sampathkumar, 2017). This policy will impact vulnerable women and girls in crisis and emergency situations who require comprehensive reproductive healthcare, including access to safe abortion (Banwell, 2019).

Let us consider the impact of the defunding of UNFPA for women and girls affected by the conflict in Syria. In 2016, UNFPA provided services to victims of GBV both within and beyond the conflict zone (UNFPA, 2017a). Victims included women, men and children. Women and girls of reproductive age, who were victims of child and/or forced marriage, were exposed to forced and unprotected sex (more on child marriage shortly). This also placed them at an increased *risk* of unwanted pregnancies (see Save the Children, 2014). In cases of unwanted pregnancies, the defunding of UNFPA has impacted their access to safe abortion should they require it. The defunding of UNFPA also has implications for female victims of wartime rape in Syria.

Research shows that rape has been used as a weapon of war in Syria (UN General Assembly, 2013b; UN SRSG-SVC, 2015; Human Rights and Gender Justice, MADRE, The WILPF, 2016). The Women's Media Centre has documented 162 stories on rape and sexual violence in Syria between March 2011 and March 2013 (Wolfe, 2013). While other reports have documented the abduction (for purposes of sexual slavery) and rape of Yazidi women by ISIS (see Human Rights Council [HRC], 2016; Human Rights Watch [HRW], 2015a). Details of the impregnation (resulting in unwanted pregnancies) of Yazidi women and girls are also included in these reports. While some women were forced to take birth control during their captivity, this was not the case for all women and some were impregnated following rape (HRC, 2016).

A number of women gave birth while they remained in captivity, some gave birth after they had been released and others gave their babies away (HRC, 2016). Trying to retrieve accurate data on the number of women and girls who were raped and impregnated during the Syrian conflict is challenging. This is due to abortion laws in Syria. In this context, abortion is only permitted if the woman's life is in danger.

For women and girls who do not meet Syrian abortion law requirements, there was a reluctance to discuss pregnancies resulting from rape, especially when survivors wanted to terminate those pregnancies (HRC, 2016). This is supported by Stoter who states: '[t]he women hardly talk about pregnancy. Many pregnant women seek abortions to avoid being stigmatized after spending months in sexual slavery by IS militants' (Stoter, 2015).

Despite the law surrounding abortion in Syria, survivors have sought and undergone abortions. Those working in the medical profession report that they have provided girls with abortion pills or performed abortions themselves (Stoter, 2015). This is corroborated by the UK select committee who interviewed survivors about access to safe abortion following rape and forced impregnation (House of Lords, 2016). The WMC also includes cases of women seeking to terminate pregnancies resulting from rape.

The head of the UNFPA, Dr Babatunde Osotimehin, has voiced her concerns about the number of pregnant Syrian refugees who are displaced (see Spencer, 2016). According to reports, 500,000 pregnant Syrian women remain in the country or neighbouring regions (van der Mensbrugghe, 2016). As van der Mensbrugghe (2016) points out:

> More than ever, access to abortion services is a critical form of medical care for these wartime rape victims, as well as a protected right under the Geneva Conventions. Yet safe abortion services remain woefully lacking.

As a result of the conflict, which began in 2011, the maternal mortality ratio in Syria has increased from 49% to 68% per 100,000 (see Centre for Reproductive Rights, 2017). These maternal deaths are attributed to the delays and overall challenges in accessing necessary reproductive healthcare, including access to safe abortion (Centre for Reproductive Rights, 2017). Those working within and beyond the conflict zone have highlighted the importance of providing contraception as both a safety and survival mechanism. A lack of access to contraception, including emergency contraception, leaves victims dealing with both the physical and psychological consequences of rape and, in cases of forced impregnation, the unwanted pregnancy that follows (see Women on Waves, n.d.).

As a reminder: in 2017, the Trump administration defunded UNFPA. This resulted in a funding gap of $16 million in Syria (Merelli, 2017). In their annual review of Syria for 2015, UNFPA note that 4.2 million of the 13.5 million people who required humanitarian aid within the conflict zone, were females of reproductive age (UNFPA, 2015). Of the five million women and girls who have been displaced and affected by the conflict, 430,000 require reproductive healthcare. They will be impacted by these funding cuts. The increased risk of unwanted pregnancies for victims of sexual violence-related pregnancies is also addressed in the report and UNFPA explain how cuts to funding impedes their ability to deliver the necessary reproductive healthcare to these female survivors (UNFPA, 2015).

With the support of US funds, UNFPA set up a survivors' centre in Duhok, Iraq. Among other things, it provides reproductive healthcare to Syrian women and girls who were raped and held captive by ISIS. This centre will be impacted by the defunding of UNFPA (Cauterucci, 2017). Likewise, the maternity hospital in the Za'atari refugee camp in northern Jordan, which is run by UNFPA, will also be impacted by US funding cuts (Cauterucci, 2017). This hospital offers reproductive healthcare to Syrian women and girls who face challenges such as 'lack of proper medical care, poor access to reproductive health services [and]unwanted pregnancies'. In terms of reproductive healthcare, the clinic provides 'family planning, post abortion care and counselling, prevention and management of sexually transmitted infections [and] clinical management of rape'. In addition, the clinic provides services for girls who have been exposed to forced and/or unprotected sex as a result of forced marriage (European Commission, n.d.).

And finally, UNFPA provides support for 19 safe spaces across Jordon. The list of services provided by these safe spaces includes emergency reproductive healthcare, which can include abortion (Sutton, Daniels, & Maclean, 2017). They also ran Minimum Initial Service Package training workshops and distributed reproductive healthcare kits (these were mainly rape kits) to Syrian refugees in Lebanon (Masterson, 2013).

In relation to the conflict in Syria, the defunding of UNFPA has impacted the lives of women and girls who are seeking to terminate sexual violence-related pregnancies. To reiterate, denying females' access to safe abortions, which results in unwanted pregnancies – themselves a result of forcible impregnation – should be considered a form of structural violence. It is a type of violence that is obscured by a security agenda that focuses narrowly on rape and sexual violence.

While UNFPA is a UN agency, it delivers vital reproductive healthcare services in developing countries. In the context of economic globalisation – where world economies are interdependent (Shangquan, 2000) – the defunding of UNFPA has a detrimental impact on developing countries who rely upon this support from UNFPA to deliver requisite reproductive healthcare to their citizens. Indeed, in the context of Syria, as we will see, economic crises, extreme droughts, increasing engagement with neoliberal policies, as well as the impact of the current conflict, have all 'devastated the economy' (Gobat & Kostial, 2016, p. 10). This means that the country continues to rely on foreign aid to deliver, among other things, reproductive healthcare (see Banwell, 2019).

We now move on to consider the second example of structural GBV in Syria: denial of education.

Child Marriage and the Denial of Education

Before we delve into this example, I want to outline the relationship between child marriage and the denial of education. The relationship between these two phenomena is circular; the destruction of education facilities and the chaos of the armed conflict have led to an increase in early and forced marriage in Syria (used mainly as a social and economic coping mechanism). The use of early and forced marriage prevents girls from accessing/completing their education. The importance of education, particularly for vulnerable populations, is included in goal 4 of the UN Sustainable Goals. This includes women and girls in conflict-affected areas. Let us review this in more detail.

At the age of 14 Malala Yousafzai was shot in the head by a member of the Taliban for her beliefs about women's right to education. In 2014, Boko Haram abducted 276 girls from a school in Chibok, Nigeria. This denial of education, and the violence used to achieve this, constitutes both physical and structural violence as outlined in the DEVAW (defined in the previous chapter; see also John, 2016). Visible cases such as Malala and the Chibok girls – which involved direct physical violence and the use of arms – have received international attention. Whilst they draw attention to the global problem of violence against women and girls, they overshadow more subtle forms of structural violence that impact women and girls' access to education (John, 2016). As John (2016, p. 195) highlights:

> While such attention is important and necessary, there is an on-going, less direct and less physical but equally powerful and painful violence that continues to slowly, and less visibly, disrupt and prevent girls and women from their rightful education endeavors – this is the hidden hand of poverty, patriarchy and power struggles which constitute systemic and structural violence.

Here, I broaden what is meant by GBV by examining the impact of both physical/direct and structural violence on girls' access to education within the Syrian conflict zone.

According to the Syrian Network for Human Rights (2013), 1,000 schools have been used to detain and torture civilians. Girls' access to education is further compromised by the use of explosive weapons in civilian-occupied zones (UNFPA, 2017b). In their global analysis of attacks on schools between 2011 and 2015, Save the Children reported that over half of these occurred in Syria (Save the Children, 2015). And a report published by the World Bank in 2017 noted that 53% of schools had been damaged in Syria, while 10% had been completely destroyed (as cited in Save the Children, 2018). Various reports detail the level of damage and destruction to Syrian schools since the conflict began in 2011. This information is collated by The International Center for Transnational Justice (hereafter ICTJ) in their 2018 report – *'We didn't think it would hit us': Understanding the impact of attacks on schools in Syria.*

This deliberate targeting of education facilities has implications for GBV. Not only does this destruction to property curtail girls' future career prospects – thereby maintaining their subordinate position, which speaks to the definition of structural violence outlined in this book – it can also be linked with other forms of GBV: early and forced marriage (International Center for Transnational Justice [ICTJ], 2018; Save the Children, 2014; the United Nations Children's Education Fund [UNICEF], 2014; UNFPA, 2017b; Women's Refugee Commission [WRC], 2016).

As a result of the crisis in Syria, practices of early and forced marriage have increased (Bartels et al., 2018; Mourtada et al., 2017; UNICEF, 2014).

Child marriage, in many cases, is used to alleviate extreme poverty among Syrian girls (HRC, 2016; Inter-agency, 2013; The Freedom Fund, 2016; Spencer et al., 2015; WILPF, 2016). Despite these attempts to provide for and protect their daughters, family use of child marriage is problematic. It involves young girls marrying much older men, which increases the risk of sexual exploitation and abuse (Save the Children, 2014). It also, as noted above, impedes access to education (UNICEF, 2014; WRC, 2016). Females who enter into marriage at a young age are required to leave school in order to care for their husbands or to begin their childbearing and childrearing responsibilities. As articulated by a Syrian woman from Daret Azza sub-district, in Aleppo: '[s]ome say that when a 14-year-old girl is made to marry, she must leave school and be controlled by a man who will prevent her from leaving the house' (as cited in UNFPA, 2017b, p. 67).

This denial of education is both situational (resulting from the conflict) and cultural (rooted in patriarchal beliefs about gender roles and gendered divisions of labour). And, as noted above, the relationship is circular. Before unpacking this in more detail, it is important that we clarify what is meant by child marriage.

Child marriage refers to the marriage of a girl or boy under the age of 18. It includes both formal marriages and informal unions (the latter involves children living together as though married; UNICEF, 2016 as cited in Bartels et al., 2018). It is a practice that affects both genders, with girls making up the majority of cases. Broadly speaking, early marriage encompasses child marriage. Forced marriage is a marriage where one, or indeed both parties, have not provided their full and free consent to the union (Bartels et al., 2018). This can and does include children under the age of 18 (Bartels et al., 2018). Forced marriage was a key feature of the 1991–2002 civil war in Sierra Leone where thousands of women and girls were abducted by insurgents and taken into the bush and forced to marry their kidnappers (Haenen, 2013). Referred to as bush-wives, these women and girls were victims of rape, forced impregnation, forced pregnancy and forced abortion (Gong-Gershowitz, 2009; Haenen, 2013; see also O'Brien, 2016). Forced marriage may also involve various forms of productive and domestic labour and may be used to punish and humiliate the enemy as well as reproduce the nation (Aijazi & Baines, 2017, p. 466).

Child marriage and forced marriage are global issues (Girls not Brides, 2017), however, my focus is on Syria. Whilst it is true that child and forced marriage can cause long-term physical and mental harms,[7] in order to move beyond examples of interpersonal violence, as per the current security framework, my focus is on structural violence, specifically girls' lack of access to education.

Child marriage is considered a human rights violation (this is recognised by a number of Conventions; see Bartels et al., 2018, p. 2 for a detailed list).

---

[7]This may include but is not limited to, an increased risk in intimate partner violence, sexually transmitted diseases and sexual exploitation and abuse (Save the Children, 2014).

In addition, various UN documents and international conventions provide guidance to States on how they can meet their human rights obligations in relation to early and forced child marriage. These include, but are not limited to, *The Committee on the Elimination of Discrimination against Women; The Committee on the Rights of the Child; The Human Rights Committee; The Committee on the Elimination of Racial Discrimination; The Committee on Economic, Social and Cultural Rights; and The Committee against Torture.* To follow on from my discussion of unwanted pregnancy as a form of torture, in a recent statement, the Special Rapporteur on Torture and Other cruel, Inhuman or Degrading Treatment or Punishment, argued that child and forced marriage should be considered forms of GBV that amount to torture. Finally, child, early and forced marriages were included under Goal 5 of the UN Sustainable Development Goals (United Nations General Assembly, 2016).

Early Marriage in Syria

Empirical research has found that early marriage – a long accepted practice in Syria – has increased since the conflict began, changing from a cultural practice to a coping mechanism (Bartels et al., 2018; ICTJ, 2018; UNFPA, 2017b; see also Mourtada et al., 2017). Child marriage is of particular concern for 'Syrian girls in refugee communities in Jordan, Lebanon, Iraq and Turkey' (Girls not Brides, 2017). In Jordan, for example, registered marriages involving girls under the age of 18 have increased from 12% in 2011 to 18% in 2012 and from 25% in 2013 to 32% in 2014 (Girls not Brides, 2017; see also UNICEF, 2014). As a result of the conflict, and increasing engagement with neoliberal policies, employment and livelihood opportunities for Syrians have diminished. Let me provide some historical context. During the 1980s, armed conflict and economic crises plagued the Arab region. As a result, Syria experienced a reduction in social spending. This ultimately led to the collapse of the economy and the withdrawal of public services and subsidies (Alsaba & Kapilashrami, 2016; Banwell, 2018). From 2000 onwards, the government adopted the neoliberal model. This involved transferring the control of the economy from the public to the private sphere (Abboud, 2017; Gobat & Kostial, 2016). This facilitated the rise in poverty and unemployment levels (Gobat & Kostial, 2016).

Despite the efforts of host countries, accommodating the influx of refugees fleeing the war in Syria has been challenging. HRW (2016a, 2016b) outlines some of the practical and institutional barriers Syrian refugees face in Lebanon and Jordan when trying to enrol their children in school. In Lebanon, these include: the imposition of additional school enrolment requirements; strict regulations relating to legal residency; employment-related restrictions (which impacts families' ability to pay for school-related costs, such as travel and school equipment) and classes being taught in unknown languages (HRW, 2016a). In Jordan, these barriers include 'refugee registration polices' that require children to provide identification cards to enrol in school as well as 'certification and documentary requirements' that many refugees do not have (HRW, 2016b).

Concerns about the lack of access to education, as a result of the conflict, were captured during focus group discussions with Syrian refugees:

> We were all pro-education; the priority was education before marriage. We wanted our daughters to reach at least the secondary education level. Things have changed now. Many young girls are resorting to early marriage due to their fear of the ambiguous future. I married off two daughters after the war, one was 18 and the other one was 12.

> 'We wished to study and get married, but now the situation is different' (as cited in Mourtada et al., 2017, p. 58).

During these focus group discussions, many of the participants admitted that they were against child marriage, but with the chaos of the conflict and the displacement that followed, some recognised the potential advantage of early marriage, particularly in relation to protecting a woman's honour (referred to as al Sutra) (Mourtada et al., 2017, p. 58). In the words of one participant:

> Fear of insecurity is a major factor. They are marrying early because of al Sutra. We have war. Many women are afraid of being raped, and if a married woman is raped, she is more likely to be forgiven by her husband but if an unmarried woman is raped, it will destroy her life. (as cited in Mourtada et al., 2017, p. 58).

Research by Save the Children (2014) has found that forced marriage – reportedly taking place in refugee camps – is used to restore family honour following rape. As one GBV expert noted (as cited in UNFPA, 2017b, p. 20):

> Forced marriage of a young girl to her cousin at a certain age existed before the crisis, but this practice has increased during the crisis because of the need to seek protection, the lack of men, the worsening economic situation, or because the girls are exploited, or threatened at gunpoint.

In addition to the use of early and forced marriage as a coping mechanism, research has also found that families are also relying on temporary marriages to protect their daughters from abduction. Ironically, however, these temporary marriages expose young girls to sexual exploitation and abuse as many are only married for a few hours before the marriage is annulled. In cases where the girls become pregnant, the lack of official registration of these marriages means that 'husbands' are exempted from any parental responsibility for the child (UNFPA, 2017b).

In this example, we move between a macro- and meso-level analysis. Here, using the feminist political economy approach, we can unpack how neoliberalism, at the macro-level informed/informs State-level economic policies and practices in Syria which, along with State-level cultural and patriarchal practices, heightens girls' exposure to GBV in the form of child marriage. This, and the concomitant denial of education, facilitates structural GBV. Regrettably, the preoccupation with wartime rape and sexual violence occludes this type of violence.

We will now move on to consider the final example of structural violence within and beyond the Syrian conflict zone: denial of formal employment opportunities; resulting in coerced sexual activities.

Survival Sex in Syria

Forced prostitution, trafficking and sexual slavery, outlined and defined in the previous chapter, form part of the landscape of coerced sexual activities in Syria (see The Freedom Fund, 2016; Shaheen, 2017). However, in order to cover the range of coerced sexual activities during war/armed conflict, as well as the multiple and complex causal factors, I will focus on survival sex in the context of Syria. Drawing on my analysis of forced prostitution (see previous chapter) as a form of structural violence, survival sex – which does not include the term 'forced', but is the result of poverty and unemployment – will also be understood as behaviour that emerges from a lack of alternative means to support oneself and/or family. It is examined here against the backdrop of a security agenda that constructs women as always and already vulnerable victims. By broadening our analysis of the violence(s) of war/armed conflict – to consider, in this instance, women's use of survival sex – we can begin to see women as three-dimensional characters; both victims and agents, who exercise relative autonomy (discussed in the previous chapter). This is not to underestimate the extreme conditions under which women make these coerced decisions.

As noted above, armed conflict and economic crises have resulted in the collapse of the formal economy in Syria resulting in mass poverty and unemployment. In 2015, poverty levels reached 83.5% in Syria, with extreme poverty reaching 69.3% (Gobat & Kostial, 2016; The Syrian Centre for Policy Research [SCPR], 2015). Exacerbated by the drought (see Gupta, 2016; Richani, 2016), and the increasing engagement with neoliberal policies, these conditions were heightened within the conflict zone (Banwell, 2018). Here, loss of property and employment, as well as the destruction of health and education services, has affected more than two-thirds of Syrians (Gobat & Kostial, 2016). In their review of six cities (Aleppo, Deraa, Hama, Homs, Idlib and Latakia) - which covers agriculture, health, education, housing, transport and energy – The World Bank's Syria Damage Assessment note that '[t]he conflict has set the country back decades in terms of its economic, social, and human development' (as cited in Gobat & Kostial 2016, pp. 21, 23). Here, I want to focus on the impact of the drought in more detail.

As Femia and Werrell (2012) note, the human and economic cost of the drought in Syria is substantial (see Al-Riffai et al., 2012 for a detailed assessment of the impact of the drought). As a result of the impact to livestock and agriculture, thousands of Syrians – particularly those in the northeast of the country, who rely on agricultural farming – have lost their livelihoods (Gupta, 2016;

Richani, 2016; Sohl, 2010). At least a million were left 'food insecure' and, as unemployment levels increased, millions of Syrians found themselves living in abject poverty (Gobat & Kostial, 2016; Gleick, 2014; Richani, 2016; Sohl, 2010). Over a million farmers fled to the cities in search of employment, however finding work was extremely difficult (Femia & Werrell, 2012; Gupta, 2016). This influx of people placed an increased strain on Syria's 'economically-depressed cities' where the '[p]oor have been forced to compete with poor not just for scarce employment opportunities, but for access to water resources as well' (Femia & Werrell, 2012; see also Gobat & Kostial, 2016). According to reports, 36,000 households from Al-Hassake Governorate (this amounts to around 200,000–300,000 people), for example, have moved to urban areas such as Damascus and Aleppo (Sohl, 2010). Accommodating this displaced population, as well as the million refugees fleeing from war-torn Iraq, further diminishes access to limited resources, particularly employment (De Châtel, 2014; Kelley et al., 2015; Sohl, 2010; see also The New Humanitarian, 2009).

It is within this context that the illicit economy flourishes (Gobat & Kostial, 2016). Informal economies were discussed in detail with reference to Iraq. Here, I will provide a brief reminder. In conflict zones, illicit economies consist of three types: coping, combat and criminal (Peterson, 2009). Coping economies revolve around survival, while combat and criminal economies are driven by military objectives and profit-making activities (Peterson, 2009). As noted by the Syrian Center for Policy Research (SCPR) in 2015, due to extreme poverty, and the lack of employment options, a huge number of Syrians were forced to work in the informal economy (as cited by Gobat & Kostial, 2016; see also De Châtel, 2014). This can be broken down by gender. Men from the various warring factions in Syria turned to combat and criminal activities (Banwell, 2018). They engage in activities such as kidnapping (HRW, 2015a; United Nations General Assembly, 2013b; WILPF, 2016); trafficking for sexual purposes (Freedman, 2016; The Freedom Fund, 2016; WILPF, 2016); economic and aid blockages (HRW, 2014c; United Nations General Assembly, 2015a); extraction and smuggling of oil (Gupta, 2016; Richani, 2016); trading in weapons (WILPF, 2016); and the smuggling of women and girls (Freedman, 2016; HRC, 2016). Conversely, Syrian women resorted to coping economies in the form of survival sex.

As established, in the absence of their husbands, who are missing or have been killed during the conflict, women become the head of the household. Faced with an increasing lack of employment opportunities, which were exacerbated by the drought, Syrian women have been providing sexual services in exchange for food and accommodation for their families (Amnesty International, 2016; Banwell, 2018; Spencer et al. 2015; The Freedom Fund, 2016; UNFPA, 2017b; United Nations High Commissioner for Refugees [UNHCR], 2015). As articulated by a GBV expert working on the ground in Syria: '[t]here are many cases of "sex for money", more than before, because of the economic situation and the absence of the male factor for various reasons' (as cited in UNFPA, 2017b, p. 30).

As well as the lack of access to formal employment, women are also denied access to the labour market in their host communities. The combination of the conflict, rising unemployment levels and the increased cost of living, resulting from the drought, has meant that many Syrians have fled to neighbouring regions such as Jordan and Lebanon in order to survive (Banwell, 2018). In these host communities, many female Syrian refugees are forced into the informal economy when restrictions are placed upon their right to access formal employment in these settings (Anani, 2013; Banwell, 2018; The Freedom Fund, 2016; UNHCR, 2015). In Lebanon, for example, many refugees resort to 'survival sex' to pay for increased living costs (The Freedom Fund). In 2012, the International Rescue Committee, in collaboration with ABAAD-Resource Center for Gender Equality, conducted a rapid assessment of GBV in Syria (see Anani, 2013). Survival sex was identified as one example of GBV experienced by Syrian women and girls (Anani, 2013). In the words of one focus group participant: '… if you want other help from other NGOs you should send your daughter or your sister or sometimes your wife… with full make-up so you can get anything… I think you understand me' (as cited in Anani, 2013, p. 76). More recently, The Freedom Fund (2016) found that Syrian refugee women were providing sexual favours in return for rent, food and employment in Lebanon.

In addition, empirical research has found that Syrian women seeking refuge in Europe are also impacted by this type of structural GBV (see Freedman, 2016). In this context, women provide sexual services to fund their travel to Europe (Freedman, 2016). Indeed, for women in refugee camps across Calais in France, coerced sex is a common survival strategy (Freedman, 2016). In other cases, women and girls find themselves victims of sexual harassment. Human Rights Watch (HRW) (2015b), for example, reported incidents of sexual harassment of female refugees in detention in Macedonia where women were offered preferential treatment in exchange for sex. Asma, a 20-year-old Syrian woman, shares her experience of being harassed by a police officer:

> He tried whatever he could to get me alone in a room with him. He used to approach me and whisper to me that I am very beautiful and that he would help me out, that he would personally look into my case. (HRW, 2015b, p. 17)

Coerced sexual behaviour, in the form of survival sex, relies on an understanding of coercion as a condition of unemployment (see previous chapter) and, as such, conceptualises survival sex as a form of structural violence. In Syria macro- and meso-level exploitative systems such as neoliberalism resulted in an increase in poverty and unemployment levels. These, in turn, were exacerbated by the drought. As a result, both genders were forced into the informal economy. Departing from the other examples in this chapter (and indeed coerced sexual activities in Iraq) the macro-level in this instance, not only takes into account economic and political foreign policy agendas, as well as global drivers, it also considers environmental forces. Indeed, moving beyond the fetishisation of wartime rape and sexual violence – to consider women's engagement with coerced sexual activities – necessitates that we extend the diagnostic framework to consider how climate variability and the extreme weather events it leads to (in this case, droughts), diminishes employment opportunities which, in turn, leads to coping, combat and criminal coping informal economies. As demonstrated, these are demarcated along gendered lines. This expansion of the analytical framework enables a holistic analysis of the causes and consequences of the structural and interpersonal violence(s) of war/armed conflict.

Conclusion

This chapter has exposed the shortcomings of the securitisation of wartime rape and sexual violence. By moving beyond examples of interpersonal violence to address structural forms of GBV in relation to the Syrian conflict, the discussion broadens our understanding of the violence(s) of war/armed conflict. All three examples of structural violence – denial of reproductive healthcare, resulting in unwanted pregnancies; denial of education, exacerbated by the use of child marriage (and vice versa); and denial of employment opportunities, leading to survival sex – are linked to broader macro- and meso-level economic, cultural and political policies and practices. In all three examples, we see how these exploitative systems and institutions (economic globalisation, neoliberalism, patriarchy) are exacerbated during conflict, thereby, at the very least, maintaining, but all too often, increasing women and girls' exposure to GBV. In case of survival sex, this form of structural violence can be linked to extreme weather events, such as droughts, caused by climate variability. The political economy approach was utilised to examine these examples of structural violence. In the next chapter, returning to examples of interpersonal violence, we expand our discussion of the use of the visual in representations of armed conflict. Here, focusing on male victimisation – thereby posing a challenge to the title of this book – I unpack female perpetrators of sexualised violence and torture.

Chapter 5

War-on-terror Femininity and the Sexualised Violence(s) at Abu Ghraib

Introduction

In 2016, while staying in New York City (NYC), I attended Laura Poitras's immersive installation, Astro Noise, at the Whitney Museum of American Art. Curated by Jay Sanders, this experience builds upon themes found in Poitras' earlier work documenting life in post-9/11 America. Among other things, the collection addresses: the war on terror, the US drone programme, Guantánamo Bay and themes of occupation and torture (Laura Poitras Astral Noise). In one of the video installations of Astro Noise, we watch New Yorkers respond to the smoking pit of Ground Zero (the relevance of this will become clear shortly). Despite its critical appraisal, unlike my experience at the 9/11 Memorial and Museum site later that same day, this installation did not leave a lasting impression. At Ground Zero, I watched teenagers take 'selfies' of themselves next to the North and South Pools before asking the adults with them: 'What happened here?', 'What are the pools for?', 'Whose names are these?' While '[t]aking selfies at horror sites, like concentration camps, Ground Zero or disaster-stricken areas, has become a growing trend on social media websites…' (Hodalska, 2017, p. 407) – and can be placed within the broader landscape of dark tourism, which involves travel to sites of tragedy and death – what I witnessed at Ground Zero was not quite the same. For these teenagers, there was a tacit understanding that they were at a memorial site of some sort. However, they were unaware of the exact details. They had not chosen to explicitly engage in dark tourism. In this instance, they appeared to have happened upon a 'horror site'. The details of what, when and who the memorial site was paying tribute to, did not seem to matter. Taking a picture (with a smile on their faces) and being 'seen' at or being superimposed onto history, is what mattered. Whose or what history was less important. Incidentally, the teenagers I observed, continued to take 'selfies' once they had

Gender and the Violence(s) of War and Armed Conflict:
More Dangerous to be a Woman?, 107–134
Copyright © 2020 by Stacy Banwell. Published by Emerald Publishing Limited.
This work is published under the Creative Commons Attribution (CC BY 4.0) licence.
Anyone may reproduce, distribute, translate and create derivative works of this work
(for both commercial and non-commercial purposes), subject to full attribution to the original
publication and authors. The full terms of this licence may be seen at http://creativecommons.org/
licences/by/4.0/legalcode" Knowledge Unlatched Open Access
doi:10.1108/978-1-78769-115-520201007

learned of the mass death and destruction that had taken place at this site. As Hodalska (2017, p. 416) notes, '[s]elfies taken at places of horror are ghoulish souvenirs, mobile memories'.

These are not the only 'mobile memories' we can associate with 9/11 and the war on terror that followed. As we will see in this chapter, seven US soldiers also used mobile phone cameras to pose with smiling faces; only this time it was to document the sexualised violence and torture of Iraqi prisoners. To be clear, I am not equating teenagers taking 'selfies' at Ground Zero with the behaviour of the American soldiers. What happened at this memorial site, on the 11th September 2001, was the catalyst for the war on terror. On this now historic day, the Islamic terrorist group al-Qaeda hijacked four US passenger planes. Two of the planes were crashed into the North and South towers of The World Trade Centre in NYC. The third crashed into the Pentagon while the fourth crashed into a field. In response to these attacks, the US launched the war on terror. Part of this campaign involved the invasion and occupation of Iraq (see Chapter 2). The sexualised violence and torture committed at Abu Ghraib (a prison in Iraq) falls within this 'war'. What took place at this prison was captured on mobile phone cameras by the soldiers involved. Thirteen years later, mobile memories, in the form of 'selfies' at the Ground Zero memorial site, still form part of the post-9/11 story. It is this that I reflect upon here.

Outline of the Chapter

This chapter provides a gendered analysis of the war on terror. This is a macro-level foreign policy agenda launched by the Bush administration following the 9/11 terrorist attacks. It is not limited to the US. Other nations, most notably the UK, also joined in this global fight against terrorism. As this chapter will focus on a particular enactment of the war on terror – the invasion and occupation of Iraq and the sexualised violence and torture at Abu Ghraib – I will limit the focus to US involvement. As such, at the meso-level, I will examine the US military, as well as militarised femininity. At the micro-level, the chapter will unpack the involvement of female soldiers in the violence(s) that took place. American exceptionalism is at work across all three levels. It is also worth noting that the events at Abu Ghraib took place against the backdrop of the neoliberal agenda discussed in Chapter 2. While these three levels of analysis are dealt with implicitly, the explicit focus of this chapter centres on challenging wartime gender essentialism and ontological constructions of females as always and already innocent victims. Adding to my discussion in the previous chapter – where, in response to the fetishisation of rape and sexual violence, I examined structural forms of GBV – this chapter considers women as perpetrators of the violence(s) of armed conflict.

The chapter begins by outlining the terminology and the analytical frameworks employed throughout the chapter. This is followed by a gendered analysis of the war on terror. The body of the chapter – which addresses the involvement of three women in the sexualised violence and torture at Abu Ghraib – is divided into three main parts. The first section, which draws on Visual Criminology and literature on photography and war, examines a selection of images of the violence(s) that took place at Abu Ghraib. The categories addressed include gender and sovereign violence; gender, ethics and appropriate responses to images of suffering (specifically the postmodern meme: 'doing a Lynndie'); and finally, the limitations of the Abu Ghraib images. The second section, which draws inspiration from Feminist Criminology, unpacks mainstream media accounts of women's involvement in sexualised violence and torture, paying particular attention to the case of Lynndie England. The main themes explored here are female agency, gender and performance, female sexuality, as well as class and the maternal militarised body. In a reversal of Spivak's infamous quote, referred to in Chapter 3, the images of the tortured and abused male Iraqi bodies suggest that 'brown men needed to be protected from…white [women]' (Holland, 2009, p. 249). If we follow this line of thinking, we are able to revise our understanding of globalisation masculinities (Chapter 2) to consider how femininities feature within this enactment of American foreign policy. The final section unpacks the subversive possibilities of war-on-terror femininity with reference to the conviction that crime is a resource for doing gender. Previous themes, such as western civilising missions, hypermasculinity and the US empire (Chapters 2 and 3), are revisited in this chapter.

Terminology and Analytical Frameworks

In this chapter, I will use the terms sexualised violence and torture to refer to the violence(s) committed at Abu Ghraib.

I outlined Halbmayr's (2010) notion of sexualised violence in Chapter 1. Here, it is employed to understand men's experiences of 'humiliation, intimidation and destruction' (Halbmayr, 2010, p. 30). The US government refused to refer to these acts as torture, choosing instead to refer to them as abuse. Furthermore, attempts were made to distance the US government from the actions of individual soldiers. Nevertheless, I posit that these acts of violence were carried out by men and women who represented the US military; therefore, these acts of interpersonal violence were enacted against the backdrop of the military institution. In other words, this violence emerges from an interpersonal-institutional nexus.

In this chapter, I use the term war-on-terror femininity to enrich our understanding of women's involvement in sexualised violence. It is adapted from Sjoberg and Gentry's (2007, p. 86) notion of militarised femininity. According to their typology, the female soldier is:

> […] brave, but needs the men around her to survive … She is sexy, but not sexual. She can fight, but the kind of fighting she can do is sanitized: she cannot engage in cruelty or torture. She is never far from her maternal instincts. The ideal-type of militarized femininity expects a woman to be as capable as a male soldier, but as vulnerable as a civilian woman.

While this offers a more generic depiction of the female solider, my war-on-terror femininity is context specific: it exists within the milieu of American exceptionalism and the fight against terrorism. Within this articulation, the female solider is not *expected* to be sexy. She *is* violent, aggressive and can engage in cruelty and torture as part of this wider US geopolitical agenda. This brand of feminism includes the use of sexual violence. While she may be maternal (this will be discussed later), this does not belie her duty to serve her country. She remains subservient to the white male soldier but is not *required* to be as vulnerable as a female civilian. Above all, she is superior to the Iraqi terrorist 'other'.

As noted above, I will be analysing the (interpersonal-institutional) violence(s) at Abu Ghraib against the backdrop of American exceptionalism. This concept, as defined by Kramer and Michalowski (2011, p. 105),

> [...] generally portrays the United States as a nation of exceptional virtue, a moral leader in the world with a unique historic mission to spread universal values such as freedom, democracy, equality...

And with regards to states of exception more broadly, as Aradau and van Munster (2009, p. 688) point out, 'Guantánamo Bay, Abu Ghraib, extraordinary rendition, migration camps [and] surveillance practices' are all examples of extraordinary measures that are presented as necessary and justified in the fight against terrorism. This chapter provides a gendered analysis of American exceptionalism.

Three of the seven soldiers involved in the sexualised violence and torture at Abu Ghraib were women: Megan Ambuhl, Lynndie England and Sabrina Harman.[1] In order to analyse their involvement in the war on terror, this chapter draws on the sub-disciplines of Feminist and Visual Criminology to critically examine gender and the sexualised violence committed at Abu Ghraib. What follows is a brief and partial overview of both subjects, starting with Feminist Criminology (for a more detailed account, see Renzetti, 2013).

Feminist Criminology

Feminist Criminology has demonstrated that gender, alongside other intersecting factors such as age, race, class, ethnicity and sexual orientation, is central to understanding criminal offending, victimisation and experiences of/treatment by the Criminal Justice System. While Feminist Criminology can be divided into different strands – liberal, Marxist, radical, postmodern and black feminist thought – for my purposes here, reference to the broad aims of Feminist Criminology will suffice.

Over the years, feminists have sought to highlight the inadequacies and fallacies of much criminological work pertaining to the criminal and/or deviant behaviour of women. The general tenet of their argument is that women have either been overlooked within the literature or, when included, have been misrepresented or presented in distorted and negative ways, and/or depicted in terms of sexist stereotypes based upon their supposed biological (Lombroso & Ferrero,

---

[1]The male soldiers were Javal Davis, Ivan Frederick, Charles Graner and Jeremy Sivits.

1893/2004) and psychological (Kanopka, 1966) nature. In sum, their criticisms of mainstream criminology centre around three main issues: excluding, marginalising and distorting (mis-representing) women (Banwell, 2007). Since the 1980s, inquiries (both theoretical and empirical) into the relationship between feminism, gender and crime have flourished. Chesney-Lind (2006) and Cook (2016) provide a more thorough review of this work than is possible here.

In the twenty-first century, Feminist Criminology interrogates the relationship between patriarchy and female offending (Parker & Reckenwald, 2008). It continues to unpack intersecting inequalities in the lives of criminal women and girls (see Burgess-Proctor, 2006; Button & Worthen, 2014; Erez, Adelman, & Gregory, 2009; Potter, 2006). It also examines the blurred boundaries between females' victimisation, their offending behaviour (Banwell, 2010; Peters, 2006; Wesely, 2006) and their treatment within the Criminal Justice System (Franklin, 2008; Pollack, 2007). Feminist criminology has also broadened its analysis to address 'transnational dimensions of crime' (Henne & Shah, 2016, p. 4; see also Henne & Torshynski, 2013; Kim & Merlo, 2014).

Questions of how agency, choice and victimisation feature in the lives of women and girls caught up in the Criminal Justice System, alongside the broader structural, institutional, political and economic constraints that inform these lived-experiences – in sum, their pathways into crime – remain key concerns for the discipline. Finally, from a methodological point of view, feminist criminology embraces the reflexive tradition and draws upon a range of methodological tools in pursuit of this agenda (Burman, Batchelor, & Brown, 2001; Henne & Shah, 2016; Mason & Stubbs, 2010). Having outlined the basic tenets of Feminist Criminology, let us move on to consider Visual Criminology.

Visual Criminology

In recent years, Criminology has become concerned with the visual (for a review of this work, see Brown, 2014; Carrabine, 2011, 2012; Henne & Shah, 2016; Young, 2014; see also *The Handbook of Visual Criminology* edited by Brown & Carrabine, 2017 and the special edition of *Theoretical Criminology*, 2014). The goal of this work is to understand 'how crime and punishment are represented visually' (Henne & Shah, 2016, p. 6). Criminologists have argued that the study of visuality as a formation of social power is capable of producing specific visions of hierarchical systems such as race, gender and sexuality (Brown, 2014; Brown & Carrabine, 2017). That said, Visual Criminology is not limited to the visual. It is also interested in the material reality of people's lives, paying attention to 'affective and sensory' elements (Brown, 2017).

Using a variety of methods to document and analyse visual representations of crime and punishment – including photodocumentary, photo-ethnography, data visualisations, graffiti and dark tourism (see Brown, 2017) – visual criminologists, as Brown (2017) notes, push the boundaries of conventional crime and media studies to interrogate the role of the image more thoroughly. Images may be produced by the researcher or, as is more common, researchers analyse existing visual materials (Pauwels, 2017).

From the beginnings of the discipline, criminologists have used images in their analyses of crime and criminality. Ranging from Lombroso's biological determinism (and the use of photographic evidence to identify criminals, see Finn, 2017), to the ethnographic work of the Chicago School (and Cultural Criminology more broadly), as well as Foucauldian analyses of sovereign punishment (and critical work on Criminal Justice responses to crime), scholars have engaged with visual representations of crime across spatial, social, cultural and political planes (see Brown, 2017; Carney, 2017; Ferrell, 2017; Finn, 2017).

The outline provided above speaks to the more generic elements of Visual Criminology. For the remainder of this section, I will focus on specific elements that align with the focus of this chapter: gender, American exceptionalism and the war on terror. Certain scholars have acknowledged the importance of the relationship between visuality, empire and the State, particularly in relation to colonial and imperial practices (see Mirzoeff, 2011; Schept, 2016; see also Marchant, 2019). Simply put, visuality (in this context) – as highlighted in the Introduction – is not intrinsically visual but takes on a narrative form. It involves, to paraphrase Schept (2016), the creation, representation and normalisation of State power (I will return to this shortly). For Schept (2016), however, the use of the image in the production of State power has not taken centre stage within Visual Criminology. That said, Visual Criminology has explored the relationship '…between aesthetics and ideologies…optics and politics' and whether or not visuality 'achieve[s] recognizability and legibility' (Brown & Carrabine, 2017). Allied to this, Visual Criminology is interested in unpacking the ethical, normative and moral consequences of looking and seeing (Brown & Carrabine, 2017; Gies, 2017).

Now that I have outlined the general principles of Feminist and Visual Criminology, let us move on to unpack women's role(s) within the war on terror.

Gender and the War on Terror

For some criminologists, the US-led war on terror is an example of American exceptionalism (Aradau & van Munster, 2009; Rothe & Muzatti, 2004).[2] What is missing is a gendered analysis of this 'extraordinary' fight against terrorism. Militarised masculinities play a key role in US empire building. With reference to the (interpersonal-institutional) violence(s) at Abu Ghraib, I want to examine how war-on-terror femininity might also form part of this neo-imperialistic story. What follows then, is an exploration of the war on terror through a gendered lens.

Three narratives emerge when we consider women and the war on terror:

1. The woman in need of rescue and protection (reads as the generic 'third-world' Muslim woman; see Mohanty, 1988).
2. The woman in danger: militarised femininity and the ideal female soldier.
3. The fallen woman: female perpetrators of sexualised violence.

---

[2]For a discussion of these issues in relation to the British State, see Mythen and Walklate 2006 & 2008.

The first two 'stories' will be addressed briefly here while the remainder of the chapter interrogates the third narrative.

1. The 'Third-world' Muslim Woman in Need of Rescue and Protection

In both Iraq and Afghanistan, US intervention was justified on the grounds that both missions were part of a broader campaign to rescue and liberate Muslim women from 'barbaric' Islamic regimes (Holland, 2009; Khan, 2014; Nayak, 2006; Riley, 2013; Shepherd, 2006; Sjoberg, 2006a; Stabile & Kumar, 2005; Steans, 2008; Tétreault, 2006).

In the Introduction, I talked about western efforts to instil gender equality in Afghanistan. Part of this mission involves the liberation of Afghan women. The mutilated face of Bibi Aisha on the front cover of *Time Magazine* in July 2010 is a perfect illustration of western civilising missions. The image is graphic. We see a hole where the nose has been cut off. The headline reads: 'what happens if we leave Afghanistan'. In the article that follows, written by Aryan Baker (a news reporter for Pakistan and Afghanistan, Heck & Schlag, 2012), we learn that Bibi Aisha was an 18-year-old Afghan woman who ran away from her husband and his family who, under orders from the Taliban, cut off her nose and sliced her ears. Bibi was rescued by US forces in Afghanistan and was taken to the US to receive reconstructive surgery (Heck & Schlag, 2013; Khan, 2014). This narrative, as Khan (2014, p.102) notes:

> [...] leads to a logical conclusion: NATO and the United States should stay in Afghanistan to continue to rescue women from the Taliban who want to brutalise them. Logically, [w]estern forces are set up as saviors of the Afghan woman. (see also Rasul & McDowell, 2010)

The violence involved in US interventions in the middle-east is obscured. Here, drawing on Schept (2016, p. 5), we return to the relationship between visuality, empire and the State:

> Visuality, then, is the mechanism by which the quotidian violence underwriting authority is made illegible and un-seeable... [it masks] the inherent violence of [S]tates in a vocabulary that leaves intact the very logics, infrastructures and institutions necessary for the violence to occur in the first place.

In the previous chapter, I talked about *sighting* and *citing* women. Unlike the image of President Trump signing the anti-abortion Executive Order, where woman is absent, in this picture the woman is present. Bibi is both *sighted* and *cited*. However, she is still marginalised. Her story is not simply about fighting gender injustice; about the violence enacted upon her, its (geo)political scope is greater than this: victory in the battle against the evil forces of Islamic terrorism. This agenda is based on ethnocentric and orientalist ideas about women, Islam and the middle-east. Orientalism, as coined by Said (1979), is based upon ontological and epistemological distinctions between the 'orient' and the 'occident', where the west dominates, restructures and has authority over this threatening, dangerous, mysterious 'Other'. For Said (1979, p. 300), orientalism is the systematic attempt to distinguish 'between the West, which is rational, developed, humane, superior, and the Orient, which is aberrant, undeveloped, inferior'. Furthermore, the Orient is considered as a 'hotbed of terrorism, ignorance, poverty, oppression, racism and misogyny' (Nayak, 2006, p. 46).

To explore this case in more detail, I turn to Walklate's (2017) work on the power of the visual to communicate ideas about victimhood and suffering (see also Gies 2017 who discusses mediating suffering in relation to staged imagery of killing and torture).

In the chapter *Mediated Suffering*, Walklate (2017) draws on three images to discuss the concepts of 'pain, horror and resilience'. The first is an image of a woman running towards a funeral procession. The funeral is for her cousin who died in Afghanistan. This is reviewed under the subheading *Pain?* This is followed by the image of a woman in Norway covered in blood following the attacks by Anders Breivik in 2011. This section is entitled *Horror?* The final image, dissected under the title *Resilience?,* is of a march in Paris in response to the Charlie Hebdo attacks. The image features a banner with 'Not Afraid' written on it. Walklate (2017) argues that all three, produced in the aftermath of 9/11, 'carry the marks of that moment in time in how they have been mediated and responded to'. Through her analysis, we see how suffering is '…reshaped, commodified, and packaged for its public and didactic salience' (McEvoy & Jamieson, 2007, p. 425 as cited in Walklate, 2017).

To this canon of post 9/11 images, we can add the photo of Bibi Aisha. I argue that the image of Bibi Aisha offers a 'mediated' illustration of pain and horror vis-à-vis the generic 'third-world-woman'. In this example, the orchestration of female suffering was used by the US administration to sell the war on terror to the American people. As Stabile and Kumar (2005, p. 778) note:

> As long as women are not permitted to speak for themselves, they provide the perfect grounds for an elaborate ventriloquist act, in which they serve as the passive vehicle for the representation of U.S interests.

As an illustration of how gender can serve American exceptionalism, Bibi Aisha is only one example of the various ways in which women were used to justify this global campaign (see Stabile & Kumar, 2005; Steans, 2008 for a more detailed analysis).

2. The Woman in Danger

The next narrative I want to draw upon is a variation of the first. However, in this instance, the woman in danger was a US soldier deployed in Iraq . Her name was Jessica Lynch. News stories reported that 19-year-old Lynch had 'gone down fighting', that she had been injured in battle and then sexually violated in captivity (Sjoberg, 2007, p. 86). However, this was a fabricated story (by the Pentagon) of capture, detention and sexual violation. The reality was far more banal: Lynch's gun had malfunctioned. She did not 'go down fighting'. Her injuries were not battle-related. She was not captured *per se;* rather she willingly surrendered. She was held but received medical care (Bragg, 2003 as cited in Sjoberg, 2007; see also Lobasz, 2008; Mason, 2005).

After nine days, US soldiers rescued Lynch from the Iraqi hospital where she was being held (Lobasz, 2008). Lynch was portrayed as helpless, as needing male soldiers to rescue her (Sjoberg, 2007). As Lobasz (2008, p. 319 emphasis in the original) notes:

> [...] Lynch was represented not only as a woman in need of res-
> cuing, but as a *virtuous and good* woman in need of rescuing.
> Depicted as an innocent small-town girl who wanted nothing more
> than to teach kindergarten...Lynch both needed and deserved to
> be rescued.

While the story of Bibi Aisha was used to legitimise the continued presence of US forces in Afghanistan, it can be argued that the fabricated rescue mission of Jessica Lynch formed part of US efforts to revitalise support for the war on terror in Iraq. Like with Bibi Aisha, Lynch's story was central to the war on terror narrative. Conversely, our final 'story', concerning women's involvement in sexualised violence and torture, did very little to justify the invasion and occupation of Iraq. In fact, this comparison – between victim and perpetrator in the form of Lynch and England – has formed the basis of numerous academic articles on the subject of women's role in the US military (see Howard III & Prividera, 2008; Lobasz, 2008; Mason, 2005; Sjoberg, 2007). Here, as captured in the title of Lobasz's (2008) article, *The woman in peril* (Lynch) is compared with '*the ruined woman*' (England). Lynch embodies women's normative role within the US military, while England represents the subversion of it.

3. Abu Ghraib and Female Perpetrators of Sexualised Violence

In April 2004, *60 Minutes II*, a CBS American news programme, broadcast a breaking report detailing the sexual abuse and torture of Iraqi prisoners by US soldiers at Abu Ghraib (Howard III & Prividera 2008; Murphy, 2007). The show released images of hooded naked detainees being piled on top of one another to form a pyramid, while other images depicted forced simulated sexual acts (Holland, 2009). Later, in May 2004, Seymore Hersh also reported on the story in *The New Yorker*. This was followed by published photographs of the violence(s) in the *The New York Times*, *Newsweek* and *The Washington Post* (Tucker & Triantafyllos, 2008). US soldiers, over the course of three months, took an estimated 1,800 photographs of the sexual abuse and torture of Iraqi detainees (Murphy, 2007; Richter-Montpetit, 2007).

Hersh's article in *The New Yorker*, *Torture at Abu Ghraib*, was based on the classified report by Major General Antonio Taguba (Holland, 2009). And although, as Sjoberg (2007) notes, there were eight official investigations into the sexualised violence and torture, only those written by General Taguba in 2004 and by Major General George Fay in 2005 are in the public domain. Among the acts of physical, mental and sexual abuse listed in the Taguba (2004, pp. 16–17) report are: the use of military dogs to intimidate detainees; various acts of physical violence, including jumping on prisoners' feet; forcing prisoners to pose in sexually explicit positions for the camera; forced nakedness, forced masturbation and 'forcing naked male detainees to wear women's underwear'; the sodomising of a detainee; and 'threatening male detainees with rape'. This is corroborated by Fay and Jones (2005) who also found that military personnel engaged in the improper use of isolation.

Seven US military soldiers – the seven 'rotten apples' (named earlier) – were found guilty of various violations of the Uniform Code of Military Justice (UCMJ), including numerous counts of dereliction of duty, as well as the maltreatment of prisoners between May 2004 and September 2005 (Caldwell & Mestrovic, 2008, p. 276). No senior officers within the US military were charged or tried for their crimes (Howard III & Prividera, 2008, p. 288). Janis Karpinski, the female general in charge of Abu Ghraib, was 'formally admonished and quietly suspended' (Hersh, 2004). For my purposes here, I will provide details of the three women who were involved as well as Charles Graner, the supposed ringleader of the violence(s) and England's boyfriend at the time of the scandal.

In 2004, Megan Ambuhl, following a plea deal, pleaded guilty to a single charge of dereliction of duty. She was dismissed from the army and did not serve any prison time (CNN, 2013). In 2005, Sabrina Harman was demoted and sent to prison for her role in the sexualised violence and torture at Abu Ghraib. Following her sentence, she received a bad conduct discharge from the army (CNN, 2013). In the same year, as part of a pretrial agreement, Lynndie England pleaded guilty for her involvement, while claiming that she did not understand that her actions were wrong. This resulted in a mistrial. During her second trial, England was found guilty of 'four counts of maltreating detainees, one count of conspiracy and one count of committing an indecent act' (CNN, 2013). She received a three-year prison sentence but was released after serving half of this time. Charles Graner was sentenced to 10 years in prison. He also received a dishonourable discharge from the army (CNN, 2013).

In Chapter 1, I talked about the tendency to argue that perpetrators of excessive and brutal violence dehumanise their victims prior to carrying out their acts of violence. Accounts of the sexualised violence at Abu Ghraib are no exception. A number of writers have argued that the sexualised violence and torture at Abu Ghraib was enacted upon dehumanised victims (Apel, 2005; Spens, 2014). My position on this remains the same: dehumanisation was not a precursor to this violence. What happed to the detainees at Abu Ghraib may have dehumanised them, *after the fact*, but this violence was not enacted upon dehumanised bodies. It was inflicted upon bodies that were identified and marked as enemies of the State. Bodies that 'required' punishment as part of a western civilising mission. In the context of Abu Ghraib, moving beyond dehumanisation allows us to appreciate the racial (and by extension, ethnocentric and orientalist), political and gendered meanings and motivations behind this sexualised violence (see also Richter-Montpetit, 2007; Tétreault, 2006).

Images of Sexualised Violence and Torture at Abu Ghraib

I opened this chapter with a discussion about teenagers smiling and taking 'selfies' at Ground Zero. Following on from this, the images that I have chosen to analyse include England and Harman smiling for the camera as they pose in front of abused and exposed Iraqi men (see Figs. 1, 2, 4 & 5). I have also included the somewhat paradoxical image of Harman treating an injured solider. On the one hand, Harman is performing the normative feminine role of caring. On the other hand, she is grinning and posing, with a thumbs-up, in front of a naked man who has been bitten by a military dog (see Fig. 5). There are no published images of Megan Ambuhl, and apart from the details regarding her dismissal from the army, there is no real focus on her involvement, other than the fact that she was one of the three women who engaged in acts of sexualised violence.

Before we unpack the individual images in detail, I want to consider Foucault's work on sovereign violence and how this applies when women are at the forefront of the analysis.

In his chapter, *How Does the Photograph Punish?*, Phil Carney draws on Foucault's work on sovereign punitive violence where ceremonial/spectacular punishment is enacted upon the body of the criminal by the State (see Foucault, 1977). He focuses in particular, on Foucault's reference to the punitive act of marking in the form of branding, scarring and flogging. Here, Foucault distinguished between a 'real' and a 'virtual' marking of the body. The former leaves a visible mark on the physical, anatomical body, while the latter is a mark upon a person's status. Here, the individual's social, symbolic body is humiliated and shamed. In both cases, the person is '...marked by an element of memory and recognition' (Foucault, 1972-3/2015, p. 7). Here, we might think of the serial number tattooed onto the bodies of Jews in the concentration camps during the Holocaust as both an actual and a virtual mark.

The bite mark, seen in the final image in this collection, speaks to Foucault's notion of actual marking. In this photograph, there is a visible, material imprint of the violence that was inflicted. In terms of virtual marking, as noted above, male detainees – as part of the catalogue of violence(s) at Abu Ghraib – were forced to wear pink underwear on their heads. In this instance, their bodies were virtually and symbolically marked. Their humiliation and shame were captured in a photograph and then shared for others to consume their degradation. In this second example, these men have been emasculated and feminised by this act of sexualised violence. As Halbmayr (2010, p. 30) notes, this affects a person's 'physical, emotional and spiritual' status.

In the examples Foucault (1977) refers to, while we might question the *nature* of the violence inflicted upon the subject, we are less inclined to question the *legitimacy* of the State's right to inflict such violence. In other words, we do not question the sovereign authority of the State to punish these particular individuals. This does not translate to the situation in Abu Ghraib. Based on the well-rehearsed arguments that this was an illegal invasion; constituting a State crime (Kramer & Michalowski, 2005, 2011; Whyte, 2007), we might question the sovereign authority of the US and the sexualised violence and torture committed against these detainees. Here, it will be useful to return to American exceptionalism and the war on terror. It has been argued that in this context the normal rules of war did not apply. Given that detainees at Abu Ghraib were presented as persons under control and not prisoners of war (POW), it was argued that the third Geneva Convention (that offers protection to POW) did not apply (Caldwell & Mestrovic, 2008). Nevertheless, I still want to interrogate these spectacles of State violence; especially given the involvement of women and the departure from traditional representations of this type of violence. As Caldwell (2012, p. 70) notes:

> In a modernist patriarchal society... 'sovereign' is associated with masculinity such that power is aligned with the masculine symbolic or phallic power, as this is the ultimate measure for self-determination.

Against this backdrop, how do we theorise women's involvement in this State violence?

In terms of locating the individual agency and responsibility of the three women involved in this sexualised violence and torture, Richter-Montpetit (2007, p. 39) believes that these actions followed a pre-constructed 'heterosexed, racialised and gendered script' that can be placed within the broader 'war on terror' campaign. In other words, these women (and indeed the men) were simply props. They did not make 'individual' decisions to engage in this violence. They were part of the larger US war machinery. For Richter-Montpetit, *Operation Iraqi Freedom* was a colonial endeavour. The racialised violence enacted by US soldiers on Iraqi detainees were 'acts of colonial violence rooted in the desire to enact "Whiteness"' (Richter-Montpetit, 2007, p. 45). Caldwell (2012) comes to a similar conclusion in her book *Fallgirls: Gender and the Framing of Torture at Abu Ghraib*. The book, as the title suggests, presents the women as scapegoats. As Caldwell (2012, pp. 102–103 emphasis in the original) argues: the '...female soldiers were *used* for the humiliation of Iraqi male prisoners ... and were *framed* as objects complying with male organized torture scenarios'. Others (see Gronnvoll, 2017; Sjoberg, 2007), however, have argued that the women played a specific role: to feminise and emasculate the enemy. As Sjoberg states (2007, p. 95):

> Sexual abuse of Iraqi men by American women communicates (whether it was intended to or not) a disdain for Iraqi masculinities so strong that subordinated American femininities are the appropriate tool for their humiliation.

Using these insights as my point of departure, I will now provide my own interpretation of women's involvement in sovereign violence.

What Is the Appropriate Response to These Images?

In Fig. 1, England has a cigarette in her mouth and is smiling for the camera. In keeping with my discussion of taking 'selfies' at memorial sites, this is a more

Fig. 1. Lynndie England Either Doing the 'Thumbs-up' Gesture or Signalling That She Is Holding a Pistol Aimed at the Penis of the Hooded Naked Iraqi Detainee at Abu Ghraib (en.wikipedia.org, 2003).

playful image of Lynndie compared with the infamous picture of her with the detainee on a leash. My decision to use the term 'playful' to describe England in this image will become apparent when we discuss the phenomenon of 'doing a Lynndie' in due course. This first image will be unpacked in relation to gender, ethics and appropriate responses to suffering and violence.

Writers have expressed concern about the inability of images to move people, both in general, but specifically in relation to the photos that were taken at Abu Ghraib (Butler, 2007; Carrabine, 2011; Kennedy & Patrick, 2014; Sontag, 1979, 2003). In her book *On Photography*, Sontag declared that images of suffering and violence had lost their ability to alarm (Sontag, 1979). In her next book, *Regarding the Pain of Others*, published in 2003, Sontag concedes that habitual viewing of horrifying images does not always result in compassion fatigue. Others have raised similar concerns to those raised by Sontag in her earlier work. Bulter (2007), for example, in her article, *The Digitalization of Evil*, grapples with ideas about what is grievable, which lives matter and whose lives are represented in the aftermath of war. With reference to Abu Ghraib, Butler tries to understand the process by which these images and their distribution were normalised. Her argument is that the so-called enemy, depicted in these images, was '…not idiosyncratic, but shared, so widely shared, it seems, that there was hardly a thought that something might be amiss here' (Butler, 2007, p. 958). Furthermore, the images, Butler argues, came to be perceived as banal because they were catalogued alongside the soldiers' 'holiday' photos:

> In these instances, it would seem that the photos are part of a record of everyday life, and that everyday life has to be understood

in this context as consisting in a certain sequential interchange-
ability of such images. (Butler, 2007, p. 960)

In this context then, the actions of these soldiers are normalised and not
regarded as 'morally alarming' (Butler, 2007). Here, the exceptional becomes
the quotidian.

It is a common argument that repeated viewings of images of war, violence
and atrocity, eventually lead to compassion fatigue (Kennedy & Patrick, 2014).
When the images of the sexualised violence and torture at Abu Ghraib surfaced
in 2004, various newspapers expressed their shock and horror at what had taken
place, particularly given the involvement of women (see Åhäll, 2017). But do these
images still have the same impact? I always provide students with a trigger warning
when teaching on this subject. I also do the same when presenting at conferences.
In fact, in December 2018, I presented a paper at *The Evil Women* conference
in Vienna. The title of my paper was *The feminine-as-monstrous: Using the
whore narrative to unpack representations of militarized femininity gone awry*. As
per my usual practice, I forewarned the audience that I would be showing violent images. In this particular presentation, I was showing images of Lynndie
England and Sabrina Harman. No one in the audience seemed concerned. In fact,
the person who presented after me (with no visual cues) received more outrage
for his teaching practices than I did for showing images of sexualised violence
and torture. Is this compassion fatigue or do images of female violence no longer
shock us? Carrabine's (2011, p. 19) work on this is instructive. He reminds us
that images of suffering and violence are deeply embedded in human storytelling
therefore, '"human outrage" is not the "natural response" to images of torture'.
Furthermore, such images have to be placed within the broader cultural context.
While for some, this means addressing the consumption of violent pornography and video games within American culture (see Sontag, 2004), the cultural
context I am interested in is the war on terror, which created simplistic binaries
between good and bad; rescuers/liberators versus dictators/extremists. Perhaps for
some, the violence that we see in these images can be regarded as a just and necessary response to the threat posed by 'dangerous terrorists'. This is compatible
with the rhetoric of American exceptionalism. Recall the image of Bibi Aisha.
Although her story relates to Afghanistan, a similar rhetoric (the protection of
women) was applied to the case of Iraq. Maybe for some, the men in these images
are a synecdoche for men in the middle-east. The kind of men who cut off wom-
en's noses.

Perhaps due to some, or all of these reasons, the images of Abu Ghraib
did not shock as much or, as universally, as one would assume.[3] This may also

---

[3]In his book, *The Abu Ghraib Effect* (2007), Stephen Eisenman provides evidence to
support the notion that the images did not cause as much outrage as one might have
expected. First, despite the four investigations into what happened at Abu Ghraib,
as noted earlier, only a few charges and convictions followed. Second, US congress received as little as 12 hours of sworn testimony concerning the violence(s) at

explain why they have been appropriated and recontextualised in numerous ways (Carrabine, 2011, p. 25). Some of these reimagining's have offered critical analyses of this violence (see Carrabine for a discussion of Phil Toledano's 2008 virtual exhibition), while others fall short. The most obvious example being the 'doing a Lynndie' phenomenon. This involves posing like England, as captured in the image above, and taking a photograph. According to Hristova (2013), 827 photos of the 'Lynndie pose' were uploaded to the British blog, *Bad Gas*, following the release of the Abu Ghraib images in May 2004. Most of the submitted photos are, Hristova (2013) argues, mundane; taken in the context of people's everyday lives. These are the instructions for visitors to the site:

1. Find a victim who deserves to be 'Lynndied'.
2. Make sure you have a friend nearby with a camera ready to capture the 'Lynndie'.
3. Stick a cigarette (or pen) in your mouth and allow it to hang slightly below the horizontal.
4. Face the camera, tilt your upper body slightly forward but lean back on your right leg.
5. Make a hitchhiking gesture with your right hand and extend your right arm so that it's in roughly the same position as if you were holding a rifle.
6. Keeping your left arm slightly bent, point in the direction of the victim and smile (Know Your Meme, Lynndie England Pose, n.d.).

The gesture is also included in the Urban Dictionary as: 'the act of pointing and laughing at an unaware victim while holding a cigarette half-cocked in your mouth and being photographed. Much like Lynndie England' (as cited in Hristova, 2013, p. 431).

Let us unpack this phenomenon in more detail with reference to semiotics, postmodernism and the uses of memes. For our purposes here, a brief overview of these subjects is provided.

The Lynndie England Pose as Postmodern Meme

The term meme, from the Greek mīmēma, meaning that which is imitated (Grundlingh, 2018), was coined by Richard Dawkins in his 1976 book *The Selfish Gene* (Boudana, Frosh, & Cohen, 2017; Cannizarro, 2016; Grundlingh, 2018; Krsteva, Donev, & Iliev, 2018; Marchant, 2019; Milner, 2012). Internet memes, to paraphrase Huntington (2013), are considered a subversive form of communication within participatory media culture (see also Gradinaru, 2018). As everyday artefacts, memes recycle, mimic and parody popular culture (Kuipers, 2005 as cited in Huntington, 2013; Marchant, 2019). They also appropriate and transform cultural texts (Milner, 2012). Milner (2012, p. iii) defines internet memes

---

Abu Ghraib. Third, candidates did not discuss the images during the 2004 Presidential election campaign. And finally, George W. Bush was re-elected.

as 'amateur media artefacts, extensively remixed and recirculated by different participants on social media networks'. Also, in the words of Krsteva et al. (2018, p. 136):

> [M]emes can be viewed as postmodern hybrid creations combining the visual and the written modes of expression. They make use of different artistic forms, genres, modes and techniques. The visual and the written parts form one unit often using radical parody, irony, kitsch, quotations and other stylistic devices. The result is a new media item of rich semiotic content, a metaphor ready to be seen by more media consumer than ever before.

A number of scholars have used ideas from semiotics to examine the use and meaning of memes (Cannizarro, 2016; Grundlingh, 2018; see also Gradinaru, 2018). Semiotics is interested in unpacking the meaning attached to cultural objects and how that meaning is conveyed through signs. Signs contain the signifier, the physical form, as well as the signified, the concept (Hall, 1997 as cited in Huntington, 2013; see also Gradinaru, 2018). Within postmodern thinking, the relationship between signifier and signified is viewed as arbitrary (Gradinaru, 2018). For writers such as Lacan, Barthes and Derrida, the meanings of signs are fluid, '...signs do not need to be fixed in any particular signified, the "free play" of signifiers being the only authentic semiotic movement' (Gradinaru, 2018, p. 295). While Gradinaru (2018, p. 304) bases her discussion on GIFs, we can apply her thinking to memes to posit that memes change the meaning of the initial sign, modifying the signification and transforming 'the originals into floating signifiers' (Gradinaru, 2018, p. 304). Or, as articulated by Boudana et al. (2017, p. 1226), 'the signifiers are disconnected from their historical signifieds and reassigned according to the users' will and wit'.

Boudana et al. (2017, p. 1212) unpack the use of postmodern memes in relation to iconic photographs. For them, iconic images consist of three traits:

> (a) the recognition of these photos by a large public, (b) their repetition and recycling across media platforms, and (c) their broad social and moral significance, beyond the referential meaning of the originally reported event.

In their research, they review 34 different memes of the iconic photograph *The Napalm Girl*, taken by Nick Ut in 1972. This image depicts children fleeing the Napalm attack during the Vietnam War. In terms of the various appropriations of this photograph, in the form of memes, the authors note:

> [T]hese appropriations reveal a fundamental paradox: the more a photograph is recycled, the more it may influence the public – yet the more the original referential context may be lost in the process. (Boudana et al., 2017, p. 1214)

In terms of appropriations, there are two types: 'politically oriented' or 'pop-culture-oriented' (Shifman, 2013, p. 372 as cited in Boudana et al., 2017, p. 1225). The former, on the whole, are sardonic, while the latter, are more humorous (Boudana et al., 2017). While some memes aim to revolt and subvert, others can be viewed as 'a solipsistic, self-referential, closed…and ultimately dysfunctional approach to community that accepts offending others as a normal part of everyday experience' (Kien, 2013, p. 560 as cited in Boudana et al., 2017, p. 1227).

Based on the criteria outlined by Boudana et al. (2017), the photograph of Lynndie England, shown in Fig. 1, can be categorised as iconic. The 'doing a Lynndie' meme falls under pop-culture-oriented appropriation. To explore this postmodern phenomenon, I visited the *Know Your Meme* website and looked up 'the Lynndie England Pose'. The site includes background information on the 'doing a Lynndie' pose, as well as the instructions that were posted on *Bad Gas*. It also includes details of how the phenomenon spread, the original photograph of Lynndie (as shown in Fig. 1), as well as some brief information about her involvement in the sexualised violence and torture at Abu Ghraib. Details of her sentencing are also provided. What I find most problematic is the 'notable examples' that are included of people 'doing a Lynndie'. In total, there are hundreds of thousands of posted images, however, I have limited my analysis to the ones included in the 'notable examples' section. Of the six that are included one stands out in particular. It is of a young boy doing the pose, pointing at an overweight woman sat opposite him in a chair. He appears to have a pencil in place of the cigarette. It is not clear why he is smiling sardonically at the woman. Perhaps he is mocking her for being overweight. Whatever the reason, the woman looks back at him with disdain. In keeping with the original image, the boy is smiling. Unlike in the original, where the men's faces are obscured by the hoods they have been made to wear, we see the woman's response to the boy's mocking pose. It is not clear why this woman/victim 'deserves to be Lynndied'. Regardless of the appropriation, if the boy is indeed mocking this woman due to her size, this is problematic in and of itself. The fact that this is a parody of sexualised violence and torture adds to the discomfort this image elicits.

The sign in this case is the object of the photograph. In the original photograph, the image of Lynndie England pointing at the naked Iraqi prisoners is the signifier. The signified is American exceptionalism and the war on terror. I believe that 'the original referential context' of this image – the use of sexualised violence and torture as part of the war on terror – is lost in these mimetic performances. While the uncoupling of signifier and signified within postmodern signs can, in some cases, challenge and disrupt in ways that are positive, this is not the case with the 'doing a Lynndie' meme.

I would like to make one final comment on this image and the 'doing a Lynndie' phenomenon. To do so, I will return to where I started the chapter: dark tourism and taking selfies at memorial sites.

Dark Tourism and Taking Selfies at Memorial Sites

Based on the Urban Dictionary definition, what is missing from these re-enactments (i.e. the Lynndie pose) is the intersubjective meaning behind the violence in the original image. To reiterate, the violence(s) witnessed in the images at Abu Ghraib, were enacted upon discursively constructed (as opposed to dehumanised) bodies; where racial, gendered and political meanings were inscribed prior to, and post, these acts of sexualised violence. Reminiscent of my argument about sexualised violence against Jewish women presented in Chapter 1, there is an intersubjective dynamic to this violence. Both the victim (the racially inferior terrorist 'other') and the perpetrator (the white knight of the US empire) are consumers of this political economy of violence. It is hard to imagine how these broader narratives surrounding the original Lynndie pose are captured in these re-enactments/performances. The question for me is: in what way, if any, is 'doing a Lynndie' similar to what I witnessed at Ground Zero? The answer, I believe, is that both involve superimposing individuals onto key moments in American geopolitical history. In both cases, the specific context and meaning of the original events are lost in these frivolous retellings. And yet herein lies the paradox. Both examples – 'doing a Lynndie', talking selfies at Ground Zero – involve actions that are at once ahistorical (apolitical even), while simultaneously existing within, and responding to, a specific moment in history: the 2001 terrorist attacks. Now we will move on to consider the second image in this collection.

Masculinities, Femininities and the War on Terror

In previous chapters (Chapters 2 and 3), I have talked about globalisation masculinities. These include: masculinities of conquest and settlement, masculinities of empire and masculinities of postcolonialism and neoliberalism (Connell, 1998, 2005). Masculinities of empire, postcolonialism and neoliberalism were

Fig. 2.   James Graner and Sabrina Harman Pose Behind a Pyramid of Naked Iraqi Detainees at Abu Ghraib (en.wikipedia.org., 2003–2004).

applied to the invasion of Iraq. Furthermore, I argued that this intervention was informed by a hyper-masculine agenda to re-masculinise the US after 9/11 (see Chapter 3). Paradoxically, in the context of the invasion of Iraq, this hyper-masculine campaign relied upon war-on-terror femininity in the form of Ambuhl, Harman and England. It is this paradox I wish to unpack. I will do so with reference to Connell's (2005) hierarchy of masculinities framework. Readers will recall from Chapter 2 Connell's (2005) four types of masculinity: hegemonic, complicit, marginalised and subordinate. As the most dominant form of masculinity, hegemonic masculinity is positioned above the others. Complicit, marginal (those unable to meet the requirements of hegemonic masculinity) and subordinated masculinities (those prevented from achieving hegemonic masculinity) are always positioned below hegemonic masculinity. Within this hierarchy, femininities are also placed below masculinities. As Connell and Messerchmidt (2005, p. 848) articulate: '[g]ender is always relational, and patterns of masculinity are socially defined in contradistinction from some model (whether real or imaginary) of femininity'. Indeed, hegemonic masculinity was formulated alongside hegemonic femininity. The latter was then renamed 'emphasised femininity' to denote the asymmetrical relationship between masculinities and femininities (Connell & Messerchmidt, 2005).

Below (see Fig. 3.) I offer a visualisation of this gender hierarchy.

Drawing on this visual representation of the gender hierarchy, my notion of war-on-terror femininity, and Sjoberg's (2007) ideas about subordinated femininities and inferior masculinities, we can map the image of Graner and Harman (see Fig. 2.) onto this pyramid and reformulate this illustration of the gender hierarchy in the following way:

At the top of the pyramid, we have Graner, arms folded, relaxed, playful, representing the patriarch and hegemonic masculinity. Then we have Sabrina. She is both literally and figuratively placed below him. She represents emphasised femininity which, in this context, is reimagined as war-on-terror femininity. This femininity is above subordinated and inferior masculinities, which are positioned at the bottom of the hierarchy and represented by the hooded men. This photo,

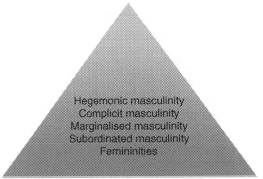

Fig. 3.   Visual Representation of Connell's (2005) Gender Hierarchy.

viewed in this way, at once reproduces Connell's gender hierarchy while, at the same time, challenges it. Unlike in the illustration of the gender hierarchy – where women are always and already inferior to all types of masculinity – in Figure 2, Sabrina is positioned above inferior Iraqi men. However, she remains subordinate to the white, western man. What we see here is a temporary, context specific enactment of hypermasculinity that – within the contours of American exceptionalism – relies upon war-on-terror femininity.

Who Was the Real Sabrina Harman?

In her book, *The Cruel Radiance: Photography and Political Violence*, Linfield (2012) asks: '[w]hy are photographs so good at making us *see* cruelty?' Her answer is '…because photographs bring home the reality of physical suffering with a literalness and an irrefutability that neither literature nor painting can claim' (Linfield, 2012, p. 39 emphasis in the original). This is particularly true when, as argued earlier, the bodies being looked at are subjected to real and virtual marking. Or, indeed, when images of violence and torture have been 'carefully choreographed with the visual experience of viewers in mind' (Gies, 2017). As Gies (2017) explains, '[t]he audience encoded within the images occupies the position of helpless onlookers, but it is also assigned an instrumental role in the degradation of victims'.

And yet for some, the photos of sexualised violence and torture at Abu Ghraib do not tell the whole story. Philip Gourevitch (writer), in collaboration with

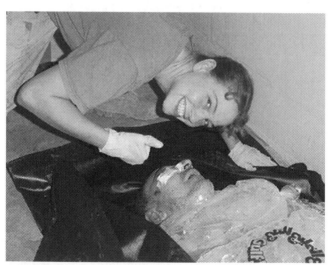

Fig. 4.   Sabrina Harman Giving the 'Thumbs-up' While Smiling Over the Dead Body of Manadel al-Jamadi Who Died During Interrogation at Abu Ghraib. His Body Bag Has Been Opened So Graner and Harman Can Take Photos of Themselves (wikimedia.commons.org, 2003a).

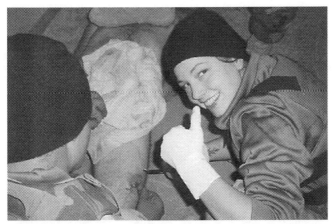

Fig. 5.   Sabrina Harman Gesturing a 'Thumps-up' While Stitching a Wounded Detainee Who 'Has Been Bitten by a Military Dog' at Abu Ghraib (wikimedia. commons.org, 2003b).

filmmaker Errol Morris, created the documentary *Standard Operating Procedure* (2008). Gourevitch believed that in order to get a fuller picture of what happened at Abu Ghraib we need to speak to the perpetrators. In this section, I will draw on an interview transcript with Sabrina Harman, as well as other pictures of Harman in relation to the war on terror, to see if these offer a more comprehensive portrait of her and her involvement in what occurred at Abu Ghraib.

In 2013, I wrote a review for the aforementioned book by Caldwell. In my review, I suggested that the book fell short of delivering a more nuanced account of gender and the sexualised violence and torture at Abu Ghraib. I argued: '[m] uch like analyses which simply demonize the women involved, the case presented here – that these women were exploited and coerced participants – is every bit as reductionist' (Banwell, 2013, p. 216). I found the denial of female agency in these acts of violence problematic and concluded my review with the opinion that *Fallgirls* was a misguided attempt to '…excuse these women because current gender stereotypes are incompatible with their existence' (Sjoberg, 2007, p. 96). Here, I want to revisit Caldwell's book to unpack the final two images in the collection (Figs. 4 & 5).

Under the image of Harman tending to the detainee who has been bitten (see Fig. 5), Caldwell (2012, p. 108) includes the following caption: 'Harman giving stiches and giving instrumental care'. She also includes, in a sub-section titled *Maternal Sabrina and Friendships*, a number of photos of Harman smiling with Iraqi families in their homes. We also learn that Harman, who cared for some of the prisoners at Abu Ghraib, was described by many as a maternal caregiver. In addition to this supplementary information, Caldwell includes the transcript of her conversation with Harman in 2007 (Caldwell, 2012, pp. 173–174):

Caldwell: In Al Hilla, did you purchase a family mattress and a refrigerator? Why? What did this family mean to you?

Harman: Yes, because she made me…lunch and I wanted to return the favor. They were important to me and I was around them for almost everyday for three months. I don't know, it's hard to explain without coming off as anti-American. They had nothing and were still happy because they had each other. Their situation seemed horrible but they made it work and never complained about it to me. If I got their kids clothes and small toys like a soccer ball they were so happy while kids in the U.S. would be so pissed if they didn't get an Xbox. I don't know, they were just amazing people that I learned a lot from.

Does this knowledge change our reaction to these images of Harman (Fig. 4 &5); to her involvement generally? To return to Gouervitch, was he correct to suggest that images alone do not tell the whole story? As I said at the outset, with regards to this final image (Fig.5), the smile and the 'thumbs up' gesture appear incongruous with the care that Harman is providing this detainee. Given her relationship with the Iraqi families, is Caldwell right in her assessment that these women did not 'choose' this violence? Even now, five years after I wrote my review, I find this denial of female agency problematic. I believe it is possible for Harman to occupy both positions: as a caring person (a civilian) who looked out for people in need and as an individual (a solider) who engaged in sexualised violence and torture. One does not, and should not, negate the other. I believe that my concept of war-on-terror femininity (where violence and torture are prescribed) resolves the paradox of Sabrina Harman, particularly if we accept that Harman *chose* to enact this type of femininity. Finally, despite portrayals of Harman as maternal, this does not (and did not) interfere with her duty to serve her country and play her role in the geopolitics of the war on terror.

The final part of the chapter will draw on Feminist Criminology to explore Lynndie England's involvement in the sexualised violence and torture at Abu Ghraib.

Feminist Criminology and Discursive Representations of Female Violence

As noted earlier, Feminist Criminology is interested in unpacking how agency, choice and victimisation feature within the lives of criminal women. Spanning the national and the transnational, Feminist Criminology addresses interlocking inequalities relating to age, race, class, gender, sexuality and patriarchy, to name but a few. In the spirit of this work, I will now unpack the various accounts of Lynndie England's involvement in the (interpersonal-institutional) violence(s) at Abu Ghraib. I will begin with existing media accounts, before considering the subversive possibilities of war-on-terror femininity.[4]

---

[4]For a more detailed exploration of women's political violence and their involvement in terrorism, as well as the narratives used to explain their violence(s), see *Mothers,*

Crazy in Love

Demonised, sexualised and, indeed, infantilised, England was believed to have acted under the influence of her then boyfriend, Charles Graner (Lobasz, 2008). For some, this narrative denied her agency and reduced her moral and criminal culpability (Sjoberg, 2007). Interestingly, both the media *and* England relied upon this narrative. In her own words, Lynndie claimed: '...he wanted me in the picture, and I was like, "no way"'. And '...Graner kept being persistent, "Oh, come on, just take the picture, take the picture"' (Dateline NBC, 2 October 2005 cited in Howard III & Prividera, 2008, p. 298). And: 'I was so in love with him that I trusted his decisions and I did whatever he wanted' (Howard III & Prividera, 2008, p. 299). The idea that England was coerced and manipulated by her boyfriend is an all-too familiar trope within 'stories of violent women'. However, if we turn to Feminist Criminology, a number of scholars within the discipline have demonstrated how women's violence can be explained by gender oppression and/or patriarchy, particularly in cases of battered women who kill (see e.g. Banwell, 2010; Dunn & Powell-Williams, 2007; see also Batchelor, 2005). In England's case, rather than dismiss her claims about Graner simply as a ploy to reduce her culpability, we might argue that she acted under the heteropatriarchal influence of this man, but still exercised her own agency, albeit in a way that was mediated by a number of interlocking oppressions (these are discussed below).

Not-woman

Other media stories focused on Lynndie's gender or, more accurately, on her distortion of it (see Holland, 2009). Numerous references were made to her tomboyish features and her masculine appearance (Holland, 2009; Tucker & Triantafyllos, 2008). This is how a Washington newspaper described England: '[s]he has short-cropped hair, a tight, muscular body and that don't-mess-with-me-expression' (as cited in Gronnvoll, 2012, p. 376). As articulated by Holland (2009): '[s]he was represented as being inappropriately masculine as well as inappropriately female, a gender abnormality with one foot in each of these seemingly dichotomous categories'. These portrayals are reminiscent of the views of Lombroso and Ferrero who, in their 1893 book, *The Criminal Woman*, argued that the true biological nature of a woman is antithetical to crime. Therefore, the female criminal is not only abnormal, she is biologically like a man. As succinctly put by Hart (1994) in a more recent comment on gender and crime (Hart, 1994, p. 13, as cited in Gilbert, 2002, p. 1293):

Monsters, Whores (Sjoberg & Gentry, 2007) and its follow-up, *Beyond Mothers, Monsters, Whores* (Gentry & Sjoberg, 2015). See also *Women as Wartime Rapists: Beyond Sensation and Stereotypes* (Sjoberg, 2016). Drawing on a range of case studies (the Armenian genocide, the Nazi genocide, the genocides in Rwanda and the former Yugoslavia, as well the DRC) Sjoberg dissects women's role in sexual violence.

> Masculinity theory pursues its circular reasoning by arguing that women are less likely to engage in criminal activity because they are not men. Boys will be boys, say masculinity theorists; and girls will be girls, unless they do become criminals, in which case they are likely to be masculinized women.

Put simply, a woman who is capable of aggression and violence becomes constituted as the masculine woman, the 'other' (Gilbert, 2002). Also, as Campbell argues:

> Her actions are forced into a masculine model of aggression, judged to be male, and the woman is seen as having violated not just the criminal law but the "natural law" of proper female behavior. (Campbell, 1993, p. 144)

In a similar way to the superficial reading of the woman-as-dupe narrative discussed above, this not-woman characterisation refuses to take women's violent behaviour seriously. By placing women's actions outside of their gender, the association of femininity/the feminine with non-violence is reaffirmed. Conversely, my war-on-terror femininity – which accepts that women can be violent and aggressive, while at the same time maternal – disrupts these gender binaries.

Class

In other accounts, the focus was on England's white working-class background: '[a]s the fallen woman, England was not simply to be removed from the military caste but to be (re)placed into the white working-class Appalachian culture from which she originated' (Howard III & Prividera, 2008, p. 302). Through numerous news sources, we learn that England was poor and grew up in a trailer behind a sheep farm (see Howard III & Prividera, 2008). She is described as an 'uncivilized hillbilly', as someone who is backward, 'other' and poor (Mason, 2005). Unlike in the case of Jessica Lynch, whose whiteness and Appalachian background were used to describe poor yet determined Americans (Tucker & Triantafyllos, 2008, p. 92), in England's case these two facts were reformulated and used as evidence of her uncivilised and savage nature (Mason, 2005; see also Lobasz, 2008). In the words of Mason (2005, p. 43):

> As representatives of Mountain country life, hillbillies can thus reflect either heroism – bravery and loyalty to traditional ways – or a deviance, sadism and primitivism that is said to fly in the face of modern progress.

In a piece on *The War on Poverty in Appalachia*, professor Ronald Eller (2014) reviews the history of politics, poverty and inequality in Appalachia. Often regarded as the symbol of the failure of the War on Poverty, introduced by President Lyndon Johnson in the 1960s, Appalachia was (and is) associated with the white poor. Eller also explores the racial tensions that emerged from the War on Poverty in Appalachia. Disparaging comments relating to England's Appalachian background are common, and apart from the work reviewed above, few have given serious academic thought to how her poor, working-class, rural upbringing might have informed her decision to join the Army in the first place, as well as her willingness to take part in the violence inflicted upon the bodies of 'brown' terrorist 'others.' From a feminist perspective, Lynndie's age, race, class and gender (or her supposed inappropriate performance of the latter) should not be interpreted in reductive ways that seek to explain her behaviour away, rather, they should be understood as interlocking constraints that informed her decisions. Indeed, an analysis which focuses solely on individualised explanations of women's violence is one which ultimately depoliticises women's experiences and does not attend to, or take into account, the structural constraints which inform their violent behaviour.

Sexuality

Details of England's sexual history and her various sexual partners were revealed as evidence of her deviance and her culpability for her crimes. Mainstream news stories focused on her 'dysfunctional, adulterous sexual relationship with Charles Graner' (Holland, 2009, p. 252). According to Jennifer Wells in the *Toronto Star*: '[g]etting naked, it now appears, was not a shy pursuit for the 21-year-old England. Included in the not-yet-released Abu Ghraib archive … were videos and still photos of England. Said one senator: "[s]he was having sex with numerous partners. It appeared to be consensual"' (as cited in Gronnvoll, 2017, p. 378). In another news article, we are told that England appeared 'in sexually explicit pictures with other soldiers' and engaged in 'raunchy behavior before and after [her] company journeyed to Iraq' (Gronnvoll, 2017, p. 379). Here, we can apply Sjoberg and Gentry's (2007, 2008) whore narrative, specifically the first category, erotomania. Erotomania is based on the idea that violent women have an insatiable appetite for sex. It is this pathological relationship with sex that causes them to be violent. In my reading of England's sexual history, stories about her sexual behaviour are incidental to, rather than explicable of her violent behaviour.

The Maternal Militarised Body

The final narrative I want to explore is that of the militarised maternal body (see Managhan, 2012). In her book, *Sexing War/Policing Gender: Motherhood, Myth and Women's Political Violence*, Åhäll (2017) argues that stories about violent women's agency are informed by normative constructions of motherhood and maternal reproduction. Women, and their maternal bodies, she argues, are not only judged and valued for their appearance, but also for the actions in which they engage. With specific reference to England, Åhäll argues that revelations that England was pregnant when news of the sexualised violence and torture surfaced not only underscored the tension between her role as a future mother and her current role as a soldier, but also drew more attention to the fact that *women* had taken part in the violence(s). For some news outlets, England's pregnancy softened her image during her trial:

> England arrived at military court this morning, seven months pregnant and dressed in combat fatigues. Nothing like the young woman in these pictures, where she is seen humiliating Iraqi Prisoners. (World News Tonight, 3 August 2004, as cited in Howard III & Prividera, 2008, p. 304)

In her review of news media representations, Åhäll (2007) cites numerous examples where Lynndie is transformed from monster to mother, a woman who is no longer capable of torture and sexual abuse. Implicit in some of these stories is the belief that motherhood is the reason England finally accepts responsibility for her actions. For others, however, her pregnancy and her subsequent status as a mother, rather than providing a recuperative narrative, serve as reminders of her confusing and dangerous sexual/gender identity (Holland, 2009). I will return to this shortly, first let us consider how war-on-terror femininity serves as a recuperative narrative.

Violence as a Resource for Achieving War-on-terror Femininity

Conventional femininity has not been associated with crime or violence therefore, for women and girls, their criminal and/or violent behaviour cannot be regarded as a resource for achieving this type of femininity. However, I would argue that within my construction of war-on-terror femininity, violence can, in this instance, be considered a resource for achieving this type of femininity. For Sjoberg and Gentry (2007, p. 87), women who behave like England and Harman '…have committed a triple transgression: the crime they are accused of, the transgression against traditional notions of femininity, and the transgression against…militarized femininity…'. Conversely, my notion of war-on-terror femininity offers a resolution to the paradox that is violent femininity. War-on-terror femininity does not negate their individual agency, it simple locates their violence within the wider US geopolitical agenda.

Within the discursive representations of England and Sabrina provided and discussed above, both women conform to and defy conventional femininity. With regards to the former, in keeping with traditional ideas about women as passive and weak, England's claim that she took part because Graner told her to and she wanted to impress/please him confirms this stereotype of women (it also underscores gender oppression in a patriarchal society). Likewise, in the photo where Harman tends to an injured detainee, and in her stories about her time with Iraqi families, traditional femininity is upheld. Yet, by virtue of taking part in sexualised violence and torture, both resist these normative expectations. Instead, they perform a subversive femininity: war-on-terror femininity.

Conclusion

Within discussions of militarised femininity, and the war on terror in Iraq, as noted earlier, comparisons between Jessica Lynch and Lynndie England abound (Lobasz, 2008; Sjoberg, 2007; Tucker & Triantafyllos, 2008). I want to close with my own comparative analysis. In 2018, I presented a paper at the European Society of Criminology conference in Sarajevo. During my stay, I attended the Crimes against Humanity Museum. Among many of the images and artefacts was a picture of a pregnant refugee being helped into a migrant boat by a man. This image encapsulates the narrative of 'the woman in need of rescue and protection' outlined at the start of this chapter. Here, I want to contrast this image with the image of a pregnant Lynndie England standing trial for the crimes she committed at Abu Ghraib. As noted above, maternal representations of England received mixed responses. In juxtaposing these two images of the maternal body, vis-à-vis war/armed conflict, I want to highlight that women's relationship to war is not always as its victims; as those in need of protection. Women can be perpetrators too. As perpetrators (in the context of the war on terror) they are not *required* to forsake their gender identities, rather they might interrupt and challenge gender boundaries, thus at once being maternal, caring and violent, and perhaps, most importantly, superior to subordinated masculinities. The irreconcilable image of a maternal body standing trial for sexualised violence forces us to confront the reality that women are in fact violent: the maternal, life-giving body is also a body that inflicts harm and violence. Indeed, in certain contexts, this behaviour is required of women.

Alas, these ideas are not as forthcoming within mainstream accounts of violent women. Whether as victims or perpetrators – be it the generic third-world-woman (Bibi Aisha), the all-American girl next door (Jessica Lynch) or the monstrous feminine (Lynndie England) – women are objectified, fetishised and reduced to two main archetypes: the fallen woman and the woman in need of rescue. Both tropes deny agency. The former suggest that the violent woman is devoid of womanhood (which is, of course, constructed as non-violent), the latter presents women as weak and vulnerable *because* of her womanhood. In order to move beyond these reductive narratives, albeit within the specific context of American exceptionalism, my notion of war-on-terror femininity – which, at once resists, complies with and mediates conventional femininity (and indeed militarised femininity) – offers a way out of this conundrum.

In this chapter, I have challenged hegemonic understandings of gender roles and of the gender hierarchy. Utilising the sub-disciplines of Feminist and Visual Criminology, I have unpacked gender and the war on terror, specifically the sexualised violence and torture at Abu Ghraib. What took place at this prison forms part of the broader narrative of American exceptionalism. In this chapter, I used my concept of war-on-terror femininity to resolve the paradox of women's involvement in this hyper-masculine response to 9/11. In a detailed analysis of four images of women involved in sexualised violence and torture, I have examined the legitimacy of sovereign violence; deliberated over ethics and just responses to sexualised violence and torture; reimagined conventional understandings of the gender hierarchy, and interrogated the truth-telling capabilities of images. Mainstream media accounts of Lynndie England were reviewed against the basic tenets of Feminist Criminology and war-on-terror femininity was offered as a resolution to reductive explanations of women's violence. Continuing with our challenge to gender essentialism – specifically the assumption that women are always and already the victims within the theatre of war/armed conflict – the final chapter addresses the victimisation of men and boys.

Chapter 6

Glocalisation Masculinities and Violence(s) Against Men and Boys in Darfur

Introduction

On the subject of sexual violence, O'Brien (2016, p. 386) makes the following observation:

> There is a long history of the use of sexual violence as a weapon of war and during mass atrocities such as crimes against humanity and genocide. While men are also subject to sexual violence, the majority of victims of sexual violence committed during mass atrocities are women, particularly in relation to sexual violence crimes beyond basic rape.

This statement is indicative of the way in which many scholars, policymakers, global advocacy groups, and the news media approach the topic of conflict-related sexual violence (CRSV). Male victims are mentioned, but they are on the periphery, presented as though they are footnotes to the main subject of female victimisation. From an empirical standpoint, based on the recorded data that we have, O'Brien (2016) is correct in her assessment: females do make up the majority of victims of *rape and sexual violence* (Henry, 2016; Leatherman, 2011; Sjoberg & Peet, 2011; Touquet & Gorris, 2016; True, 2012; see also Boesten, 2017; Davies & True, 2015 for a critical review of the data/research on this). However, as argued in Chapter 4, rape and sexual violence do not represent the full range of CRSV and sexual gender-based violence (SGBV) committed during, and in the aftermath of, war/armed conflict. Furthermore, returning to the

Gender and the Violence(s) of War and Armed Conflict:
More Dangerous to be a Woman?, 135–157
Copyright © 2020 by Stacy Banwell. Published by Emerald Publishing Limited.
This work is published under the Creative Commons Attribution (CC BY 4.0) licence.
Anyone may reproduce, distribute, translate and create derivative works of this work
(for both commercial and non-commercial purposes), subject to full attribution to the original
publication and authors. The full terms of this licence may be seen at http://creativecommons.org/
licences/by/4.0/legalcode" Knowledge Unlatched Open Access
doi:10.1108/978-1-78769-115-520201008

point I made in the Introduction, rather than base our evaluation on differences in numbers and prevalence, the experiences of both males and females can be understood through unpacking the gendered meanings of the violence(s) that are enacted and suffered.

Another trend within the scholarly literature on gender and wartime rape and sexual violence, as identified by Grey and Shepherd (2013, p. 120), is the absent presence logic. They explain:

> In these cases, although the writer does not expressly say that sexual violence is targeted predominantly at women, where a gender is ascribed to the victim, it is almost invariably female.

In the previous chapter, I referred to Butler's (2007) work on *The Digitalization of Evil* and her investment in uncovering whose lives matter and whose lives are griveable. In a similar vein, Grey and Shepherd (2013, p. 122), in their analysis of the visibility of male victims of CRSV (both within policy and academic discourses), ask two key questions: 'whose bodies are visible?' and 'whose bodies matter?' In response to these questions they suggest that the silencing of men's experiences, alongside 'the absent presence of masculinity', results in the 'denial of the materiality of the violated male body'.

Writers argue that these exclusionary politics within international relations and international security are based, in part, on essentialist assumptions about men and women. Here, hegemonic (also normative) understandings of gender associate men/masculinity with aggression, violence and agency and women/femininity with victimisation, vulnerability and passivity (see Carpenter, 2005, 2006; Grey & Shepherd, 2013). Thus, male victimisation is both materially and ontologically disruptive. This explains why the vulnerability of the penis – when it is disempowered through sexualised violence – is so destabilising (Clark, 2017). In her analysis of the human security framework, Carpenter (2005) comes to the conclusion that women and children, through their association with innocence and vulnerability, serve as a proxy for 'civilian'. It is they who must be protected during war/armed conflict. This blueprint has meant that CRSV and SGBV against men and boys, especially those identified as 'combatants', is obscured from this security paradigm (Carpenter, 2005).

Let us expand upon this discussion of the human security framework and consider the role of biopolitical violence within this securitisation narrative. To do so, we will draw on the work of Foucault (1978) and Wilcox (2015).

In order to unpack Foucault's 'biopolitics of the population' (1978), it is useful to place these ideas within his broader work on power and governmentality (Adams, 2017). For Foucault (1977, 1978), power is not treated as a possession; rather it is an economy that is dispersed throughout society, in practices, institutions and technologies (Foucault, 1977, 1978). Societies, he argued, assigned themselves the task of administering life. This political power over life, to paraphrase Foucault (1978), evolved in two basic forms. The first centred on the body as a machine and the second, on the body as a biological entity. Bodies are supervised, Foucault (1978, p. 139 emphasis in the original) continues:

[...] through an entire series of interventions and *regulatory controls: a biopolitics of the population.* The disciplines of the body and the regulations of the population constituted the two poles around which the organisation of power over life was deployed.

For Foucault (1978), biopolitics is about regulating and preserving the life of populations. It is '...a power that exerts a positive influence on life, that endeavours to administer, optimise, and multiply it, subjecting it to precise controls and comprehensive regulations' (Foucault, 1978, p. 137). Within this line of thinking, the security of the nation-state is dependent upon the survival of the population. Expert discourses, created by the nation-state, decide which bodies/populations are vulnerable and require intervention (see Wilcox, 2015). Here, the body gains meaning through discourse.

Drawing inspiration from Foucault's work (1978) on biopower and biopolitics, Wilcox (2015, p. 17) argues that contemporary practices of violence are constituted with reference to biopower. Biopolitical violence sees bodies as either populations that must be eliminated or populations that must be protected. Put simply, biopolitical practices of security are concerned with preserving certain human bodies whilst dealing death and destruction to others. Bodies, Wilcox (2015) argues, are not pre-political; they come into being through practices of international war and security. Humans, then, '...are not only vulnerable to violence as natural bodies...they also are vulnerable because they exist only in and through their constitution in a social and political world' (Wilcox, 2015, p. 167). In other words, discourses of human security, in the context of biopolitics, decide which bodies need to be rescued and kept alive (Wilcox, 2015). As demonstrated in Chapter 4, women and girls have been identified as populations that need to be protected, particularly from wartime rape and sexual violence. This is reflected in the *Stop Rape Now* campaign (first discussed in the Introduction), whose mission statement is to end '...sexual violence during and in the wake of conflict' and '... respond effectively to the needs of survivors'. Here, CRSV is described as '...a present-day emergency affecting millions of people, *primarily women and girls*' (see the Stop Rape Now website. Emphasis added).

This gendered 'rape-security nexus' (Hirschauer, 2014, p. 3) is also present within a number of UN Security Council Resolutions (UNSCRs). UNSCR 1325, passed in 2000, was the first to 'take special measures to protect women and girls from...rape and other forms of sexual abuse...in situations of armed conflict...' (UNSCR 1325, 2000, p. 3). This pledge was reiterated in 2008 with UNSCR 1820, which emphasised 'that women and girls are particularly targeted by the use of sexual violence' (UNSCR 1820, 2008, p. 1; see also UNSCR 1888, 2009a and 2106, 2013a). It is only when UNSCR 2106 was passed in 2013, that men and boys are recognised, for the first time, as victims of CRSV. Not only is this essentialised protection narrative present within policy documents, as demonstrated in previous chapters, it is also represented in visual form. In Chapter 4, I reviewed the Amnesty International poster – 'rape is cheaper than bullets'. This poster formed part of their campaign to raise awareness about the use of rape as a weapon of war *against women and girls*. And in the previous chapter,

I discussed the mutilated face of Bibi Aisha which formed part of the justificatory narrative for the war on terror. In both examples, women and girls, by virtue
of being female, are regarded as requiring protection. Men and boys – whether
implicitly or explicitly – are identified as perpetrators. Within the biopolitics of
violence, the equation between maleness, masculinity and aggression disqualifies
them from requiring protection.

As noted in the Introduction, the title of this book is taken from a statement
made by Major General Patrick Cammaert. This former United Nations force
commander reproduces the essentialist gender binaries outlined above. Granted,
his analysis compares civilian women with male combatants. Here, the irony of
his point – that war/armed conflict is more dangerous for civilian women than
it is for male soldiers – holds more currency. In this chapter, I unpack the risks
and dangers faced by men and boys during, and in the aftermath, of war/armed
conflict.

Outline of the Chapter

The main focus of the second half of this chapter is the genocide in Darfur
(2003–2005). I have chosen this case study for the following reasons. First and
foremost, the SGBV that takes place within this conflict is interconnected at
the macro-, meso- and micro-levels. Each of the chapters in this book has
sought to address gender and the violence(s) of war/armed conflict at these
three levels of analysis. Darfur offers the final example in the collection of
case studies reviewed throughout the book. It also connects the violence(s)
of armed conflict to environmental as well as institutional and interpersonal
causal factors. This is important for, as argued in Chapter 4, by broadening the
diagnostic framework – to consider climate variability and extreme weather
events within analyses of armed conflict – we can extend our understanding
of the causes and consequences of conflict violence. This will assist in our
endeavors to combat such violence. I will expand upon all three levels in due
course. Second, as discussed below, existing definitions of the violence(s) of
war/armed conflict often omit the specific harms men and boys suffer. Using
the example of Darfur, I examine categories of genocidal and reproductive
violence that are not explicitly addressed within policy discourse. Finally, this
case study allows me to revisit Connell's (2005) gender hierarchy and reimagine her notion of globalisation masculinities.

I begin my analysis of Darfur with a detailed review of the origins of the
conflict, outlining the various explanations that have been offered. This is followed by an examination of gender roles in Darfur. I argue that gender roles
and gendered hierarchies within Sudanese culture more broadly form the backdrop to this conflict; informing both the motivations of perpetrators, and the
experiences of victims. I then explore the violence(s) that took place during
this genocide: sex-selective killing, rape and genital harm. In a similar vein to
Chapter 4, as far as possible, this chapter will draw upon the narratives of vic-
tims/survivors (both male and female) from the empirical data gathered during
this period. In my analysis of the genocide that took place during the conflict

I return to the gender hierarchy discussed in the previous chapter, specifically the process of feminising and emasculating male victims. Unlike in the previous chapter – where the focus was on the motivations and representations of female perpetrators – here I explore male victimisation to unpack the messages this violence communicates to, and about, men and masculinity. Two iterations of Connell's (1998, 2005) globalisation masculinities (discussed in Chapters 2, 3 and 5) are explored in my analysis of Darfur. In the first instance, I draw upon Connell's thesis to explore the gender hierarchy (see Chapters 2 and 5) that led up to, and informed the violence(s) that took place during the conflict in Darfur. In the final part of the chapter, I draw upon feminist understandings of the local-global nexus to rethink globalisation masculinities. Drawing on Howe's (2008) notion of glocalisation, and Connell's globalisation masculinities, I use my notion of glocalisation masculinities to unpack the violence(s) that took place during this conflict (more on this below). The chapter begins however with a review of the literature on CRSV against men and boys. In this section, I identify key themes within the literature. Before that let us consider the terminology used in this chapter.

Terminology

As noted in Chapter 2, CRSV encompasses the following:

> [R]ape, sexual slavery, forced prostitution, forced pregnancy, forced abortion, enforced sterilisation, forced marriage and any other form of sexual violence of comparable gravity perpetrated against women, men, girls or boys that is directly or indirectly linked to a conflict. (United Nations (UN), 2018b, p. 3)

Interestingly, the types of CRSV that men and boys may suffer (forced masturbation, genital violence, forced rape) are not explicitly listed in the definition above. They would fall under 'any other form of sexual violence'. Apart from rape and enforced sterilisation, all other types of violence refer to violence against women and girls.

GBV is violence that is directed against an individual based on socially ascribed gender differences. SGBV reflects the sexual(ised) nature of this violence. Based on this definition, men and women can be both perpetrators and victims. However, as Carpenter (2006, p. 86) notes:

> Given the intention behind and inclusiveness of these definitions, it is very interesting that the concept of [GBV] has been linked almost exclusively to the issue of violence against women in the human security sector…

Indeed, numerous international instruments conflate GBV with violence against women and girls (Carpenter, 2006; Christian, Safar, Ramazani, Burnham, & Glass, 2011; Gorris, 2015; see Linos, 2009 for a more detailed review).

In this chapter, the types of CRSV committed against men and boys (discussed in the various sections) includes: rape (both oral and anal); sexual torture and genital mutilation; enforced sterilisation (through castration); and sexual exploitation and abuse (SEA). SGBV will refer to sex-selective killings. Grey (2017) uses the term reproductive violence to describe violence(s) that violate an individual's reproductive autonomy. In my discussion of Darfur, I use this term to refer to acts of genital harm carried out on Darfuri men. Rape and the sex-selective killing by soldiers and the militia group, the Janjaweed,[1] are understood as acts of genocidal violence.

I will be replacing Connell's notion of globalisation masculinities with my notion of glocalisation masculinities. To recap, globalisation masculinities include the following: masculinities of conquest and settlement, masculinities of empire and masculinities of postcolonialism and neoliberalism (Connell, 1998, 2005). Howe (2008) uses the term glocalisation to convey the negative impact certain macro-level systems and structures (such as globalisation, capitalism and neoliberalism) has on meso- and micro-level everyday experiences. This is referred to as the global-local nexus. With reference to Darfur, I employ this term to examine the intersections between the macro-, meso- and micro-levels. In this example, the macro-level refers to climate variability and the extreme weather conditions it produces which, in this example, resulted in extreme droughts in Darfur. As will be demonstrated, drought and desertification, which also precluded men from performing hegemonic masculinity, resulted in violent clashes over natural resources in Darfur. Here, we can trace the relationship between a macro-level phenomenon, such as climate variability, and the genocidal violence that took place at the local level in Darfur. At the meso-level, I unpack how State-led Arabisation policies impacted the gender hierarchy in Darfur. The institutionalisation of local Arab Sudanese masculinities subordinated African Darfuri men. Rape and sexual violence were used to achieve this. Finally, at the micro-level, I review the use of genocidal and reproductive violence by the Janjaweed and the government of Sudan. Here, we see how individual men carried out localised acts of conquest and expulsion.

This chapter acknowledges that the violence(s) that took place during the armed conflict in Darfur (against males and females) were genocidal. There have been disagreements about this. Most notably *The UN International Commission of Inquiry on Darfur*. Written in 2005, it '...concluded that the Government of the Sudan [had] not pursued a policy of genocide' (as cited in Hagan, Rymond-Richmond & Parker, 2005, p. 534). Scott Anderson, who wrote an article in *The New York Times* also refused to acknowledge that genocide was committed in Darfur (as cited in Hagan et al., 2005; see their article for a more detailed review of these denials). Despite this, a number of scholars provide detailed and compelling evidence to support the argument that genocide was committed in Darfur (see Ferrales, Brehm, & McElrath, 2016; Hagan et al.,

---

[1]The Janjaweed are an Arab militia. The term itself means '...men with guns on horses or camels...colloquially used by Africans to mean devil on horseback...' (Hagan et al., 2005, p. 530).

2005; Hagan & Rymond-Richmond, 2008; Kaiser & Hagan, 2015). When referring to the conflict in Darfur, I understand and position the violence(s) that took place as genocidal.

A Brief Review of the Literature

Throughout history and across conflicts globally (e.g. Colombia, Peru, Rwanda, Darfur, Sri Lanka), men are systematically targeted for execution (Carpenter, 2005). Battle-aged men and boys (those likely to become combatants) become targets of political violence (Carpenter, 2005, 2006; Jones, 2000, 2002). In the words of Carpenter (2006, p. 88):

> The empirical record suggests that, of all civilians, adult men are most likely to be targeted in armed conflict. The singling out of men for execution has now been documented in dozens of ongoing conflicts worldwide…More often than women, young children, or the elderly, military-age men and adolescent boys are assumed to be 'potential' combatants and are therefore treated by armed forces…as though they are legitimate targets of political violence….

Despite this evidence – which points to the deliberate and systematic targeting of civilian men and boys – historically their experiences have been obscured from the human security framework (Carpenter, 2005). Gender essentialism, biopolitical and ontological constructions of women as vulnerable and in need of protection – and the concomitant equation of women with civilian- explain this marginalisation of men within the security paradigm.

Apart from Carpenter's work in the early 2000s, historically, research on male victims of CRSV has received far less attention, particularly when compared with the copious amount of information on female victims. Generally speaking, policy makers, academics, advocacy groups, as well as the news media, are guilty of this oversight (Apperley, 2015; Christian et al., 2011; Gorris 2015; Grey & Shepherd, 2013; Lewis, 2009; Linos, 2009; United Nations Office for the Special Representative of the Secretary-General on Sexual Violence in Conflict [UN SRSG-SVC], 2013; Sivakumaran, 2007, 2010; Solangon & Patel, 2012; Vojdik, 2014). Despite receiving limited attention, both within and outside academia, CRSV against men and boys has been documented in over 25 conflicts over the last three decades (Gorris, 2015; Linos, 2009; Solangon & Patel, 2012; Touquet & Gorris, 2016; UN SRSG-SVC, 2013; Vojdik, 2014). As Sivakumaran (2007, p. 257) notes, sometimes the violence is sporadic and haphazard, at other times it is systematic. She lists the following conflicts where sexual violence against men and boys has taken place: Uganda, Sierra Leone, Kenya, Liberia, Sudan, the Central African Republic, Zimbabwe, the DRC and South Africa; El Salvador, Chile, Guatemala and Argentina; Iraq, Afghanistan, Syria, and Sri Lanka; Greece, Northern Ireland, Chechnya, Turkey and the former Yugoslavia (see also Christian et al., 2011; Trenholm, Olsson, Blomqvst, & Ahlberg, 2013). This list is by no means exhaustive but should give readers a sense of the scope.

More recently, scholars from a range of disciplines have begun to write about CRSV against men and boys (Carpenter, 2005, 2006; Gorris, 2015; Grey & Shepherd, 2013; Lewis, 2009; Linos, 2009; Touquet & Gorris, 2016; Sivakumaran, 2007, 2010; Solangon & Patel, 2012; Vojdik, 2014). Extending beyond academic scholarship, in 2013, the office of the *United Nations Special Representative of the Secretary-General on Sexual Violence in Conflict* held a workshop to examine the consequences of sexual violence against men and boys in conflict situations. And, at the time of writing, empirical research has uncovered the sexual exploitation and abuse (SEA) of unaccompanied and separated refugee boys in Greece (Digidiki & Bhabha, 2018; Freccero, Biswas, Whiting, Alrabe, & Seelinger, 2017).

As we know, conflict results in mass displacement. The current refugee crisis in Europe is characterised by an unprecedented number of children seeking asylum. This includes unaccompanied and separated children[2] (Digidiki & Bhabha, 2018; Freccero et al. 2017; Mason-Jones & Nicholson, 2018). According to Freccero et al. (2017), of the 63,000 unaccompanied and separated children applying for asylum in the European Union in 2016, 89% were males (see also Digidiki & Bhabha, 2018). These 14–17-year-old boys, many of whom are in Greece, do not have access to accommodation or employment opportunities while they await decisions on their cases (Digidiki & Bhabha, 2018). Many of these children, Freccero et al. (2017) report, are kept in police cells alongside adults. This exposes them to a number of risks, including SEA. In Athens, for example, SEA of young males takes place in public spaces such as parks and squares, as well as bars, where boys receive payment in exchange for sexual services (Freccero et al., 2017; See also Digidiki & Bhabha, 2018; Mason-Jones & Nicholson, 2018).

As noted by Freccero et al. (2017, p. 2), the SEA of unaccompanied and separated children 'is both a human rights violation and an urgent public health concern.' Outlining the various physical and psychological harms associated with this type of abuse, and the barriers refugees and migrants face in seeking the necessary medical treatment within these crisis/emergency settings, Freccero et al. (2017) argue that prevention is vital. Resonant with the arguments around gender essentialism and the gendered nature of the human security framework presented above, these researchers found that, despite the predominance of adolescent boys within the population of unaccompanied and separated children, their experiences did not inform policy discussions or humanitarian responses (SEA and coerced sexual activities were discussed in relation to women and girls in Chapters 3 and 4).

Invisible Victims

Males who have experienced CRSV are often referred to as unrecognised and/or invisible victims (Gorris, 2015). This is due to underreporting and inadequacies in international law. Under-reporting, due to shame, fear, stigma and the criminalisation of homosexuality, hinders our ability to access accurate data on the

---

[2]The UN High Commissioner for Refugees (UNHCR) defines an unaccompanied child as a person under the age of 18 'who is separated from both parents and [is] not being cared for by an adult who, by law or custom, is responsible to do so' (UNHCR, 1997, p. 1).

number of male victims (see Christian et al., 2011; Lewis, 2009; Solangon & Patel, 2012; Vojdik, 2014). Homosexuality is a crime in over 70 countries (Vojdik, 2014). This criminalisation discourages male victims from coming forward (Apperley, 2015; Clark, 2017; Gorris, 2015; Storr, 2011; Touquet & Gorris, 2016; UN SRSG-SVC, 2013; Vojdik, 2014). Added to this, international law often re-labels rape and sexual violence against males as 'torture' or 'mutilation' (Carlson, 2006; Siva-kumaran, 2010; Vojdik, 2014; see also Oosterhoff et al., 2004). And yet, despite these criticisms concerning the terminology of international law, Grey and Shep-herd (2013) commend the Ad Hoc Tribunals for the Former Yugoslavia (ICTY) and Rwanda (ICTR), as well as the Special Court for Sierra Leone, for pros-ecuting male-to-male sexual violence and for recognising and taking seriously the experiences of male victims (see also Lewis, 2009; Sivakumaran, 2007, 2010; Vojdik, 2014). All three prosecuted individuals for committing acts of sexual violence against men (Grey & Shepherd, 2013).

The Impact of These Violence(s)

The impact of CRSV and SGBV on men and boys during war/armed conflict can be physical, emotional, psychological, psycho-sexual and psycho-social (Chris-tian et al., 2011; Lewis, 2009; UN SRSG-SVC, 2013). The consequences can be both short- and long-term (Christian et al., 2011; Lewis, 2009; Solangon & Patel, 2012). As well as the visible and immediate physical impact of these violence(s) – such as tearing, bruising and lacerations – males are also at a greater risk of contracting sexually transmitted diseases, including HIV and AIDS (UN SRSG-SVC, 2013; see also Lewis, 2009). Emotional responses may include shame, guilt, fear, frustration, humiliation, anger and powerlessness; as well as ambiguity about gender identity and sexuality (Solangon & Patel, 2012). They may suffer from various mental health problems such as depression, anxiety, Post-traumatic stress disorder (PTSD), substance misuse, phobias and suicidal thoughts (Solangon & Patel, 2012; UN SRSG-SVC, 2013). Psycho-sexual impacts relate to the inability of male victims to begin or maintain sexual relationships. Likewise, psycho-social consequences relate to problems continuing with pre-existing or new relationships (UN SRSG-SVC, 2013). Both also relate to difficulties men may face in carrying out physical labour resulting from their physical injuries. This hinders their abil-ity to provide for their families financially, further emasculating and undermining their role as breadwinners/providers (UN SRSG-SVC, 2013, pp. 13–14).

As noted in Chapter 2, rape, pillage and looting were key features of the conflict in the DRC. Accounts from male survivors in the DRC revealed both the emotional and financial impact this had on men and their families (Chris-tian et al., 2011). In the words of a survivor and a local NGO in the DRC, respectively:

> It's a risk to go out and sell things as I might have to face the Interhamwe [sic] [rebels] again and that I might be killed. But then staying at home without food and dying is the other option. So we have to risk our lives. (as cited by Christian et al., 2011, p. 240)

Men in our culture, is the chief of the family, when he is raped, he cannot accept it since he was not made to be that way. Women are raped and it's acceptable as they are meant to have sex with men, but men are not meant to have sex with men. And that's why men are shameful. This can happen to women but not to men and this happens most of the time in villages. This they cannot share with others ... They leave their house and go into the bushes...They will have to stay there with another group as they will not have any friends in the community. They will be poor, isolated and humili-ated. (as cited in Christian et al., 2011, p. 238)

Male survivors in the DRC lost everything they owned: their homes, their animals and their household supplies. This impacted their ability to fund their travel to hospital to receive medical treatment and/or to pay for the medical care they required (Christian et al., 2011). These survivors also talked about their inability to work and provide for their families following their assaults. Men revealed the shame and fear they felt and their concerns regarding risk of revictimisation. This prevented them from earning a living (Christian et al., 2011). As a result, maintaining the household became the responsibility of their wives. This inevitably put a strain on their marriages. As Christian et al. (2011, p. 239) note:

The roles the male survivors report post-sexual assault demon-strates a change in the gender roles in their household that not only impacts the survivors but also the family and wider community.

The Meanings Communicated Through These Violence(s)

In an interview with Will Storr (2011), relating to male sexual violence during the Ugandan conflict, Salome Atim (an officer for the Refugee Law Project) made the following statement:

In Africa no man is allowed to be vulnerable... You have to be mas-culine, strong.... You should never break down or cry. A man must be a leader and provide for the whole family. When he fails to reach that set standard, society perceives that there is something wrong.

Similarly, Sivakumaran (2007, p. 270) states: '[t]he concept of hegemonic mas-culinity is that of a heterosexual male; to deviate from this heteronormative male standard is to be "less" masculine'.

Writers have demonstrated that male-to-male sexual violence communicates a message of subordination to the victim. Whether through rape, castration, sexual mutilation and/or torture, the male and/or female perpetrator, deprives the victim of their manhood and their masculinity (Baaz & Stern, 2009; Christian et al., 2011; Clark, 2017; Ferrales et al., 2016; Lewis, 2009; Solangon & Patel, 2012;

Vojdik, 2014). With reference to the vulnerability of the penis, Clark (2017, p. 3) observes:

> This 'side' of the penis is rarely seen. Within contemporary discourses on sexual violence...the penis is typically framed as a weapon" [as illustrated in Chapter 4]. It is a hard, aggressive object that penetrates and tears, causing pain and suffering...the exposure of [the vulnerability of the penis] challenges phallocentric masculinity by stripping the phallus of its power and strength... hence its dominance.

In the remainder of her article, Clark (2017) urges to think of the penis in a two-dimensional way: as a weapon that harms and as an object that is harmed. Here the penis is both a symbol of phallocentric masculinity, as well as the target of its material and symbolic destruction.

As well as the feminisation and emasculation of individual males, Sivakumaran (2007, p. 274) argues that rape and sexual violence can also emasculate the group to which the man/boy belongs. She says:

> In much the same way as sexual violence against women may symbolize to offender and victim alike the destruction of the national, racial, religious or ethnic culture...sexual violence against men symbolizes the disempowerment of the national, racial, religious or ethnic group. Specifically, [t]he castration of a man is considered to emasculate him, to deprive him of his power. The castration of a man may also represent the symbolic emasculation of the entire community.

In Chapter 1, I discussed the notion of woman-as-nation. I argued that, during war/armed conflict, women and their bodies become the receptacles through which national, racial, ethnic and religious identities are reproduced. Comparable to this attack upon 'woman-as-nation', an attack upon men disempowers the national, racial, religious or ethnic group to which he belongs. Here, we might think of man-as-protector. The violated male has failed to protect the nation/community to which he belongs. In cases of enforced sterilisation (through castration) and other types of genital mutilation, this violence is more than symbolic. It can also be genocidal as it 'prevents births within the group' (The Convention on the Prevention and Punishment of the Crime of Genocide, 2014; see Chapter 1 for the full definition). Violence that is intentionally aimed at the male reproductive organs, with the aim of affecting their ability to procreate, can be considered genocidal. This was the case during the conflict in the former Yugoslavia. As explained by one perpetrator, while he was beating the testicles of his victim, 'you'll never make Muslim children again' (as cited in Sivakumaran, 2007, p. 273). These themes of feminisation, emasculation, reproductive and genocidal violence will be discussed (with reference to the genocide in Darfur) in more detail below.

Darfur

Background to the Conflict

While Sudan and South Sudan have been plagued by civil war, my focus is on the conflict in Darfur. Despite the signing of a peace agreement in 2006, violence and unrest continue in the Darfur region of Sudan (United Nations, 2007, 2017). This section, however, will focus on the period between June 2003 and January 2005. This was when the armed conflict, between the Sudanese Government, the allied Janjaweed militia and armed rebel groups, was at its height (de Waal, Hazlett, Davenport & Kennedy, 2014). For some, the conflict in Darfur can be attributed to cultural and economic clashes between the African and Arab populations in the region (Olsson & Siba, 2013). In the words of Olsson and Siba (2013, p. 301):

> [T]he ...conflict in Darfur...has deep roots within the social fabric of Darfur itself. It represents a rapid escalation of a conflict that has long divided different groups in Darfur over land use and competition for scarce natural resources, particularly water.

For others, however, the systematic neglect and marginalisation of Darfur by the government of Sudan was the catalyst to the onset of the conflict (Ferrales et al., 2016). Below I consider the social, cultural, political, environmental and economic factors that contributed to the outbreak of violence (see also Salih, 2008). I also examine the gendered nature of this genocide.

It is estimated that at least 35,000 civilians were killed during this time (de Waal et al., 2014). And by 2007, the UN reported that over 200,000 people had been killed and more than 2 million displaced from Darfur since the conflict began in 2003 (United Nations, 2007). Ferrales et al. (2016) and others (see Kaiser & Hagan, 2015) have examined the gendered nature of genocidal violence in Darfur. Drawing on this work, Connell's notion of the gender hierarchy and globalisation masculinities, as well as Grey's (2017) notion of reproductive violence, I explore the gendered nature of the genocide in Darfur. I do so by focusing on the experiences of men and boys. Women and girls were also targeted during this genocide. For a review of their experiences, see Hagan and Kaiser (2015).

Situated in the far western province of Sudan, bordering Chad, Libya and the Central African Republic, Darfur – translated from Arabic meaning 'home or land of the fur' (de Waal, 2005, Salih, 2008) – is separated into three federal states (Salih, 2008). These are: Shamal Darfur (in North Darfur), Janub Darfur (in South Darfur) and Gharb Darfur (situated in West Darfur) (Salih, 2008, p. 1). They cover roughly 500,000 sq. km (Olsson & Siba, 2013, Salih, 2008). To put this into context, this about the size of Spain (Olsson & Siba, 2013). It is estimated that 6.5 million people live in Darfur (Olsson & Siba, 2013). While Darfur comprises a number of ethnic groups, the population is either categorised as 'African' or 'Arab' (Olsson & Siba, 2013).

Historically, these self-identified tribes (African and Arab) lived in relative harmony in the Darfur region of Sudan (Ferrales et al., 2016; Hagan et al., 2005;

Olsson & Siba, 2013). All Darfuri residents are Sunni Muslims (Salih, 2008). The two main resources in Darfur are surface supplies, such as animals and agricultural crops and underground materials, such as oil and minerals (Salih, 2008, p. 2). Traditionally, the African population in this region relied upon subsistence farming. This is land they historically shared with Arab cattle herders (Hagan et al., 2005; Kaiser & Hagan, 2015). As the largest indigenous ethnic groups, the Fur and Masalit (African tribes) controlled most of the land in the area (as dictated by the customary land tenure system in Darfur). These land areas, referred to as dars, are controlled by the communal leaders of the African tribes (Olsson & Siba, 2013, p. 301). Under this system, Arab nomads, lacking their own dars, rely upon the land of African tribes. They make seasonal movements to access water and land for their herds (Olsson & Siba, 2013, pp. 301–302; see also De Juan, 2015).

Historically, when there was no shortage of land, this system ensured that there were no major clashes between the two groups (Olsson & Siba, 2013; Kaiser & Hagan, 2015). However, waves of drought and desertification put pressure on this system. Increases in migratory movements by Arab nomads (as a result of the environmental changes in the region) resulted in violent clashes between the Arab groups and the African tribes, the Fur and Masalit (De Juan 2015). The Arab groups who had been excluded from the dars during the period leading up to the conflict, joined government forces and other Arab militias to attack and destroy villages, thereby displacing African tribes from their lands (De Juan, 2015; see also Kaiser & Hagan, 2015; Salih, 2008). From this standpoint, as Olsson and Siba (2013, p. 302) point out, the conflict is regarded as a 'struggle over natural resources'. I will return to this in the latter part of the chapter when we review glocalisation masculinities in Darfur.

In terms of the national political landscape, from the 1970s onwards the government began engaging in nation-building policies. This led to a coup in 1989, leaving President Omar al-Bashir in charge of the country. Under his rule, Sudan implemented policies of Arabisation and Islamisation during the 1990s (Ayers, 2012; Castro, 2018; Hagan & Rymond-Richmond, 2008; Kaiser & Hagan, 2015; Sharkey, 2007). This 'Arab-Islamic supremacist [imperialist] ideology' (Hagan & Rymond-Richmond, 2008, p. 880) privileged those regarded as Arab and demeaned those viewed as African. Also, to paraphrase, Hagan & Rymond-Richmond (2008, p. 880), although Darfur is Muslim, this State-led agenda distinguished between Arabs and black Africans, privileging and offering preferential treatment to Arabs over Africans. These policies of forced assimilation resulted in the denial of women's independent status, the banning of tribal dancing, alcohol, bartering practices and traditional dress codes (Hagan & Rymond-Richmond, 2008). These customs were replaced with Arab traditions. This included speaking Arabic (Hagan & Rymond-Richmond, 2008; see also de Waal, 2005). Added to these cultural and political measures, Darfur (Darfuri Arabs, to be precise) became militarised during this time through the spread of small arms provided by the Libyan government (de Waal, 2005; Sharkey, 2007). As Salih (2008, p. 3) notes, this accumulation of arms occurred during the first wave of drought and desertification which plagued the region during the late 1970s and early 1980s.

Within this economic and political milieu, tensions and instability increased culminating in attacks by Darfuri rebel groups against the Sudanese army in 2003 (Castro, 2018; de Waal et al., 2014; Olsson & Siba, 2013; Salih, 2008). The two main rebel groups were The Sudan Liberation Movement/Army (SLM/A) and the Justice and Equality Movement (JEM) (Abusharaf, 2006; Salih, 2008). The main grievance of the SLM/A was the 'marginalisation' of the Darfur region. They argued that it had been neglected politically and economically by the Sudanese government. They also argued that Darfuris had been denied basic rights such as access to healthcare and education (Salih, 2008, p. 7). In response to these attacks by the rebel groups, the Sudanese government engaged in a campaign of terror against civilians in Darfur (Salih, 2008). The Janjaweed, as well as Sudanese soldiers, began destroying 'African' villages in Darfur (Ferrales et al., 2016). This involved land attacks (with the use of bombs); sex-selective killing of men; the raping of women; the possession and destruction of property; as well as the theft of food, land and resources (Hagan et al., 2005; Kaiser & Hagan, 2015; Salih, 2008).

The targets of this genocidal violence were 'African' tribes: the Masaleit, Zaghawa and Fur (Ferrales et al., 2016, p. 568). The goal of the Arab-dominated Sudanese government was to displace non-Arab African groups by destroying their farms and their villages (Hagan et al., 2005). Two million Africans were displaced and 200,000 fled as refugees to Chad during this two-year period (Hagan et al., 2005). Racial epithets accompanied these attacks. The perpetrators were reported to have said: 'this is the last day for blacks' or 'we will kill all the black-skinned people' (as cited in Hagan et al., 2005, p. 543). Based on the literature examined here, it is possible to argue that the conflict in Darfur is the result of a combination of factors: government neglect and marginalisation, clashes over resources and State-led racialised and racist policies. Gender also played a part. It is to the latter that we now turn our attention.

The Role of Gender in Sudanese Culture

Gender roles and gendered hierarchies informed the motivations of perpetrators and the experiences of victims during the genocide (see Kaiser & Hagan, 2015). Sudanese gendered identities (within the context of tribal farming communities) are based upon idealised notions of masculinity and femininity (Kaiser & Hagan, 2015). Women's roles are confined to the domestic sphere and their reproductive capabilities (Kaiser & Hagan, 2015). Following the forced assimilation policies of the 1980s, women's access to labour opportunities (indeed, their rights generally) were restricted, resulting in women's economic dependence on their husband (Abusharaf, 2006; de Waal, 2005). Such policies also buttressed heteropatriarchal ideas about the role of Sudanese men as providers and protectors of their families (Kaiser & Hagan, 2015; Willemse, 2007).

In the previous chapter, I reviewed Connell's (2005) gender hierarchy and her four types of masculine identity: hegemonic, complicit, marginalised and subordinate. Hegemonic masculinity, as the most dominant form of masculinity, is positioned above the others and femininities are always and already positioned below masculinities. Within this framework, hegemonic masculinity is fundamentally based on heterosexuality. Sudan is no exception. The construction of hegemonic masculinity within Sudanese culture reproduces heteronormative ideas about gender and sexuality, where homosexuality is marked as subordinate, inferior and deviant. Indeed, a third offence of homosexuality is punishable by death in Sudan (Ferrales et al., 2016).

As a result of the economic hardship and diminishing resources, men who belonged to the Fur began to migrate both domestically and internationally (Ferrales et al., 2016; see also De Juan, 2015; Salih, 2008). This impacted their ability to safeguard their families. It also prevented them from marrying within their community/tribe (Ferrales et al., 2016). According to Willemse (2007, 2009), this led to a widespread crisis in masculinity which precipitated the violence that followed. Here, we see how poor socioeconomic conditions, caused by drought and desertification, impeded Darfuri men's ability to perform hegemonic masculinity (this struggle to perform gender role expectations was highlighted in Chapter 2 with reference to men's experiences in the DRC). This inability to achieve hegemonic masculinity repositions men's status within the gender hierarchy, associating them with marginalised masculinity. In this instance, we see how external factors, in the form of extreme weather events, inform how and whether men are able to perform/achieve idealised notions of masculinity. In other instances, we see how the State draws on national, political and ethnic/racialised ideologies to manipulate the gender hierarchy. Below I explain this State-led agenda in more detail.

Departing from conventional interpretations of globalisation masculinities, (Connell, 1998, 2005), particularly in relation to conquest and settlement – where colonial and imperial endeavours are enacted by an outside State/colonial power – here I want to narrow the geopolitical lens to think about conquest and settlement within a State, where one group has decided that the other is an 'outsider' that needs to be expelled. While socioeconomic conditions relocate certain men within the gender hierarchy (as highlighted above), ethnopolitical Arabisation policies in Sudan base hegemonic masculinity on the Arab, Sudanese (heterosexual) male. Here, localised enactments of conquest, through Islamisation, marginalise African Sudanese men in Darfur. As will be demonstrated in more detail below, during the conflict in Darfur, rape and sexual violence were used by Arab soldiers and the Janjaweed to subordinate (and indeed emasculate) African Darfuri men. I posit that CRSV and SGBV were used to both maintain the Arab version of the gender hierarchy and to enact a localised version of masculinity of conquest and settlement. Let us consider CRSV and SGBV against Darfuri men in more detail.

CRSV and SGBV Against Darfuri men and boys

Based on the narratives of 1,136 Darfuri refugees, Ferrales et al. (2016) analyse CRSV and SGBV against Darfuri men and boys. They draw on data collected by the US State Department through the *Atrocities Documentation Survey.* Their analysis demonstrates the ways in which the violence(s) of this genocide emasculated (through homosexualisation and feminisation) the targeted group.

Their qualitative thematic coding of this data identified the following acts of violence: sex-selective killing, rape, sexual assault and sexualised violence against the body (these are discussed in more detail below). Their coding distinguished between primary victimisation – violence targeted directly against the victim, such as rape and sex-selective killings – and proximate victimisation, which involves witnessing the victimisation of others.

'They Focused on the Men and Shot Men'[3]: Sex-selective Killing

Darfuri men were targeted for extermination by the Janjaweed and the government of Sudan (Ferrales et al., 2016; Kaiser & Hagan, 2015). In the words of a Fur woman: '[m]en were targeted. Some women were hit at random. But men were targeted and shot' (as cited in Kaiser & Hagan, 2015, p. 87). Another respondent commented:

> I also saw the bodies of about 25 young boys – it seemed they were targeting the men and boys because I heard them say 'a puppy can become a dog'. (as cited in Ferrales et al., 2016, p. 578)

As noted above, in Sudanese culture, men are regarded as the protectors and bearers of their ethnic group (Ferrales et al., 2016). Therefore, as representatives of their African group, the deliberate targeting of males by members of the Arab tribes – 'killing members of the group' – amounts to genocide (see The Convention on the Prevention and Punishment of the Crime of Genocide, 2014). As one example of the violence(s) that took place during this genocide, some argue that the routine killing of Darfuri African farmers was an act of ethnic cleansing informed by two factors: racialised/racist ideologies and shortages in food and water (Kaiser & Hagan, 2015). As well as this genocidal sex-selective killing, men were targeted for various acts of sexualised violence.

Rape as Both Primary and Proximate Victimisation

Groups of soldiers and the Janjaweed would rape Darfuri men either through penile penetration or penetration using objects like sticks (Ferrales et al., 2016). Victims were raped anally and orally. As one 21-year-old Masaleit woman witnessed: '[f]our men were raped in the village... These men were then shot and killed... After they killed the men, they raped them anally with sticks' (as cited in Ferrales et al., 2016, p. 573). They would also insert penises into the mouths of dead victims. In the words of a Fur woman: 'I saw a young boy and his father dismembered while still alive. They cut off their penises and put them in their mouths' (Ferrales et al., 2016, p. 574). Darfuri men were also forced to watch the raping of 'their' women. As one survivor articulated:

---

[3]Masaleit woman cited in Kaiser and Hagan (2015, p. 87).

I saw ladies in the village [as I lay wounded] being raped right in front of everyone, even their fathers and their children…We could do nothing, nothing. We had no way to fight'.(Ferrales et al., 2016, pp. 575–576)

Rape not only disempowers individual men who have been emasculated and feminised, it also signifies their inability to fulfill their role as 'protector'. This communicates a message of symbolic elimination/destruction to the wider group (Ferrales et al., 2016). Proximate victimisation, that results in the displacement of men, transforms symbolic destruction/elimination into a material reality. This results in the 'physical destruction in whole or in part' of a group and thus amounts to genocide (see the full definition of genocide in Chapter 1). As articulated by a 36-year-old Zaghawa man:

I ran away because I couldn't stand to see the women hurt in [the] family…The men gathered in [the] yard to try to defend [them]. The soldiers shot them. The men had nothing to protect the village. (Ferrales et al., 2016, p. 576)

Here, we can rethink Connell's notion of globalisation masculinities. In this context, conquest and settlement are intrastate endeavours, rather than the colonial or imperial actions of an outside State/nation. Put simply, those who identify as Arab use rape to displace those identified as African in order to take over their land. Rape is also used to influence the gender hierarchy. Informed by State-led Arabisation policies, rape (inducing both primary and proximate victimisation) subordinates men within the gender hierarchy.

Reproductive and Genocidal Violence

The definition of genocide (1948) includes the following element: '[i]mposing measures intended to prevent births within the group' (The Convention on the Prevention and Punishment of the Crime of Genocide, 2014). Enforced sterilisation, through castration, is an example of this. Genital harm, through various acts of sexual torture, can also thwart men's reproductive capabilities. When enacted deliberately and systematically, this also counts as a form of genocide. It is both a physical and symbolic attack upon men, masculinity and the 'national, ethnical, racial or religious group' to which they belong (The Convention on the Prevention and Punishment of the Crime of Genocide, 2014).

In her article on the International Criminal Court and forced pregnancy, Grey (2017) applauds the progress that has been made in terms of the acknowledgement and prosecution of rape and sexual violence as war crimes and crimes against humanity. Echoing my own concerns about the selective focus on these crimes, Grey (2017) laments the invisibility that continues to shroud other types of SGBV. She states: '[v]iolence which involves a violation of reproductive autonomy or which is directed at people because of their reproductive capacity, henceforth "reproductive violence", is one example' (Grey, 2017, p. 906). Grey's (2017) notion of 'reproductive violence' was discussed in previous chapters (Chapters 1 and 4). Grey (2017) makes it clear that her focus is on females' experiences of reproductive violence, stating that these harms are often more acute for women and girls.

Reproductive violence, like other types of CRSV, according to Grey (2017), impacts primarily on women and girls. She goes on to argue that her choice to focus on women and girls reflects her 'interest in women's distinct experiences of violence and survival' (Grey, 2017, p. 909). She explains, in depth, that her article:

> [...] concentrates on reproductive violence against women and girls in situations of armed conflict. This is not because wartime reproductive violence is necessarily more serious, or more appropriate for international condemnation, than similar conduct in everyday life. However, as international criminal law has historically been applied in conflict settings, it is fitting to focus on those settings as a starting point, while noting that this body of law can also be applied in times of peace. (Grey, 2017, pp. 909–910)

I will begin by unpacking Grey's first argument, that reproductive violence is more acute for women. As I proposed from the outset, perhaps a more fruitful line of inquiry (as acknowledged by Grey herself) is to explore the unique experiences of males and females, rather than engage in this comparative analysis based on degrees of harm. To her second point, concerning her focus on situations of armed conflict rather than peacetime societies, nowhere in this rationale does Grey account for her decision to overlook males' experiences of reproductive violence (this oversight is curious given her earlier work in 2013 with Shepherd, discussed above, where Grey acknowledges the invisibility of the male violated body).

Reproductive violence, specifically the sexual mutilation of the male genitals, has occurred throughout history (Sivakumaran, 2007; Solangon & Patel, 2012; Vojdik, 2014). This further problematises contemporary work that excludes their experiences. Sexual mutilation, through castration, can be carried out as part of a genocidal campaign of enforced sterilisation. This occurred during the conflict in the former Yugoslavia. Sexual mutilation and sexual torture also took place at Abu Ghraib. However, in the case of the latter, this sexualised violence was not genocidal. In the context of Darfur, genital harm (which included injury to the testicles as well as the targeting of the penis) was widespread and systematic (Ferrales et al., 2016). As one Fur survivor recalls:

> For seven days, I was detained and tortured by government soldiers. I was made to lie on my back with my hands tied behind my back, ankles tied and they would stomp on my thighs and kick me in the genitals [and I have had] sexual problems ever since. (as cited in Ferrales et al., 2016, p. 576)

A female survivor witnessed five men bleed to death following castration, while other survivors spoke of men having organs dismembered and their 'genitals cut off' (Ferrales et al., 2016, p. 261).

It is the argument of Ferrales et al. (2016) that these acts of genital harm (as well as the other acts of CRSV and SGBV discussed above) achieve emasculation through homosexualisation and feminisation. Extending their argument, I argue that they count as forms of reproductive and genocidal violence. Genital harm, whether as an act of symbolic or genocidal violence (see discussion above) violates men's reproductive autonomy. As an act of reproductive violence (connotating homosexuality), it subordinates men within the gender hierarchy. In addition, and in a similar way to rape, reproductive violence against African men in Darfur speaks to my revised interpretation of Connell's globalisation masculinities. In terms of conquest and settlement, genital harm, and the emasculation, feminisation and homosexualisation that accompanies this act of reproductive violence, destroys the individual male and the community to which he belongs/represents. Arab males, as part of a larger State-wide policy, are able to conquer and expel African farmers (and their families) through these acts of sexualised genocidal violence.

I will conclude this chapter with a discussion of glocalisation masculinities – my second iteration of Connell's notion of globalisation masculinities.

Glocalisation masculinities, Genocidal and Reproductive Violence(s) in Darfur

According to Schilling, Saulich & Engwicht (2018, p. 434), '[t]he interlinkages between global, national and local dynamics are a recurrent theme in the literature on natural resource governance and conflict'. To capture this relationship, I draw upon (and revise) Howe's (2008) notion of glocalisation. In its original formation, this concept addresses the relationship between macro-level practices and processes (e.g. globalisation, capitalism) and their impact at the local level. Incorporating gender into the analysis leads me to the concept of glocalisation masculinities. This is understood here as the link between climate variability at the macro-level (resulting in droughts at the local level), institutionalised Arab-Sudanese policies at the meso-level and the use of genocidal violence (rape and sex-selective killing) and reproductive violence at the macro- and micro-levels. We will begin by unpacking the relationship between climate variability and conflict.

There is a growing body of scholarly work, within the Environmental Security literature, that reviews the security implications of climate change, particularly in relation to violent conflict (De Juan, 2015; Detges, 2017; Schilling et al., 2018; Von Uexkull, 2014; Work, 2018).[4] Vivekananda, Schilling, Mitra, & Pandey (2014)

---

[4]See Homer-Dixon (n.d.) who has written extensively on environmental scarcity and violent conflict. See also Klem 2003 who has written a report *Dealing with Scarcity and violent conflict* based on the 2003 conference of the same name).

define environmental security as 'the absence of risk or threat to the environment a person or community depends on and lives in' (Vivekananda et al., 2014, p. 1143 as cited in Schilling et al., 2018, p. 437). Risks are either caused by nature (e.g. flooding or landslides) or by humans. The example Schilling et al. (2018) provide for the latter is the pollution of soil and groundwater caused by mining.

Research on the links between conflict and climate change is both quantitative and qualitative (Schilling et al., 2018). The former involves analysing and comparing climate data with conflict data. This is often at regional or national levels. As Schilling et al. (2018) note, quantitative studies cover large geographic areas over long periods of time. The aim is to create a comprehensive database that can be used for correlation purposes (see also De Juan, 2015). Conversely, qualitative research is based on observations, interviews and focus group discussions. A common theme within this work is that 'drought or other extreme climatic events may serve as catalysts for conflicts over food and water and trigger regional and ethnic tensions to escalate into violent clashes' (Von Uexkull, 2014, p. 16; see also Schilling et al., 2018). The agricultural sector, which is reliant upon surface and sub-surface water supplies, is hit hardest by droughts (see Von Uexkull, 2014). This is of particular concern in Sub-Saharan Africa where (1) droughts have increased in frequency and intensity during the past 50 years (Detges, 2017; Von Uexkull, 2014) and (2) a third of the sub-Saharan African population live in drought-prone regions (Detges, 2017; Von Uexkull, 2014).

Whilst it is not possible to delineate a direct cause-and-effect relationship between climate variability and conflict, writers agree that, combined with pre-existing grievances and tensions (that may be ethnic, political, and/or religious), environmental changes, resulting in drought, are more likely to lead to civil conflict (Von Uexkull, 2014; See also Detges, 2017; Schilling et al., 2018). In the words of Von Uexkull (2014, p. 18):

> Where individual economic hardships coincide with other ethnic, class or religious cleavages in society, they may translate into perceptions of relative deprivation felt by a societal group...If economic deprivation is blamed on the government, this may translate into an increased propensity to engage in violence against the [S]tate... Where drought leads to food shortages and falling incomes, joining a rebel group is thus relatively more attractive

This is what occurred in Darfur. The drought added to existing grievances, allowing rebels to motivate actors to take action against the government (Von Uexkull, 2014). Likewise, the Sudanese government offered land to Arab militias who took up arms to fight against rebels (Von Uexkull, 2014). For those impacted by extreme weather events in Darfur, participation in the fighting was a means of securing or gaining resources (Von Uexkull, 2014; see also Castro, 2018; De Juan, 2015; Olsson & Siba, 2013).

As we have established, clashes over land and water resources caused by sustained droughts, was put forward as one of the main reasons for the conflict in Darfur. Here, I review the empirical evidence that supports this correlation.

Von Uexkull (2014) conducted a detailed empirical test on drought and conflict in Sub-Saharan Africa between 1989 and 2008 (thus including the conflict in Darfur). Using 'geo-referenced data' on conflicts in this area and 'high-resolution drought data', his results proved his hypothesis: that there is a positive correlation between drought and conflict. De Juan (2015), using a mix-method approach, also analysed the causal links between environmental change and violent conflict. Narrowing the focus to Darfur, he proposed that this happens in three stages. First there is an increase in migration caused by environmental changes. Second, this migration impacts and alters the demographics of 'high in-migration' areas and third, there are increases in competition over resources (De Juan, 2015, p. 23). Combined, these factors, De Juan (2015) argues, '...increase the risk of violent interethnic resource conflict'.

For the qualitative data, as well as anecdotal evidence, De Juan (2015) drew on visual geographical patterns. He utilised the Normalized Difference Vegetation Index (NDVI). This correlates with annual rainfall in Sudan and provides satellite imagery of the density and health of vegetation. The higher the NDVI values, the greater the health and density of the vegetation. He used this data to record environmental changes in different parts of Darfur. Using the 'African Population Database' he then linked migration patterns within Darfur to the environmental changes recorded by the NDVI. According to De Juan's (2015) data, areas most impacted by in-migration were characterised by violent clashes. For the quantitative analysis, De Juan (2015) used data collated by the US State Department's 'Humanitarian Information Unit (HIU)', which contained information on the villages that were attacked during the conflict. Linking all three data sets, his results '[lend] consistent support to the assumption that long-term environmental change has contributed to shaping the dynamics of violence in Darfur' (De Juan, 2015, p. 31). And finally, Detges (2017, p. 95) also ran an empirical test, investigating the links between drought and political violence in Sub-Saharan Africa. His findings 'support the argument that political exclusion exacerbates climate-related hardships and can thus give rise to social tensions and grievances in the wake of drought'.

It is my argument that in order to fully understand the conflict in Darfur, and the genocidal, reproductive violence(s) that were carried out, we need to unpack the relationship between all of these factors. At the macro-level, we need to consider the impact of climate variability and the extreme weather events it leads to, such as droughts. This impacts individuals and communities at the local level. As demonstrated above, these weather events can cause clashes that lead to civil war, as in the case of Darfur. However, we must proceed with caution. Environmental factors alone do not cause conflict. They work in tandem with preexisting grievances. In Darfur, at the meso-level institutionalised ethnopolitical Arabisation policies and the manipulation of the gender hierarchy were used to marginalise African Darfuri men. Gendered relations and hierarchies, as well as racialised enactments of masculinity, coalesced with resource insecurity, resulting in the uprising of the two main rebel groups: the SLM/A and the JEM. This marked the beginnings of the conflict. During the conflict, rape, sex-selective killing and reproductive violence, as tools of genocide, were used at both the macro- and the micro-levels. Sex-selective killing and reproductive violence were widespread and systematic. They formed part of a genocidal campaign of conquest and settlement. They can be placed at the macro-level. At the micro-level, these acts of genocidal and reproductive violence subordinated individual men within the gender hierarchy. These acts of violence were informed by, and in turn shaped, gender relations and the gender hierarchy in Darfur. Ethnopolitical, cultural, racial and environmental forces (as outlined above), in line with the Sudanese gender hierarchy (and local masculinities of conquest and settlement), are implicated in the CRSV and SGBV that took place during the conflict. Combined, these multilevel, interrelated factors, account for the origins and the nature of violence(s) that took place during the conflict in Darfur.

Conclusion

In this chapter, I have examined how, historically, the human security framework reproduces gender essentialism confirming the ontological construction of women (read civilian) as vulnerable, weak and in need of protection. In contradistinction, this biopolitical narrative (as illustrated in the various UNSCRs outlined above) necessarily views male victimisation as an ontological and material impossibility. The implications of this exclusion for male survivors were discussed. Challenging these reductive and essentialist assumptions, Clark (2017) confronts the uncomfortable reality of male vulnerability, specifically the vulnerability of the penis. Clark (2017) is not alone – numerous scholars have highlighted the emasculating and feminising effect of male-to-male rape and sexual violence and the difficulties men face in reporting such violence, not least due to laws criminalising homosexuality (Apperley, 2015; Christian et al., 2011; Clark, 2017; Gorris, 2015; Lewis, 2009; Solangon & Patel, 2012; Storr, 2011; Touquet & Gorris, 2016; UN SRSG-SVC, 2013; Vojdik, 2014). Others have drawn attention to the sex-selective, systematic killing of battle-aged men (Carpenter, 2005, 2006; Jones, 2000, 2002); the various types of CRSV and SGBV they are subjected to during war/armed conflict and finally, researchers have drawn attention to the SEA of unaccompanied and separated children (Digidiki & Bhabha, 2018; Freccero et al., 2017; Mason-Jones & Nicholson, 2018).

This work offers a rebuttal to the statement made by Major General Patrick Cammaert: 'it is now more dangerous to be a woman than a soldier in armed conflict'. While, as noted earlier, the statement is based upon a comparison between the experiences of civilian women and male soldiers – affording his cynicism some credence – it is still possible to take issue with this comment. Here, I return briefly to my argument about disproportionality raised in the Introduction (something I will return to in the Conclusion). My suggestion is that we move away from focusing on degrees of harm. I propose that we abandon our preoccupation with questions of who suffers more/for whom is the impact greater? I advocate that we spend more time unpacking the unique ways in which men and women suffer; that we dedicate more energy into unpacking the qualitative and material differences in how males and females experience and survive war/armed conflict. Why not examine how constructions of masculinities and femininities inform how the genders experience war/armed conflict? To assume that *all* women will suffer more or less than *all* men is reductive and homogenises the experiences of both genders.

I raised my concerns about these types of comparative analyses in relation to Grey's (2017) argument that women suffer reproductive violence more acutely than men. While I do not take issue with her claim *per se*, oftentimes these statements appear as throw away comments where no follow up comment is offered explaining why or how the author arrived at such a conclusion. Why is it women suffer more acutely? Why are men's experiences of reproductive violence less acute? On the contrary, in this chapter, I examined how and why men's experiences might be *different*.

This chapter provided an in-depth analysis of the causes and the nature of the genocide in Darfur. Acts of genocidal (rape and sex-selective killing) and reproductive violence (genital harm) enacted by the State, the military and the Janjaweed, were explained by my alternative reading of Connell's globalisation masculinities and my notion of glocalisation masculinities.

Conclusion

I started this book with the following questions: how is suffering gendered? How does gender inform both the experiences of those who victimise and those who are victimised during war/armed conflict? I promised that this would be a qualitative rather than a quantitative comparative endeavour based on the lived experiences of victims, survivors and perpetrators. My goal was to offer a critical understanding of gender essentialism within accounts of gender and the violence(s) of war/armed conflict. By placing the lived experiences of women and girls before, during and in the aftermath of war/armed conflict along a continuum of violence, victimisation and coerced sexual activities, I sought to offer a more nuanced account of their lives. At the same time, drawing on Feminist and Visual Criminology, I offered a holistic account of women's involvement in sexualised violence and torture. To complete this story, and redress existing gaps within the literature, I examined the experiences of male victims and survivors. In order to reflect in more detail on the aims and content of the book, let us revisit and expand upon the five key messages outlined in the Introduction.

1. The GBV(s) that take place during and in the aftermath of armed conflict cannot be reduced to visible acts of interpersonal violence. They also include, and are connected to, structural violence, State crimes and institutional organisations (see Chapters 2, 3, 4 and 5).

I will unpack each of these categories in more detail below.

Structural Violence

The securitisation agenda ironically, and perhaps paradoxically, undermines its own agenda: the elimination of wartime rape and sexual violence. It does so in two main ways. First, it selectively focuses on the experiences of women and girls, thereby obscuring those of men and boys. Second, it fails to address the range of violence(s) committed during war/armed conflict, thereby overlooking the range of causal factors. By ignoring structural types of violence, as well as reproductive

Gender and the Violence(s) of War and Armed Conflict:
More Dangerous to be a Woman?, 159–171
Copyright © 2020 by Stacy Banwell. Published by Emerald Publishing Limited.
This work is published under the Creative Commons Attribution (CC BY 4.0) licence.
Anyone may reproduce, distribute, translate and create derivative works of this work
(for both commercial and non-commercial purposes), subject to full attribution to the original
publication and authors. The full terms of this licence may be seen at http://creativecommons.org/
licences/by/4.0/legalcode" Knowledge Unlatched Open Access
doi:10.1108/978-1-78769-115-520201009

and genocidal violence committed against men and boys, it limits what falls under its remit of investigation/analysis.

In terms of my third example of structural violence – women's lack of access to formal employment, resulting in forced prostitution and survival sex – consider the women and girls in Iraq and Syria involved in coerced sexual activities (not to be confused with those trafficked for sexual purpose, see Chapters 3 and 4). These females occupy the following identities simultaneously: victim, survivor and actor. While force is present, in some cases so too is 'relative autonomy' (Sjoberg & Gentry, 2008; see Chapter 3). These women are three-dimensional agents.

While security actors, activists (such as Lisa Shannon) and celebrities (such as Charlize Theron and Nicole Kidman) may have good intentions, raising awareness about the plight of victims in war-torn regions, ultimately, this work – which focuses narrowly on one aspect of wartime/conflict violence – will only assist us on a cursory level. Our efforts to combat the violence(s) of war/armed conflict are impeded by the following: our tendency to speak for and about women and girls; our focus on certain types of victims (females rather than males) and our focus on certain types of violence (rape and sexual violence) at the expense of structural violence. The ways in which western discourses often distort and universalise the experiences of oppressed women and girls in the Global South were raised in Chapter 2. This was done with reference to Spivak's insightful essay, '*Can the subaltern speak*? (1988) and Mohanty's arguments about the monolithic third-world-woman (1988). Gendered civilising missions and the postcolonial feminist critique were also discussed in this chapter.

Rape and sexual violence are tools used by both males and females for different reasons in different contexts. As we have seen in the various case studies under review, these acts of violence can be strategic (the DRC, the 1971 Liberation War and the conflict Darfur, as well as opportunistic (the Holocaust and the sexualised violence committed at Abu Ghraib). While these are important distinctions to make, particularly for conversations about tackling such violence(s), let us not forget that these are only *two* examples of the violence(s) committed during war/armed conflict. We must broaden the range of wartime/conflict violence that we examine. Throughout the book, by including examples of structural violence, I have extended what counts as violence and expanded the diagnostic framework which facilitates this broader analysis.

State Crimes

As outlined in Chapter 2, State crimes violate international and domestic laws. They are committed by representatives of the State often for economic, geopolitical and ideological reasons (Mullins & Rothe, 2008, p. 83). In the context of this book, gender, in the form of globalisation masculinities, was also regarded as a motivating factor. I unpacked State crimes in relation to the armed conflicts in the DRC and Iraq. In both examples, these macro-level illegal actions were connected to acts of sexual gender-based violence (SGBV) committed against civilian women and girls.

In both examples, these State crimes were/are committed against the backdrop of masculinities of postcolonialism and neoliberalism. In the case of the DRC, transnational companies engage in the illegal exportation of minerals, using the chaos of the conflict – which involves the strategic use of wartime rape and sexual violence – to achieve their economic goals. This implicates them in State-corporate crimes. The US invaded Iraq without legal authorisation, failing to meet the legal standard of self-defence. This act of aggression has been described by criminologists as a State crime (Kramer & Michalowski, 2005, 2011; see also Whyte, 2007). As demonstrated in Chapter 3, following the US intervention in Iraq, GBV against women and girls increased. Furthermore, following the privatisation agenda of the west, women and girls were forced into the illicit economy where they either engaged in forced prostitution or were trafficked for sexual purposes. In both armed conflicts, State crimes maintain and exacerbate the use of sexual GBV against civilian women and girls within and beyond the conflict zone. Based on this, I posit that the interpersonal violence(s) that took/take place emerge from an interpersonal-*State* nexus.

Institutional Violence

While the US government attempted to distance themselves from the violence(s) that took place at Abu Ghraib – referring to those involved as 'a few bad apples' – the sexualised violence and torture was carried out by individuals working for the US military. As I argued in Chapter 5, while agency must be ascribed to those individuals who carried out these acts of interpersonal violence, they cannot be divorced from the wider context of the war on terror and its driving force: American exceptionalism. As a result, I posit that the interpersonal violence(s) of Abu Ghraib can be attributed to an interpersonal-*institutional* nexus.

2. **As both symbolic and corporeal mothers of the nation, women are at risk of reproductive and genocidal violence during war/armed conflict (Chapter 1).**

On a symbolic level, discourses of war/armed conflict construct the maternal body as a canvas upon which national, racial, ethnic and religious identities are inscribed (Cohn, 2013). Corporeally, and within 'nationalist discourses', women are the bearers of the next generation of (preferably male) fighters (Åhäll, 2017, p. 22). Perversely, in the context of the Holocaust, women's biological maternal function formed part of the Nazi genocide. In this instance, women's ability to produce future generations of Jews led to crimes of 'reproductive violence' (Grey, 2017) in the form of forced sterilisation and forced abortions. In the case of the 1971 Liberation War in Bangladesh, as representations of their nation, it is estimated that between 200,000 and 400,000 Bengali women and girls were raped by the Pakistani army. As I outlined in Chapter 1, both the physical and the social-symbolic element of genocide were present in this example. Furthermore, reproductive violence was enacted by the State through its regulation of the post-war reproductive body.

3.   Gender essentialism – that is, the equation of maleness with war-fighting and femaleness with victimisation – obscures the experiences of male victims and female perpetrators (Chapters 5 and 6).

In the Introduction, I asked the following: on what basis do we make the claim that women are disproportionately affected by war/armed conflict? Does the assumption that women are disproportionately impacted diminish how we view male suffering? How do we interpret male civilian victimisation? For my part, I believe that gender essentialism underpins the arguments laid out in the disproportionality thesis. That is, if one believes that men and boys are always and already combatants – and by extension, the perpetrators of the violence(s) of war/armed conflict – on a rudimentary level, it makes sense to view female civilians as disproportionately impacted by war/armed conflict. Therefore, it seems to me, that part of the project of redirecting our attention away from this focus on disproportionality requires that we contest the gender essentialism that underpins its logic (I will return to this shortly in the section below: 'Rethinking gender and the violence(s) of war/armed conflict').

The fifth chapter of this book focused on female perpetrators in Iraq. However, this is only one example of women's more active role in war/armed conflict. While the fighters of old and new wars are predominantly male, women have also participated in war/armed conflict either, indirectly through numerous auxiliary roles or, directly through combat roles. The Soviet Union, for example, recruited women into their army units during the First and Second World Wars, as well as the Russian Civil War (Pennington, 2010). Women in the UK and oversees served as auxiliaries in non-combat roles during the Second World. This included the 'War in the Auxiliary Territorial Service (ATS),' the 'Women's Auxiliary Air Force (WAAF)' and the 'Women's Royal Naval Service (WRNS)' (Mason, 2018). Examples of females' active participation include but are not limited to: female fighters in the Congo, Uganda, Sierra Leone (Turshen, 2016), Kurdish fighters in Syria; women in the Farabundo Martí National Liberation Front – a guerrilla movement in El Salvador (Ramos, López, & Quinteros, 2015); and female fighters of the Liberation Tigers of Tamil Eelam in Sri Lanka. This list is by no means exhaustive but should provide readers with an idea of the range and scope of women and girls' relationship to war/armed conflict. Allied to my focus on female perpetrators of the violence(s) of war/armed conflict, Chapter 6 examined the experiences of male victims. Both chapters defy gender essentialism and underscore the reductive nature of the disproportionality thesis.

4.   Climate variability intersects with gender to inform structural and interpersonal forms of violence within and beyond the conflict zone (Chapters 4 and 6).

In Chapters 4 and 6 – drawing on the conflicts in Syria and Darfur, respectively – I considered climate variability and its relationship to conflict. This broadens our analytical framework and adds depth and complexity to our understanding of both the causes and consequences of modern conflicts. These chapters outline how macro-level environmental factors coalesce with meso-level policies and practices (such as neoliberalism in the case of Syria and Arabisation in Darfur) to shape interpersonal and structural forms of violence. I explored these intersecting phenomena through a gendered lens. This adds further depth and value to the discussion. As demonstrated, in Syria and Darfur, extreme droughts, caused by climate variability, led to increases in poverty (in the former) and clashes over natural resources (in the latter). For women and girls, this implicated them in new war illicit economies. For Darfuri African males, this placed them at risk of genocidal and reproductive violence.

5. **The violence(s) of war/armed conflict take place at the interrelated macro- meso- and micro-levels (all chapters).**

In every chapter of the book, and in every case study I have reviewed, the particular form of violence under review has been explored at the macro- meso- and micro-levels. At the macro-level, I connected global economic geopolitical policies and practices, as well as environmental forces, with the interpersonal and structural GBV(s) taking place within and beyond conflict zones. In order to explore these through a gendered lens, I drew upon globalisation masculinities, specifically masculinities of postcolonialism and neoliberalism.

At the meso-level, I examined how gendered cultural practices, the gender hierarchy, as well as ethnic identity/identities, are reproduced in institutions and State-led agendas which in turn inform the violence(s) that take place during war/armed conflict. In the case of the DRC, militarised masculinity, pre-existing gender inequalities and Congolese rape laws were reviewed. The violence(s) that took place at Abu Ghraib, as part of the invasion and occupation of Iraq, can be linked to the US military institution. In the case of Syria, I demonstrated how denial of girls' education is connected to patriarchal beliefs about gender roles and gendered divisions of labour. In relation to Darfur, I explored the institutionalisation of local Arab Sudanese masculinities, which led to genocidal and reproductive violence against African Darfuri men.

Finally, at the micro level, I narrowed the focus to individual acts of violence. While agency can be ascribed to these actors, their actions are informed by the aforementioned macro- and meso-level policies, practices and drivers. In Chapters 2, 3 and 4, the feminist political economy approach was used to facilitate this three-level interrelated analysis. Across all examples, I have highlighted how these three interconnected levels interact to both produce and reproduce structural, institutional, interpersonal and State GBV(s) during war/armed conflict.

Rethinking Gender and the Violence(s) of War/armed Conflict

Having reviewed the five key messages of the book, in the next section, I will interrogate what it really means when one argues that it is more dangerous to be a woman than a soldier in armed conflict.

As a thought experiment let us, for now, accept Major General Patrick Cammaert's statement ('it is perhaps more dangerous to be a woman than a soldier in armed conflict') as accurate. In doing so, what are the conceptual and empirical grounds to support this claim? As we saw in our discussion of the Holocaust and the 1971 Liberation War in Bangladesh, as reproducers of the nation, women and girls were targeted for rape and sexualised genocidal violence. Within the political economy of new wars – where State-corporate crimes are committed and the illicit economy flourishes – women and girls become disposable commodities. As we saw in the DRC, the use of rape and sexual violence against women and girls is strategic: it is used to terrorise and displace the local population to ensure that combatants on the ground, as well as transnational organisations, have access to the minerals that end up on the global market. In this instance, females are expendable. In Iraq and Syria, females are used as commodities by profit-seeking networks who exploit the illicit economy within and beyond the conflict zone. Here, women and girls are trafficked and sold into sexual slavery. In addition to these acts of interpersonal violence, women and girls are at risk of structural violence within the political economy of new wars. As we saw, neoliberal policies, increases in poverty and a lack of employment opportunities (exacerbated by the drought in the case of Syria) forced women to engage in coerced sexual activities during these conflicts. Taken at face value, one could argue that this is evidence that it is more dangerous to be a woman than a soldier in armed conflict. However, I believe there is a more fruitful way of thinking about all of this. This requires (on a conceptual level) that we dissect the relationship between gender and war/armed conflict.

Here is the conundrum as I see it: the notion that it is more dangerous to be a woman than a soldier in war/armed conflict comes from the woman-as-nation thesis. To reiterate, within this line of thinking, females and their reproductive bodies are regarded as the vessels through which national, racial, ethnic and religious identities are reproduced. They are viewed as both symbolically and corporeally mothers of the nation. This equation is discursively constructed. To assist us in unpacking this, we need to return to our discussion of semiotics and the cultural meaning of signs (see Chapter 5). As noted earlier, signs comprise the signifier, the physical form. They also contain the signified, the concept (Huntington, 2013). My suggestion is this: the female body (the sign), through its biological reproductive function (the signifier) acts as a reproducer of the nation to which she belongs. This leads to the woman-as-nation thesis (the signified). For me then, the 'danger' lies in the semiotics of language; in gender essentialism – and by extension, the hierarchical gender binary system (more on this below). For example, if we consider gendered justificatory narratives (discussed in Chapters 3 and 5 in relation to the invasion and occupation of Iraq), these are based upon ontological constructions of women as weak, fragile beings who are in need of protection. The corollary of this is that men are strong and are required to fight on behalf of these 'beautiful souls' (see Elshtain, 1982; Lobasz, 2008; Sjoberg, 2007; Sjoberg & Peet, 2011). However, as we saw in Iraq, intervention and occupation does little to diminish GBV against women and girls. In fact, not only does it exacerbate existing types of GBV, it can lead to new types of violence, for example structural GBV(s).

Two further problems arise from this reductive framing of women and men vis-à-vis war/armed conflict: (1) the securitisation agenda which focuses on women and girls at the expense of men and boys and (2) the persistent view of female perpetrators as aberrant. Moving forward my proposal is that we take on board the work of Krylova (2016, p. 309) who seeks to understand gender outside normative and binary-bound contexts.

In her article, *Gender Binary and the Limits of Poststructuralist Method*, Krylova (2016, p. 309) proposes that we '...broaden our theoretical framework...to revisit the concept of dichotomy and differentiate it from binary connotations of difference'. Before we get to this distinction, we will begin with her interpretation of the concept of 'gender binary'. For Krylova (2016, p. 307), this is a:

> [C]oncept [that] carries a rich repertoire of connotations, which informs and influences the gender category: those of radical distinction, opposition, mutually exclusive and exhaustive differentiation, hierarchy, domination, oppression – in all their myriad historical forms.

Based on her research into female combatants during the Soviet era, specifically the memoir of Zoia Medvedeva, Krylova (2016) encourages us to move beyond the concept of gender binary towards the idea of a 'nonbinary dichotomy'. Let us explore this in more detail. Zoia was the commander of a male machine-gun platoon in 1941 in Soviet Russia (Krylova, 2016, p. 317). As a Soviet female soldier her story is not unique. Soviet women volunteered as combatants during the Second World War (Krylova, 2016). They also, following authorisation by Stalin, established an all-female team of night bombers. Referred to as 'The night Witches',[1] this '588th Night Bomber Regiment...became one of the most remarkable fighting forces of World War II'. Referring specifically to the story of Zoia, while gender forms a part of this landscape, Krylova (2016, p. 317) argues that 'it did not operate as an omnipresent binary enterprise'. Furthermore, Zoia's accounts do not describe female soldiers as feeling as though they were entering into 'a male space' (Krylova, 2016).

Here, it is worth quoting Krylova (2016, pp. 317–318) at length:

> [...] 'women-soldiers'...are not described by Zoia as a self-evident contradiction assembled out of binary parts...that is, as 'masculine women', enacting or mimicking male behaviour. Far from it, the social identity of a 'women-soldier' constitutes what the Soviet society referred to as a 'different concept of a woman'

---

[1]The Night Witches often flew their planes at night. As they approached their targets, they would idle their planes before releasing their bombs. This tactic meant that their planes made whooshing noises as they glided by. It is reported that, for their German victims, this noise was reminiscent of a witch's broomstick, hence the name 'Night Witches' (see Garber, 2013; Grundhauser, 2015).

whose feminine qualities were not seen as necessarily compromised. Rather, they were informed with new connotations of the feminine. For example…I read the presence of red poppies at her gun site (marking one's combat space with flowers was a common preoccupation among women-soldiers) not as an importation of conventional femininity into the male trenches but as women combatants' attempt to change the very meaning of the feminine, to detach femininity from its binary associations with weakness and debilitating frivolity and to visually change the gender map of combat spaces.

Based on this, Krylova believes that the term dichotomy – which does not assign negative or positive values to its parts – can assist us in moving beyond binary understandings of gender. Within this framework, we explore how differences between the genders are produced, but we also acknowledge that '…*not all dichotomies must be necessarily binary*' (Krylova, 2016, p. 320 emphasis in the original). In other words, dichotomies, unlike binaries, do not assign a positive or negative value to males/masculinity/ies and females/femininity/ies respectively. Rather, they acknowledge differences, but not in a hierarchical sense. While Krylova's proposal is drawn from a specific historical time period, the conceptual foundations of her theoretical framework need not be time or context bound. This leads me to ask: how might her 'nonbinary dichotomy' assist us in moving away from gender essentialism and the assumption that it is more dangerous to be a woman than a soldier in war/armed conflict?

First, it is important to note that I believe that the dismantling of gender essentialism – the assumption that certain behaviours are inherently male/female – needs to work in conjunction with nonbinary dichotomies. So, while we can acknowledge that there are differences in the experiences of males and females, we must regard these as socially constructed normative ideas about gender and gender roles. These gendered expectations are internalised and performed by males and females who subscribed to these conventional ideals. This is stage one. Stage two involves applying the nonbinary dichotomy which removes the positive and negative connotations that map onto the categories male/female respectively.

Now that I have clarified this two-stage approach let us continue with our application of the nonbinary dichotomy. Here, I will draw out the various elements included in Krylova's definition of the 'gender binary' cited above.

'Hierarchy, Domination, Oppression'

In the Introduction, I talked about the *bacha posh,* the Afghan girls who dress like boys because being female is considered a 'humiliation' or a 'failure' in Afghan culture. Conversely, being male is considered a 'triumph' (Nordberg, 2014, p. 39 as cited in Banwell, 2015a, pp. 587–588). However, the benefits and privileges associated with being male are short-lived: the *bacha posh* cannot present as male beyond puberty as they will be required to marry in order to fulfil their childbearing responsibilities. Similarly, within the conflict zone in Syria, young girls who enter into marriage at a young age are forced to abandon their education so they can begin their childbearing and childrearing responsibilities. While this is used as a coping mechanism by fathers to alleviate poverty and secure their daughters' financial future, it also speaks to patriarchal beliefs about the role of females within the domestic/private sphere. This is a role where access to education is secondary. Here, we see how traditional gender binaries – which are hierarchical – associate males/masculinity/ies with freedom, privilege and power and females/femininity/ies with powerlessness, a lack of freedom and a lack of decision-making power. In cases of early and forced marriage, to paraphrase Krylova (2016), we need to detach conventional femininity from its binary associations with domesticity to ensure that young girls are not denied access to education, but also not placed at an increased risk of sexual violence and exploitation from their much older husbands. This will reduce the dangers they face.

'Connotations Which Informs and Influences the Gender Category'

As reproducers of the nation females are targeted during war/armed conflict. Here, the connotations associated with the maternal body – as symbolic and corporeal mothers of the nation – means that women, as a gender category, are attacked. In this example, we need to revise the meaning of the feminine and detach it from its essentialist association with biological motherhood. Again, this will reduce the dangers women face during war/armed conflict.

'Radical Distinction, Opposition'

As noted at the outset, differentiated gender roles are performed and reproduced within the military institution. As we saw in the DRC, militarised masculinity expects men and boys to be tough and aggressive. Furthermore, they are required to perform a violent heterosexual hegemonic masculinity. In opposition, idealised militarised femininity requires females to engage in sanitised fighting (Sjoberg & Gentry, 2007).

Within my framing of 'war-on-terror femininity', as outlined in detail in Chapter 5, the female soldier is violent and aggressive. She can engage in cruelty and torture. And while I based this alternative militarised femininity on the war on terror, its subversion of binary associations of femininity with weakness, frailty and vulnerability can be applied more universally. This means acknowledging that females, like males, can and are violent and aggressive, thus challenging the equation of femaleness (and conventional femininity) with passivity and non-violence.

Mutually Exclusive and Exhaustive Differentiation

Within the gender hierarchy, femininities are always positioned below masculinities. To paraphrase Connell and Messerchmidt (2005), masculinity is defined in contradistinction to femininity. Put another way, the feminine is always inferior to the masculine. However, my 'war-on-terror femininity' and the images I reviewed in Chapter 5, challenge this. Now I want us to consider the implications of the gender hierarchy for male victimisation.

As demonstrated in Chapter 5, the three women involved in the sexualised violence and torture at Abu Ghraib were used to feminise and emasculate the enemy. Rape and reproductive (genocidal) violence against males, disempowers men on an individual level, but it can also emasculate the group to which he belongs, thereby sending a message of symbolic elimination/destruction to the group as a whole (Ferrales, Brehm, & McElrath, 2016; Sivakumaran, 2007, p.274). Going back to Krylova's reading of Zoia's memoir, if we detach femininity from this binary association with weakness and inferiority, the power of rape and reproductive violence to emasculate and feminise the enemy is diminished.

In all of these examples, '[changing] the very meaning of the feminine' (Krylova, 2016, p. 318) – that is, applying the nonbinary dichotomy – assists us in challenging reductive understandings of the roles and experiences of males and females during war/armed conflict. Critics might argue that this is a purely academic exercise, that tackling this from a conceptual standpoint will do little to address the lived experiences of those affected by the violence(s) of war/armed conflict. And yet, as we have seen throughout this book, gender essentialism and binary constructions are pervasive and have informed (national and international) discourses (i.e. the securitisation agenda), cultural practices, foreign policy agendas (justifications for invading Iraq) and the tactics of war/armed conflict (woman-as-nation, man-as-protector). Ultimately, these discursive constructions have served to reinforce the notion that it is more dangerous to be a woman than a soldier in war/armed conflict. That said, I will now consider some of the practical steps we need to take to address the GBV(s) of war/armed conflict. These are demarcated along empirical, policy, legal, institutional and cultural lines.

Research (Empirical)

As I noted earlier, despite an increase in research on the links between climate change, and violent conflict, no direct causal relationship can be found (De Juan, 2015; Detges, 2017; Schilling, Saulich, & Engwicht, 2018; Von Uexkull, 2014; Work, 2018). Rather, environmental changes, leading to extreme weather events intersect with pre-existing grievances that can lead to conflict (Von Uexkull, 2014; see also Detges, 2017; Schilling et al., 2018). Drawing on the conflicts in Syria and Darfur, I examined gender, climate variability and conflict. Additional robust qualitative and quantitative data are needed to measure the relationship between conflict, extreme weather events (caused by climate variability) and interpersonal and structural GBV(s) that occur as a result.

Writing in 2016, Ferrales et al. (2016, pp. 567–568) argued that 'research on gender-based violence against men is in its infancy and has faced several limitations, including a disproportionate focus on the former Yugoslavia'. Indeed, to my knowledge, since then there have only been a handful of articles published that address this subject (these are reviewed in Chapter 6). In fact, while researching my chapter on men and boys, I was struck by the paucity of scholarly articles on the topic of conflict-related sexual violence (CRSV) against men and boys, particularly when compared with the copious amounts of material about female victims/survivors. SGBV against men and boys, has been listed in over 25 conflicts over the past 30 years, yet this is not reflected in the amount of literature we have on this subject. To redress this, research with male survivors/victims is needed. This empirical work must address the causes, the nature and the range of violence(s) to which men and boys are subjected to. As with females, this work must extend beyond rape and sexual violence. For example, Aijazi and Baines (2017, p. 464) conducted research with demobilised men from the Lord's Resistance Army in Uganda relating to their experiences of forced marriage. As they note: '[t]he majority of scholarship on forced marriage focuses on women's experiences of harm'.

Securitisation (Policy)

As noted previously, the securitisation agenda identifies women and girls as those most at risk of rape and sexual violence. This message is reproduced in numerous policy documents, most notably in a number of UN Security Council Resolutions (UNSCRs). Up until 2013, before UNSCR 2106 was passed, men and boys had not been included within these policy documents. Going forward, we need to ensure that the language of these documents (and others that address CRSV) includes the experiences of men and boys (see, for example, the 2019 annual report by the UN Secretary General on CRSV).

National and International Laws

The ICC and Forced Pregnancy

To reiterate, the Statute of the International Criminal Court (ICC) defines forced pregnancy as: 'the unlawful confinement of a woman forcibly made pregnant, with the intent of affecting the ethnic composition of any population or carrying out other grave violations of international law' (Rome Statue of the Criminal Court, 2011, p. 4). Taking a different position, The Holy See suggests that the Statute need only 'criminalize the act of forcibly *making* a woman pregnant, but not the subsequent conduct of forcibly *keeping* her pregnant' (Grey, 2017, p. 920, emphasis in the original). They proposed the term forcible impregnation rather than forced pregnancy. However, forcible impregnation was not considered as an acceptable replacement for forced pregnancy. This is because the former only refers to forcibly making a woman pregnant, whilst the latter involves keeping the woman pregnant. Thus, this definition 'excludes situations where the victim becomes pregnant by force, but is not subsequently confined' (Grey, 2017, p. 921).

In line with Grey's (2017) notion of reproductive violence, I believe that forcible impregnation should be listed as a crime by the ICC; one that is distinct from forced pregnancy as an act of genocide. This would recognise the experiences of women who have been forcibly impregnated, denied access to a safe abortion and then forced to continue with an unwanted pregnancy (as discussed in relation to Syria). Removing the requirement that women be confined would also mean that the experiences of women and girls, such as those who were raped and impregnated during the 1971 Liberation War, would be recognised and perpetrators criminalised under international law.

Rape, Honour Killings and Trafficking Laws in the DRC, Iraq and Beyond

States that are party to international laws prohibiting rape and CRSV should incorporate these into their national laws (as argued with reference to the DRC). Corruption within the local Criminal Justice System as well as the high fees associated with prosecution (including travel costs) need to be addressed. If we can improve the system itself, including how evidence is gathered, this may incentivise victims to come forward and report their experiences. As noted in previous chapters, one of the main reasons why survivors (both male and female) remain silent is due to fear of being stigmatised by their family and/or community. As we saw in Iraq, in some cases this led to honour killings in order to remove shame and restore family honour.

While removing the internalised shame victims/survivors may feel is arguably an impossible task, this should not deter us from tackling the shortcomings of the judicial process from a practical and logistical standpoint. Nor should we abandon efforts to criminalise and/or enforce existing laws relating to honour killings. Relatedly, anti-trafficking laws need to be enforced and perpetrators prosecuted. Women and girls who have been trafficked for sexual purposes are victims and should not be criminalised, as was the case in Iraq.

In terms of men and boys, laws that criminalise homosexuality need to be revoked, thereby making it easier for male victims to come forward. Acts of reproductive violence in the form of genital harm need to be fully acknowledged and not categorised as lesser crimes when dealt with by the ICC or other courts (Grey & Shepherd, 2012).

The Military (Institutional)

As noted with reference to the DRC, the performance of heterosexual hegemonic masculinity is reinforced within the military. This is an institution that normalises rape and sexual violence. It allows individual men to subvert their marginalised position within the hierarchy of the military and society more generally. Research by Trenholm, Olsson, Blomqvst, & Ahlberg (2013, p. 212) with 12 child soldiers from a range of rebel and official State military groups in the DRC, revealed that 'starvation, the use of mind-altering substances, forced marches and sleep deprivation' were among the measures used to ensure compliance from these child soldiers. This included engaging in gang rape. Most of the boys had either been abducted or forced into the military, with some joining to alleviate lives of abject poverty. The boys recount atmospheres of subjugation within the military, designed to maintain their obedience and loyalty to authority. This was often achieved through violence, including being beaten with sticks. Their involvement in acts of sexual violence signified their commitment and conformity to the aggressive heterosexual code of the military. As I argued earlier, this culture of militarised heterosexual masculinity, that condones violence against women and girls, needs to be challenged. However, in cases of forced recruitment, where male child soldiers are forced to rape, the ICC (and international law more generally) needs to recognise and prosecute commanders who order these acts of violence.

Despite the involvement of female soldiers in sexualised violence and torture at Abu Ghraib, female violence is not embedded within the institutional code of the military. This was underscored by the need for my recuperative narrative in the form of war-on-terror femininity.

Pre-existing Gender Inequalities and Discrimination (Cultural)

As I argued in the Introduction, pre-existing gender discrimination and gendered inequalities are reproduced and exacerbated during war/armed conflict. These need to be tackled prior to, during and in the aftermath of war/armed conflict. Laws, programmes and policies that promote equality between males and females need to be upheld and/or developed. Restrictions on women's freedom of movement need to be removed. Denying females access to reproductive healthcare and/or education should be regarded and punished as acts of structural violence.

So, to finish where we began: is it more dangerous to be a woman than a soldier in armed conflict?

In the six chapters of this book my qualitative analysis of the unique lived experiences of men, women, boys and girls eschews misguided tendencies to pursue quantitative, comparative analyses to prove the disproportionality thesis. The experiences of victims, survivors and perpetrators (boys, men, women and girls) were unpacked through a gendered lens. By unpacking ontological constructions of females as weak, passive and in need of protection and, conversely, of males as always and already actors and perpetrators, I have offered a counter narrative to the reductive gender essentialism inherent in many accounts of war/armed conflict. This alternative story about gender and the violence(s) of war/armed acknowledges that males and females experience such violence in unique and gendered ways; but does not seek to quantify the material reality of those affected by war/armed conflict. Non-essentialist and nonbinary dichotomous depictions of the categories male and female are key to fully understanding those who victimise and those who are victimised during war/armed conflict.

If the female body, and its biological reproductive function, continues to stand in for the nation, and if men and boys continue (and indeed are expected) to act as fighters and protectors, gendered notions of who 'is dangerous' and who is 'in danger' during war/armed conflict will remain unchallenged.

References

Abboud, S. (2017). *The economics of war and peace in Syria: Stratification and factionalization in the business community*. Retrieved from https://tcf.org/content/report/economics-war-peace-syria/

Abusharaf, R. M. (2006). Competing masculinities: Probing political disputes as acts of violence against women from Southern Sudan and Darfur. *Human Rights Review*, 7(2), 59–74.

Acker, J. (2004). Gender, capitalism and globalization. *Critical Sociology*, 30(1), 17–41.

Adams, R. (2017). *Michel Foucault: Biopolitics and biopower*. Retrieved from http://critical-legalthinking.com/2017/05/10/michel-foucault-biopolitics-biopower/

Africa Research Bulletin. (2011). Democratic Republic of Congo: FARDC accused of rape. *Africa Research Bulletin*, 48(1), 18701.

AfriMap and The Open Society Initiative for Southern Africa. (2009). *The Democratic Republic of Congo military justice and human rights – An urgent need to complete reforms*. Retrieved from https://issat.dcaf.ch/download/2212/19164/AfriMAP-DRC-MilitaryJustice-DD-EN.pdf

Agathangelou, A. M., & Turcotte, H. M. (2015). Postcolonial theories and challenges to 'first world-ism." In L. J. Shepherd (Ed.), *Gender matters in global politics: A feminist introduction to international relations* (pp. 36–48). New York, NY: Routledge.

Åhäll, L. (2017). *Sexing war/policing gender: Motherhood, myth and women's political violence*. London: Routledge.

Aijazi, O., & Baines, E. (2017). Relationality, culpability and consent in wartime: Men's experiences of forced marriage. *The International Journal of Transitional Justice*, 11(3), 463–483.

Al-Ali, N. (2005). Reconstructing gender: Iraqi women between dictatorship, war, sanctions and occupation. *Third World Quarterly*, 26 (4–5), 739–758.

Al-Ali, N. (2018). Sexual violence in Iraq: Challenges for transnational feminist politics. *European Journal of Women's Studies*, 25(1), 10–27.

Al-Ali, N., & Pratt, N. (2009a). Introduction. In N. Al-Ali & N. Pratt (Eds.), *Women and war in the Middle East: Transnational perspectives* (pp. 1–31). London: Zed Books.

Al-Ali, N., & Pratt, N. (2009b). The United States, the Iraqi women's diaspora and women's 'empowerment' in Iraq. In N. Al-Ali & N. Pratt (Eds.), *Women and war in the Middle East: Transnational perspectives* (pp. 65–98). London: Zed Books.

Al-Riffai, P., Breisinger, C., Verner, D., & Zhu, T. (2012). Droughts in Syria: An assessment of impacts and options for improving the resilience of the poor. *Quarterly Journal of International Agriculture*, 51(1), 21–49.

Alison, M. (2007). Wartime sexual violence: Women's human rights and questions of masculinity. *Review of International Studies*, 33(1), 75–90.

Alsaba, K., & Kapilashrami, A. (2016). Understanding women's experience of violence and the political economy of gender in conflict: The case of Syria. *Reproductive Health Matters*, 24(47), 5–17.

Amnesty International. (2009a). *Rape is cheaper than bullets*. Retrieved from https://politicaladvertising.co.uk/2009/02/27/amnesty-rape-is-cheaper-than-a-bullet/

Amnesty International. (2009b). *Women's rights… Provocative new rape in conflict advert to appear in London tubes*. Retrieved from https://www.amnesty.org.uk/press-releases/womens-rightss-rightss-rightss-rightss-rightss-rightss-rights-provocative-new-rape

Amnesty International. (2016). *I want a safe place: Refugee women from Syria uprooted and unprotected in Lebanon*. Retrieved from https://www.amnesty.org/download/Documents/MDE1832102016ENGLISH.PDF

Anani, G. (2013). *Dimensions of gender-based violence against Syrian refugees in Lebanon.* Retrieved from http://www.fmreview.org/sites/fmr/files/FMRdownloads/en/detention/anani.pdf

Anonymous. (1954). *A woman in Berlin* (P. Boehm, Trans.). London: Virago Press.

Aoláin, F. N. (2000). Sex-based violence and the Holocaust: A re-evaluation of harms and rights in international law. *Yale Journal of Law and Feminism, 12*(1), 43–84.

Aoláin, F. N. (2016). The 'war on terror' and extremism: Assessing the relevance of the women, peace and security agenda. *International Affairs, 92*(2), 275–291.

Apel, D. (2005). Torture culture: Lynching photographs and the images of Abu Ghraib. *Art Journal, 64*(2), 88–100.

Apperley, H. (2015). Hidden victims: A call to action on sexual violence against men in conflict. *Medicine, Conflict and Survival, 31*(2), 92–99.

Aradau, C., & van Munster, R. (2009). Exceptionalism and the 'war on terror:' Criminology meets international relations. *British Journal of Criminology, 49*(5), 686–701.

Argibay, C. M. (2003). Sexual slavery and the "Comfort women" of World War II. *Berkeley Journal of International Law, 21*, 375–389.

Askin, D. K. (2003). Prosecuting wartime rapes and other gender-related crimes under international law: Extraordinary advances, enduring obstacles. *Berkeley Journal of International Law, 21*, 288–349.

Ayers, A. J. (2008). Beyond the ideology of 'civil war': The global-historical constitution of political violence in Sudan. *The Journal of Pan African Studies, 4*(10), 261–288.

Baaz, M. E., & Stern, M. (2009). Why do soldiers rape? Masculinity, violence, and sexuality in the armed forces in the Congo (DCR). *International Studies Quarterly, 53*(2), 495–518.

Baaz, M. E., & Stern, M. (2013). *Sexual violence as a weapon of war? Perceptions, prescriptions, problems in the Congo and beyond.* New York, NY: Zed Books.

Banwell, S. (2007). *From unspeakable to unsayable to talked about: Women's subjective accounts of their violent behaviour, an interactionist study.* Unpublished doctoral thesis. University of Wales, Bangor.

Banwell, S. (2010). Gendered narratives: Women's subjective accounts of their use of violence and alternative aggression(s) within their marital relationships. *Feminist Criminology, 5*(2), 116–134.

Banwell, S. (2013). Book review: Ryan Ashley Caldwell, 'Fallgirls: Gender and the framing of torture at Abu Ghraib.' *Crime, Media, Culture, 9*(2), 214–216.

Banwell, S. (2014). Rape and sexual violence in the Democratic Republic of Congo: A case study of gender-based violence. *Journal of Gender Studies, 23*(1), 45–58.

Banwell, S. (2015a). Book review: Jenny Nordberg, 'The underground girls of Kabul: The hidden lives of Afghan girls disguised as boys.' *Journal of Gender Studies, 24*(5), 587–588.

Banwell, S. (2015b). Globalisation masculinities, empire-building and forced prostitution: A critical analysis of the gendered impact of the neoliberal economic agenda in post-invasion/occupation Iraq. *Third World Quarterly, 36*(4), 705–722.

Banwell, S. (2016). Rassenschande, genocide and the reproductive Jewish body: Examining the use of rape and sexualized violence against Jewish women during the Holocaust. *Journal of Modern Jewish Studies, 15*(2), 208–227.

Banwell, S. (2018). Security, peace and development: Unpacking discursive constructions of wartime rape and sexual violence in Syria. *International Journal of Peace and Development Studies, 9*(2), 15–30.

Banwell, S. (2019). Gender, north–south relations: Reviewing the global gag rule and the defunding of UNFPA under President Trump. *Third World Quarterly, 41*(1), 1–19.

Bartels, S. A., Michael, S., Roupetz, S., Garbern, S., Kilzar, L., Bergquist, H., … Bunting, A. (2018). Making sense of child, early and forced marriage among Syrian refugee girls:

A mixed methods study in Lebanon. *BMJ Global Health, 3*(1), 1–12. doi:10.1136/bmjgh-2017-000509

Bass, G. (2004). Jus post bellum. *Philosophy and Public Affairs, 32*(4), 384–412.

Batchelor, S. (2005). 'Prove me the bam!': Victimization and agency in the lives of young women who commit violent offences. *Probation Journal, 52*(4), 358–375.

Batha, E. (2015, February 17). Iraqi women trafficked into sexual slavery – rights group. *Reuters*. Retrieved from https://www.reuters.com/article/us-iraq-trafficking-women/iraqi-women-trafficked-into-sexual-slavery-rights-group-idUSKBN0L-L1U220150217

BBC. (2011). *Iraq war in figures*. Retrieved from https://www.bbc.co.uk/news/world-middle-east-11107739

BBC. (2013). *Iraq 10 years on: In numbers*. Retrieved from https://www.bbc.co.uk/news/world-middle-east-21752819

BBC. (2019a). *What's happening in Syria?* Retrieved from https://www.bbc.co.uk/newsround/16979186

BBC. (2019b). *Why is there a war in Syria?* Retrieved from https://www.bbc.co.uk/news/world-middle-east-35806229

Beachler, D. (2007). The politics of genocide scholarship: The case of Bangladesh. *Patterns of Prejudice, 41*(5), 467–492.

Beasley, C. (2008). Rethinking hegemonic masculinity in a globalizing world. *Men and Masculinities, 11*(1), 86–103.

Beauchamp, Z. (2017). *The war in Syria, explained: How Syria's civil war became America's problem*. Retrieved from https://www.vox.com/2017/4/8/15218782/syria-trump-bomb-assadexplainer

Beijing Declaration and Platform for Action. (1995). *The fourth world conference on women*. Retrieved from https://www.un.org/en/events/pastevents/pdfs/Beijing_Declaration_and_Platform_for_Action.pdf

Bock, G. (1993). Racism and sexism in Nazi Germany: Motherhood, compulsory sterilization, and the state. In C. Rittner & J. Roth (Eds.), *Different voices: Women and the Holocaust* (pp. 161–186). New York, NY: Paragon House (Original work published in 1984).

Boesten, J. (2017). Of exceptions and continuities: Theory and methodology in research on conflict-related sexual violence. *International Feminist Journal of Politics, 19*(4), 506–519.

Bose, S. (2007). Losing the victims: Problems of using women as weapons in recounting the Bangladesh war. *Economic and Political Weekly, 42*(38), 3864–3871.

Boudana, S., Frosh, P., & Cohen, A. A. (2017). Reviving icons to death: When historic photographs become digital memes. *Media, Culture & Society, 39*(8), 1210–1230.

Bouvier, P. (2014). Sexual violence, health and humanitarian ethics: Towards a holistic, person-centred approach. *International Review of the Red Cross, 96*(894), 565–584.

Brown, M. (2014). Visual criminology and carceral studies: Counter-images in the carceral age. *Theoretical Criminology, 18*(2), 176–197.

Brown, M. (2017). *Visual criminology: Oxford research encyclopedia of criminology*. Retrieved from https://oxfordre.com/criminology/view/10.1093/acrefore/9780190264079.001.0001/acrefore-9780190264079-e-206

Brown, M., & Carrabine, E. (2017). Introducing visual criminology. In M. Brown & E. Carrabine (Eds.), *Routledge international handbook of visual criminology* (e-book version). Oxon: Routledge.

Browne, G. (2018). *Al Qaeda's 're-radicalization' schools lure ISIL fighters in Syria*. Retrieved from https://www.thenational.ae/world/mena/al-qaeda-s-re-radicalisationschools-lure-isil-fighters-in-syria-1.697124

Brownmiller, S. (1975). *Against our will: Men, women and rape*. New York, NY. Ballantine Books.

Burgess-Proctor, A. (2006). Intersections of race, class, gender, and crime: Future directions for feminist criminology. *Feminist Criminology*, *1*(1), 27–47.

Burke, J. (2018, April 3). 'The wars will never stop' –millions flee bloodshed as Congo falls apart. *The Guardian*. Retrieved from https://www.theguardian.com/world/2018/apr/03/millions-flee-bloodshed-as-congos-army-steps-up-fight-with-rebels-in-east

Burke, J. (2019, July 8). DRC warlord 'the terminator' convicted of war crimes. *The Guardian*. Retrieved from https://www.theguardian.com/world/2019/jul/08/drc-rebel-commander-bosco-ntaganda-the-terminator-convicted-over-war-crimes?CMP=Share_iOSApp_Other

Burman, M. J., Batchelor, S. A. & Brown, J. A. (2001). Researching girls and violence: Facing the dilemmas of fieldwork. *The British Journal of Criminology*, *41*(3), 443–459.

Buss, D. E. (2009). Rethinking 'rape as a weapon of war.' *Feminist Legal Studies 17*, 145–163.

Butler, J. (1990). *Gender trouble. Feminism and the subversion of identity*. New York, NY: Routledge.

Butler, J. (2007). Torture and the ethics of photography. *Environment and Planning D: Society and Space*, *25*, 951–966.

Button, D. M., & Worthen, M. G. F. (2014). General strain theory for LGBQ and SSB youth: The importance of intersectionality in the future of feminist criminology. *Feminist Criminology*, *9*(4), 270–297.

Caldwell, R. A. (2012). *Fallgirls: Gender and the framing of torture at Abu Ghraib*. Farnham: Ashgate Publishing Limited.

Caldwell, R. A., & Mestrovic, S. G. (2008). The role of gender in 'expressive' abuse at Abu Ghraib. *Cultural Sociology*, *2*(3), 275–299.

Campbell, A. (1993). *Out of control: Men women and aggression*. London: Pandora.

Canning, V. (2010). Who's human? Developing sociological understandings of the rights of women raped in conflict. *The International Journal of Human Rights*, *14*(6), 849–864.

Cannizzaro, S. (2016). Internet memes as internet signs: A semiotic view of digital culture. *Sign Systems Studies*, *44*(4), 562–586.

Caprioli, M., & Douglass, K. L. (2008). Nation building and women: The effect of intervention on women's agency. *Foreign Policy Analysis*, *4*(1), 45–65.

Card, C. (1996). Rape as a weapon of war. *Hypatia*, *11*(4), 6–18.

Card, C. (2008). The paradox of genocidal rape aimed at enforced pregnancy. *The Southern Journal of Philosophy*, *46*(1), 176–189.

Carline, A. (2011). Criminal justice, extreme pornography and prostitution: Protecting women or promoting morality? *Sexualities*, *14*(3), 312–333.

Carlson, E. S. (2006). The hidden prevalence of male sexual assault during war: Observations on blunt trauma to the male genitals. *British Journal of Criminology*, *46*(1), 16–25.

Carney, P. (2017). How does the photograph punish? In M. Brown & E. Carrabine (Eds.), *Routledge international handbook of visual criminology* (e-book version). Oxon: Routledge.

Carpenter, C. R. (2002). Beyond 'gendercide': Incorporating gender into comparative genocide studies. *The International Journal of Human Rights*, *6*(4), 77–101.

Carpenter, C. R. (2005). Women, children and other vulnerable groups: Gender, strategic frames and the protection of civilians as a transnational issue. *International Studies Quarterly*, *49*(2), 295–334.

Carpenter, C. (2006). Recognizing gender-based violence against civilian men and boys in conflict situations. *Security Dialogue*, *37*(1), 83–103.

Carrabine, E. (2011). Images of torture: Culture, politics and power. *Crime, Media, Culture*, *7*(1), 5–30.

Carrabine, E. (2012). Just images: Aesthetics, ethics and visual criminology. *The British Journal of Criminology, 52*(3), 463–489.

Castro, A. P. (2018). Promoting natural resource conflict management in an illiberal setting: Experiences from Central Darfur, Sudan. *World Development, 109,* 163–171.

Cauterucci, C. (2017). *How U.S funding cuts to the U.N. population fund will hurt women in Guatemala and beyond.* Retrieved from https://slate.com/human-interest/2017/04/how-u-s-funding-cuts-to-the-u-n-population-fund-will-hurt-women-in-guatemala-and-beyond.html

Centre for Reproductive Rights. (2017). *Ensuring sexual and reproductive health and rights of women and girls affected by conflict. Briefing paper.* Retrieved from https://www.reproductiverights.org/document/briefing-paper-ensuring-sexual-and-reproductive-health-and-rights

Chalmers, B. (2015). Jewish women's sexual behavior and sexualized abuse during the Nazi era. *The Canadian Journal of Human Sexuality, 24*(2), 184–196.

Chesney-Lind, M. (2006). Patriarchy, crime and justice: Feminist criminology in an era' of backlash. *Feminist Criminology, 1*(1), 6–26.

Chinkin, C., & Kaldor, M. (2013). Gender and new wars. *Journal of International Affairs, 67*(1), 167–187.

Chirot, D., & McCauley, C. (2006). *Why not kill them all? The logic and prevention of mass political murder.* Princeton, NJ: Princeton University Press.

Christian, M., Safar, O., Ramazani, P., Burnham, G., & Glass, N. (2011) Sexual and gender-based violence against men in the Democratic Republic of Congo: Effects on survivors, their families and the community. *Medicine, Conflict and Survival, 27*(4), 227–246.

Chulov, M. (2019, March 24). The rise and fall of the Isis 'caliphate.' *The Guardian.* Retrieved from https://www.theguardian.com/world/2019/mar/23/the-rise-and-fall-of-the-isis-caliphate

Clark, J. N. (2017). The vulnerability of the penis: Sexual violence against men in conflict and security frames. *Men and Masculinities,* 1–23. https://doi.org/10.1177/1097184X17724487

CNN. (2013). *Iraq prison abuse scandal fast facts.* Retrieved from https://edition.cnn.com/2013/10/30/world/meast/iraq-prison-abuse-scandal-fast-facts/index.html

CNN. (2019). *Syrian civil war facts.* Retrieved from https://edition.cnn.com/2013/08/27/world/meast/syria-civil-war-fast-facts/index.html

Cockburn, C. (2012). Gender relations as causal in militarization and war. In A. Kronsell & E. Svedberg (Eds.), *Making gender, making war: Violence, military and peacekeeping practices* (pp. 19–34). London: Routledge.

Cockburn, P. (2017, September 6). While defeat of Isis dominates global attention, Al-Qaeda strengthens in Syria. *The Independent.* Retrieved from http://www.independent.co.uk/news/world/middle-east/isis-defeatal-quaeda-syria-grow-global-attention-islamist-terrorists-jihadis-unus-west-iraq-raqqa-a7932881.html

Cohen, D. K., Green, A. H, & Wood, E. J. (2013). Wartime sexual violence: Misconceptions, implications, and ways forward. *Special report of the United States institute of peace.* Retrieved from https://www.usip.org/sites/default/files/resources/SR323.pdf

Cohn, C. (2013). Women and wars: Toward a conceptual framework. In C. Cohn (Ed.), *Women and wars* (pp. 1–35). Cambridge: Polity Press.

Collins, V. E. (2017). *State crime: Women and gender.* London: Routledge.

Connell, R. W. (1998). Masculinities and globalization. *Men and Masculinities, 1*(1), 3–23.

Connell, R. W. (2005). *Masculinities* (2nd ed.). Berkeley, CA: University of California Press.

Connell, R. W., & Messerschmidt, J. W. (2005). Hegemonic masculinity: Rethinking the concept. *Gender and Society, 19*(6), 829–859.

Connell, R. W., & Wood, J. (2005). Globalization and business masculinities. *Men and Masculinities, 7*(4), 347–364.

Cook, K. J. (2016). Has criminology awakened from its "androcentric slumber"? *Feminist Criminology, 11*(4), 334–353.

Cosslett, R. (2017, January 2). This photo sums up Trump's assault on women's rights. *The Guardian.* Retrieved from https://www.theguardian.com/commentisfree/2017/jan/24/photo-trump-womens-rights-protest-reproductive-abortion-developing-contries

Council on Foreign Relations. (2018). *Violence in the Democratic Republic of Congo.* Retrieved from https://www.cfr.org/interactive/global-conflict-tracker/#!/conflict/violence-in-the-democratic-republic-of-congo

Crawford, K. F. (2013). From spoils to weapons: Framing wartime sexual violence. *Gender Development, 21*(3), 505–517.

Crawford, K. F., Green, A. H, & Parkinson, S. E. (2014, September 24). Wartime sexual violence is not just a "weapon of war." *The Washington Post.* Retrieved from https://www.washingtonpost.com/news/monkey-cage/wp/2014/09/24/wartime-sexual-violence-is-not-just-a-weapon-of-war/

Cudd, A. E. (2008). Rape and enforced pregnancy as femicide: Comments on Claudia Card's 'The paradox of genocidal rape aimed at enforced pregnancy.' *The Southern Journal of Philosophy, 46*, 190–199.

Dakkak, H. (2007). Tackling sexual violence, abuse and exploitation. *Forced Migration Review, 39.* Retrieved from https://www.fmreview.org/sites/fmr/files/FMRdownloads/en/iraq/dakkak.pdf

Dallman, A. (2009). Prosecuting conflict-related sexual violence at the international criminal court. *SIPRI Insights on Peace and Security, 1*, 1–16.

Das, B. (2011). *Bangladesh rape victims say war crimes overlooked.* Retrieved from https://womensenews.org/2011/09/bangladesh-rape-victims-say-war-crimes-overlooked/

Davies, S. E., & True, J. (2015). Reframing conflict-related sexual and gender-based violence: Bringing gender analysis back in. *Security Dialogue, 46*(6), 495–512.

De Châtel, F. (2014). The role of drought and climate change in the Syrian uprising: Untangling the triggers of the revolution. *Middle Eastern Studies, 50*(4), 521–535.

De Juan, A. (2015). Long-term environmental change and geographical patterns of violence in Darfur, 2003–2005. *Political Geography, 45*, 22–33.

de Waal, A. (2005). Who are the Darfurians? Arab and African identities, violence and external engagement. *African Affairs, 104*(415), 181–205.

de Waal, A., Hazlett, C., Davenport, C., & Kennedy, J. (2014). The epidemiology of lethal violence in Darfur: Using micro-data to explore complex patterns of ongoing armed conflict. *Social Science & Medicine, 120*, 368–377.

Decision of the Nuremberg Special Court in the Katzenberger Race Defilement Case. (n.d.). Retrieved from https://www.ushmm.org/wlc/en/article.php?ModuleId=10007909

Detges, A. (2017). Droughts, state-citizen relations and support for political violence in Sub-Saharan Africa: A micro-level analysis. *Political Geography, 61*, 88–98.

Digidiki, V., & Bhabha, J. (2018). Sexual abuse and exploitation of unaccompanied migrant children in Greece: Identifying risk factors and gaps in services during the European migration crisis. *Children and Youth Services Review, 92*, 114–121.

Diken, B., & Lausten, C. B. (2005). Becoming abject: Rape as a weapon of war. *Body and Society, 11*(1), 111–128.

Dixon, R. (2002). Rape as a crime in international humanitarian law: Where from here? *European Journal of International Law, 13*(3), 697–719.

Duncanson, C. (2013). *Forces for good? Military masculinities and peacebuilding in Afghanistan and Iraq.* Basingstoke: Palgrave Macmillan.

Dunn, J. L., & Powell-Williams, M. (2007). Everybody makes choices: Victim advocates and the social construction of battered women's victimization and agency. *Violence Against Women, 13*(10), 977–1001.

Duroch, F., & Schulte-Hillen, C. (2015). *Care for victims of sexual violence. An organization pushed to its limits: The case of Médecins Sans Frontières.* Retrieved from https://international-review.icrc.org/articles/care-victims-sexual-violence-organization-pushed-its-limits-case

Eisenman, S. (2007). *The Abu Ghraib effect.* London: Reaktion Books.

Eller, R. D. (2014). *The war on poverty in Appalachia.* Retrieved from http://www.uky.edu/CommInfoStudies/IRJCI/EllerPovertyWarAppalachiaOhioU.pdf

Elshtain, J. B. (1982). On beautiful souls, just warriors and feminist consciousness. *Women's Studies International Forum, 5*(3-4), 341–348.

Emmanuel, K. I. (2016). Access to health care in the Democratic Republic of Congo: Major challenge for the poor. *Journal of Nursing and Palliative Care Services* (NPCS). http://hendun.org/journals/NPCS/PDF/NPCS-16-1-103.pdf

En.wikipedia.org. (2003). Retrieved from https://en.wikipedia.org/wiki/File:AG-10B.JPG#/media/File:AG-10.jpg

En.wikipedia.org. (2003–2004). Retrieved from https://en.wikipedia.org/wiki/File:Abu_Ghraib_48.jpg

End Violence Against Women. (2014). *Submission to Amnesty International's global policy consultation on sex work.* Retrieved from https://www.endviolenceagainstwomen.org.uk/wp-content/uploads/EVAW_Submission_on_Amnesty_consultation_FINAL.pdf

Enloe, C. (2000). *Maneuvers: The international politics of militarizing women's lives.* Berkley, CA: University California Press.

Enloe, C. (2010). *Nimo's war, Emma's war: Making feminist sense of the Iraq war.* London: University of California Press.

Erez, E., Adelman, M., & Gregory, C. (2009). Intersections of immigration and domestic violence: Voices of battered immigrant women. *Feminist Criminology, 4*(1), 32–56.

European Commission. (n.d.). Zaatari camp: *Taking care of women and the future generation.* Retrieved from https://ec.europa.eu/echo/field-blogs/stories/zaatari-camp-taking-care-women-and-future-generation_en

European Security Strategy. (2003). *A secure Europe in a better world.* Retrieved from https://www.cvce.eu/content/publication/2004/10/11/1df262f2-260c-486f-b414-db-f8dc112b6b/publishable_en.pdf

Farwell, N. (2004). War rape: New conceptualizations and responses. *Affilia, 19*(4), 389–403.

Fanghanel, A., Milne, E., Zampini, G., Banwell, S., Filddler, M. (Forthcoming) *Sex and Crime.* London: Sage Publishing.

Faust, A. M. (2015). *The Ba'thification of Iraq: Saddam Hussein's totalitarianism.* Austin, TX: University of Texas press.

Fay, G. R., & Jones, A. R. (2005). *Investigation of intelligence activities at Abu Ghraib.* Retrieved from https://apps.dtic.mil/dtic/tr/fulltext/u2/a429125.pdf

Fein, H. (1999). Genocide and gender: The uses of women and group destiny. *Journal of Genocide Research, 1*(1), 43–63.

Femia, F., & Werrell, C. (2012). *Syria: Climate change, drought and social unrest.* Retrieved from https://climateandsecurity.org/2012/02/29/syria-climate-change-drought-and-social-unrest/

Ferrales, G., Brehm, H. N., & McElrath, S. (2016). Gender-based violence against men and boys in Darfur: The gender-genocide nexus. *Gender and Society, 30*(4), 565–589.

Ferrell, J. (2017). 'We never, never talked about photography': Documentary photography, visual criminology, and method. In M. Brown & E. Carrabine (Eds.), *Routledge international handbook of visual criminology* (e-book version). Oxon: Routledge.

Ferris, E. (2007). Abuse of power: Sexual exploitation of refugee women and girls. *Signs: A Journal of Women in Culture and Society, 32*(3), 584–591.

FIDH. (2012). *Violence against women in Syria: Breaking the silence. Briefing paper based on an FIDH assessment mission in Jordan.* Retrieved from: https://fidh.org/IMG/pdf/syria_sexual_violence-web.pdf

Finn, J. (2017). Making the criminal visible: Photography and criminality. In M. Brown & E. Carrabine (Eds.), *Routledge international handbook of visual criminology* (e-book version). Oxon: Routledge.

Flaschka, M. (2010). Only pretty women were raped: The effect of sexual violence on gender identities in concentration camps. In S. Hedgepeth & R. Saidel (Eds.), *Sexual violence against Jewish women during the Holocaust* (pp. 77–93). Massachusetts: Brandeis University Press.

Fogelman, E. (2012). Rape during the Nazi Holocaust: Vulnerabilities and motivations. In C. Rittner & J. Roth (Eds.), *Rape: Weapon of war and genocide* (pp. 15–28). St Paul Minnesota: Paragon House.

Ford, L. (2019, April 23). UN waters down rape resolution to appease U.S's hardline abortion stance. *The Guardian.* Retrieved from https://www.theguardian.com/global-development/2019/apr/23/un-resolution-passes-trump-us-veto-threat-abortion-language-removed

Foster, A. M. (2016, March 9–11). Safe abortion in humanitarian settings: An overview of needs, gaps and resources. Paper presented at the 16th annual meeting of the IAWG on Reproductive Health in Crises. Dakar, Senegal. Retrieved from http://iawg.net/wp-content/uploads/2016/08/IAWG-16th-Annual-Meeting-6-21-16-FINAL.pdf

Foster, A. M., Arnott, G., & Hobstetter, M. (2017). Community-based distribution of misoprostol for early abortion: Evaluation of a program along the Thailand-Burma border. *Contraception, 96*(4), 242–247.

Foster, A. M., Arnott, G., Hobstetter, M., Zaw, H., Maung, C., Sietstra, C., & Walsh, M. (2016). Establishing a referral system for safe and legal abortion care: A pilot project on the Thailand-Burma border. *International Perspectives on Sexual and Reproductive Health, 42*(3), 151–156.

Foster, J. E., & Minwalla, S. (2018). Voices of Yazidi women: Perceptions of journalistic practices in the reporting on ISIS sexual violence. *Women's Studies International Forum, 67,* 53–64.

Foucault, M. (1977). *Discipline and punish: The birth of the prison* (A. Sheridan, Trans). London: Penguin.

Foucault, M. (1978). *The history of sexuality. Volume I: An introduction* (R. Hurley, Trans.). London: Penguin. Retrieved from https://suplaney.files.wordpress.com/2010/09/foucault-the-history-of-sexuality-volume-1.pdf

Foucault, M. (2015). *The Punitive Society: Lectures at the Collège de France, 1972-1973.* (G. Burchell, Trans & Ed. A.I. Davidson). Gordonsville, United States: Palgrave Macmillan (Original work published in 1972–1973).

Franklin, C. A. (2008). Women offenders, disparate treatment, and criminal justice: A theoretical, historical, and contemporary overview. *Criminal Justice Studies, 21*(4), 341–360.

Freccero, J., Biswas, D., Whiting, A., Alrabe, K., & Seelinger, K. T. (2017). Sexual exploitation of unaccompanied migrant and refugee boys in Greece: Approaches to prevention. *PLoS Med., 14*(11), e1002438. https://doi.org/10.1371/journal.pmed.1002438

Freedman, J. (2016). Sexual and gender-based violence against refugee women: A hidden aspect of the refugee "crisis." *Reproductive Health Matters, 24*(47), 18–26.

Freedman, J. (2011). Explaining sexual violence and gender inequalities in the DRC. *Peace Review, 23*(2), 170–175.

Friedman, J. (2002). *Speaking the unspeakable: Essays on sexuality, gender, and the Holocaust survivor memory*. Maryland: University Press of America.

GAPS UK. (2013). *Response to the preventing sexual violence Initiative*. Unpublished briefing paper circulated prior to the ESVC Summit.

Garber, M. (2013, July 15). Night witches: The female fighter pilots of World War II members of the 588th night bomber regiment decorated their planes with flowers ... and dropped 23,000 tons of bombs. *The Atlantic*. Retrieved from https://www.theatlantic.com/technology/archive/2013/07/night-witches-the-female-fighter-pilots-of-world-war-ii/277779/

Gentry, C. E., & Sjoberg, L. (2015). *Beyond mothers, monsters, whores: Thinking about women's violence in global politics*. London: Zed books.

George, N., & Shepherd, L. (2016). Women, peace and security: Exploring the implementation and integration of UNSCR 1325. *International Political Science Review, 37*(3), 297–306.

Gies, L. (2017). Staged imagery of killing and torture: Ethical and normative dimensions of seeing. In M. Brown & E. Carrabine (Eds.), *Routledge international handbook of visual criminology* (e-book version). Oxon: Routledge.

Gilbert, P. (2002). Discourses of female violence and societal gender stereotypes. *Violence Against Women, 8*(11), 1271–1300.

Girls not Brides. (2017). Child marriage and the Syrian conflict: 7 things you need to know. Retrieved from https://www.girlsnotbrides.org/child-marriage-and-the-syrian-conflict-7-things-you-need-to-know/

Gleick, P. H. (2014). Water, drought, climate change, and conflict in Syria. *Weather, Climate and Society, 6*, 331–340.

Global Citizen. (2017). *The details of Trump's proposed foreign aid cuts are devastating*. Retrieved from https://www.globalcitizen.org/en/content/trump-foreign-aid-cuts-report/

Global Justice Centre. (2011). *The right to an abortion for girls and women raped in armed conflict: States' positive obligations to provide non-discriminatory medical care under the Geneva conventions*. Retrieved from http://globaljusticecenter.net/documents/LegalBrief.RightToAnAbortion.February2011.pdf

Global Witness. (2016). *River of Gold. How the state lost out in an eastern Congo gold boom, while armed groups, a foreign mining company and provincial authorities pocketed millions*. Retrieved from https://reliefweb.int/sites/reliefweb.int/files/resources/River_of_gold.pdf

Gobat, J., & Kostial, K. (2016). *International monetary fund working paper: Syria's conflict economy*. Retrieved from https://www.imf.org/external/pubs/ft/wp/2016/wp16123.pdf

Goetze, K. (2008). *Special report: Sexual violence in the Democratic Republic of Congo*. Institute for War and Peace Reporting: Netherlands International Justice Programme. Retrieved from http://www.ceipaz.org/images/contenido/Sexual%20violence%20in%20the%20Democratic%20Republic%20of%20Congo.pdf

Goldenberg, M. (1998). Memoirs of Auschwitz survivors: The burden of gender. In D. Ofer & L. Weitzman (Eds.), *Women in the Holocaust* (pp. 327–339). New Heaven: Yale University Press.

Goldenberg, M. (2013). Sex-based violence and the politics and ethics of survival. In M. Goldenberg & A. Shapiro (Eds.), *Different horrors, same hell: Gender and the Holocaust* (pp. 99–127). Seattle, WA: University of Washington Press.

Gong-Gershowitz, J. (2009). Forced marriage: A "new" crime against humanity? *Northwestern Journal of International Human Rights, 8*(1), 53–76.

Gorris, E. A. P. (2015). Invisible victims? Where are male victims of conflict-related sexual violence in international law and policy? *European Journal of Women's Studies, 24*(4), 412–427.

Gradinaru, C. (2018). GIFs as floating signifiers. *Sign Systems Studies 46*(2/3), 294–318.

Gronnvoll, M. (2017). Gender (in)visibility at Abu Ghraib. *Faculty Research and Creative Activity*. Retrieved from https://thekeep.eiu.edu/cgi/viewcontent.cgi?referer=https://www.google.com/&httpsredir=1&article=1001&context=commstudies_fac

Grey, R. (2017). The ICC's first 'forced pregnancy' case in historical perspective. *Journal of International Criminal Justice, 15*(5), 905–930.

Grey, R., & Shepherd, L. J. (2012). "Stop rape now?": Masculinity, responsibility, and conflict-related sexual violence. *Men and Masculinities, 16*(1), 115–135.

Grundhauser, E. (2015, June 25). The little-known story of the night witches, an all-female force in WWII. *Vanity Fair*. Retrieved from https://www.vanityfair.com/culture/2015/06/night-witches-wwii-female-pilots

Grundlingh, L. (2018). Memes as speech acts. *Social Semiotics, 28*(2), 147–168.

Gupta, R. (2016). Understanding the war in Syria and the roles of external players: Way out of the quagmire? *The Round Table: The Commonwealth Journal of International Affairs, 105*(1), 29–41.

Gurashi, R. (2017, May 19–20). Beyond hyper capitalism: Can the sharing economy reshape sustainable development? Paper presented at the 13th International Conference of ASECU, Durres, Albania. Retrieved from http://www.asecu.gr/files/13th_conf_files/Beyond-Hyper-Capitalism-Can-the-Sharing-Economy-Reshape-Sustainable-Development.pdf

Haenen, I. (2013). The parameters of enslavement and the act of forced marriage. *International Criminal Law Review, 13*, 895–915.

Hagan, J., & Kaiser, J. (2015). Gendered genocide: The socially destructive process of genocidal rape, killing, and displacement in Darfur. *Law and Society Review, 49*(1), 69–107.

Hagan, J., Kaiser, J., Rothenberg, D., Hanson, A., & Parker, P. (2012). Atrocity victimization and the costs of economic conflict crimes in the battle for Baghdad and Iraq. *European Journal of Criminology, 9*(5), 481–498.

Hagan, J., & Rymond-Richmond, W. (2008). The collective dynamics of racial dehumanization and genocidal victimization in Darfur. *American Sociological Review, 73*(6), 875–902.

Hagan, J., Rymond-Richmond, W., & Parker, P. (2005). The criminology of genocide: The death and rape of Darfur. *Criminology, 43*(3), 525–561.

Hakamies, N., Geissler, P. W., & Borchert, M. (2008). Providing reproductive health care to internally displaced persons: Barriers experienced by humanitarian agencies. *Reproductive Health Matters, 16*(31), 33–43.

Halbmayr, B. (2010). Sexualized violence against women during Nazi 'racial' persecution. In S. Hedgepeth & R. Saidel (Eds.), *Sexual violence against Jewish women during the Holocaust* (pp. 29–44). Massachusetts: Brandeis University Press.

Hassan, N. (2007, June 24). 50,000 Iraqi refugees forced into prostitution. *Independent*. Retrieved from https://www.independent.co.uk/news/world/middle-east/50000-iraqi-refugees-forced-into-prostitution-5333575.html

Haveman, R., & Smeulers, A. (2008). *Supranational criminology: Towards a criminology of international crimes*. Antwerp: Intersentia.

Heck, A., & Schlag, G. (2013). Securitizing images: The female body and the war in Afghanistan. *European Journal of International Relations, 19*(4), 891–913.

Hedgepeth, S., & Saidel, R. (Eds.) (2010). *Sexual violence against Jewish women during the Holocaust*. Massachusetts: Brandeis University Press.

Heit, S. (2009). Waging sexual warfare: Case studies of rape warfare used by the Japanese Imperial Army during World War II. *Women's Studies International Forum, 32*, 363–370.

Henne, K., & Shah, R. (2016). Feminist criminology and the visual. *Oxford Research Encyclopedia of Criminology*. Retrieved from http://oxfordre.com/criminology/view/10.1093/acrefore/9780190264079.001.0001/acrefore-9780190264079-e-56#

Henne, K., & Troshynski, E. (2013). Mapping the margins of intersectionality: Criminological possibilities in a transnational world. *Theoretical Criminology, 17*(4), 455–473.

Henry, N. (2014). The fixation on wartime rape: Feminist critique and international criminal law. *Social and Legal Studies, 23(1)*, 93–11.

Henry, N. (2016). Theorizing wartime rape: Deconstructing gender, sexuality, and violence. *Gender & Society, 30*(1), 44–56.

Herring, E., & G. Rangwala, G. (2005). Iraq, imperialism and global governance. *Third World Quarterly, 26*(4–5), 667–683.

Hersh, S. (2004, April 30). Torture at Abu Ghraib: American soldiers brutalized Iraqis. How far up does the responsibility go? *The New Yorker*. Retrieved from https://www.newyorker.com/magazine/2004/05/10/torture-at-abu-ghraib

Highgate, P. (2007). Peacekeepers, masculinities, and sexual exploitation. *Men and Masculinities, 10*(1), 99–119.

Hirschauer, S. (2014). *The securitization of rape: Women, war and sexual violence*. London: Palgrave Macmillan.

Hodalska, M. (2017). Selfies at horror sites: Dark tourism, ghoulish souvenirs and digital narcissism. *Zeszyty Prasoznawcze, 2*(230), 405–423. Retrieved from http://www.ejournals.eu/Zeszyty-Prasoznawcze/2017/2-230/art/10331/

Holland, S. L. (2009). The enigmatic Lynndie England: Gendered explanations for the crisis at Abu Ghraib. *Communication and Critical/Cultural Studies, 6*(3), 246–264.

Holmes, J. (2007, October 11). Congo's rape war. *Los Angeles Times*. Retrieved from https://www.latimes.com/archives/la-xpm-2007-oct-11-oe-holmes11-story.html

Home Office. (2018). *Country policy and information note DRC: Gender-based violence*. Retrieved from https://assets.publishing.service.gov.uk/government/uploads/system/uploads/attachment_data/file/742590/DRC._GBV._2018.v2_ext__003_.pdf

Homer-Dixon, T. (n.d.). *Environmental scarcities and violent conflict: Evidence from cases*. Retrieved from https://homerdixon.com/environmental-scarcities-and-violent-conflict-evidence-from-cases/

Hooper, C. (2001). *Manly states: Masculinities, international relations and gender politics*. New York, NY: Columbia Press.

Horowitz, S. (1998). Women in the Holocaust literature: Engendering trauma memory. In D. Ofer & L. Weitzman (Eds.), *Women in the Holocaust* (pp. 364–377). New Heaven: Yale University Press.

Hossain, A. (2016). Why is the mass sexualized violence of Bangladesh's liberation war being ignored? Retrieved from https://womenintheworld.com/2016/03/25/why-is-the-mass-sexualized-violence-of-bangladeshs-liberation-war-being-ignored/

House of Lords. (2016). *Select committee on sexual violence in conflict. Report of session 2015–16*. Report No. 123. Retrieved from https://www.publications.parliament.uk/pa/ld201516/ldselect/ldsvc/123/123.pdf

Howard III, J. W., & Prividera, L. C. (2008). The fallen woman archetype: Media representations of Lynndie England, gender, and the (ab)uses of U.S. female soldiers. *Women's Studies in Communication, 31*(3), 287–311.

Howe, A. (2008). Violence against women: Rethinking the local-global nexus. In M. Cain & A. Howe (Eds.), *Women, crime and social harm: Towards a criminology for the global era* (pp. 37–55). Oxford: Hart publishing.

Hristova, S. (2013). 'Doing a Lynndie': Iconography of a gesture. *Visual Anthropology, 26*(5), 430–443.

Human Rights and Gender Justice, MADRE, The Women's International League for Peace and Freedom. (2016). *Human rights violations against women and girls in Syria. Submission to the UN universal periodic review of The Syrian Arab Republic.* Retrieved from https://www.madre.org/sites/default/files/PDFs/Syria%20UPR%20 submission%20Final.pdf

Human Rights Council (HRC). (2016). *They came to destroy: ISIS crimes against the Yazidis.* Report No. A/HRC/32/CRP.2. Retrieved from https://www.ohchr.org/ Documents/HRBodies/HRCouncil/CoISyria/A_HRC_32_CRP.2_en.pdf

Human Rights Watch (HRW). (1999). *World report: The Democratic Republic of Congo.* Retrieved from https://www.hrw.org/legacy/worldreport99/africa/drc.html

Human Rights Watch (HRW). (2002). *The war within the war: Sexual violence against women and girls in Eastern Congo.* Retrieved from https://www.hrw.org/reports/2002/ drc/Congo0602.pdf

Human Rights Watch (HRW). (2003). *Climate of fear: Sexual violence and abduction of women and girls in Baghdad.* Retrieved from https://www.hrw.org/reports/2003/ iraq0703/iraq0703.pdf

Human Rights Watch (HRW). (2005). Seeking justice: The prosecution of sexual violence in the Congo war. *Human Rights Watch, 17* 1(A), i–53.

Human Rights Watch (HRW). (2006). *Democratic Republic of Congo: On the brink.* Retrieved from https://www.hrw.org/news/2006/08/01/democratic-republic-congo-brink

Human Rights Watch (HRW). (2008). *Congo advocacy coalition: Update on protection of civilians in Eastern Congo's peace process.* Retrieved from https://cdn.globalwitness. org/archive/files/pdfs/congo_advocacy_coalition_update_july_2008_english.pdf

Human Rights Watch (HRW). (2011). *At a crossroads: Human rights eight years after the US-led invasion.* Retrieved from https://www.hrw.org/report/2011/02/21/crossroads/ human-rights-iraq-eight-years-after-us-led-invasion#

Human Rights Watch (HRW). (2014a). *No one is safe: Abuses of women in Iraq's criminal justice system.* Retrieved from https://www.hrw.org/report/2014/02/06/no-one-safe/ abuse-women-iraqs-criminal-justice-system#

Human Rights Watch (HRW). (2014b). *World report 2014 Iraq.* Retrieved from https:// www.hrw.org/world-report/2014/country-chapters/iraq

Human Rights Watch (HRW). (2014c). *We are still here: Women on the front lines of Syria's conflict.* Retrieved from https://www.hrw.org/report/2014/07/02/we-are-still-here/ women-front-lines-syrias-conflict

Human Rights Watch (HRW). (2015a). *Iraq: ISIS escapees describe systematic rape: Yezidi survivors in need of urgent care.* Retrieved from: https://www.hrw.org/ news/2015/04/14/iraq-isis-escapees-describe-systematic-rape

Human Rights Watch (HRW). (2015b). *As though we are not human beings: Police brutality against migrants and asylum seekers in Macedonia.* Retrieved from https://www.ecoi. net/en/file/local/1280234/1002_1442920879_macedonia0915-4up.pdf

Human Rights Watch (HRW). (2016a). *Growing up without an education: Barriers to education for Syrian refugee children in Lebanon.* Retrieved from https://www.hrw.org/ report/2016/07/19/growing-without-education/barriers-education-syrian-refugee-children-lebanon

Human Rights Watch (HRW). (2016b). *"We're afraid for their future:" Barriers to education for Syrian refugee children in Jordan.* Retrieved from: https://www.hrw.org/ report/2016/08/16/were-afraid-their-future/barriers-education-syrian-refugee-children-jordan

Human Rights Watch (HRW). (2017). *Iraq: Events of 2016.* Retrieved from https://www. hrw.org/world-report/2017/country-chapters/iraq

Human Rights Watch (HRW). (2018a). *Iraq: Events of 2017.* Retrieved from https://www. hrw.org/world-report/2018/country-chapters/iraq

Human Rights Watch (HRW). (2018b). *Democratic Republic of Congo events of 2017*. Retrieved from https://www.hrw.org/world-report/2018/country-chapters/democratic-republic-congo

Huntington, H. E. (2013). Subversive memes: Internet memes as a form of visual rhetoric. *Selected Papers of Internet Research, 14*. Retrieved from https://pdfs.semanticscholar.org/bfd2/63e65405d8807403fda06dccc70526100e2d.pdf?_ga=2.9172605.955758820.1563460049-533432257.1563460049

Institute for Security Studies Africa. (2016). *Is the illegal trade in Congolese minerals financing terror?* Retrieved from https://www.defenceweb.co.za/security/national-security/iss-is-the-illegal-trade-in-congolese-minerals-financing-terror/

Inter-agency. (2013). *Gender-based violence and child protection among Syrian refugees in Jordan, with a focus on early marriage*. Retrieved from http://www.refworld.org/docid/52cfa5d14.html

Inter-agency Information and Analysis Unit (IAU). (2008). *Gender-based violence in Iraq: The effects of violence - real and perceived – on the lives of women, girls, men and boys in Iraq*. Retrieved from http://lastradainternational.org/lsidocs/824%20gender%20violence%20in%20Iraq.pdf

Inter-agency Working Group on Reproductive Health in Crises. (2010). Inter-agency field manual on reproductive health in humanitarian settings. *Revision for field review*. Retrieved from https://www.ncbi.nlm.nih.gov/books/NBK305149/pdf/Bookshelf_NBK305149.pdf

Inter-agency Working Group on Reproductive Health in Crises. (2011). *Minimal initial service package*. Retrieved from http://iawg.net/minimum-initial-service-package/

Isenberg, D. (2011, October 19). The neoliberal wars. *Huffington Post*. Retrieved from https://www.huffpost.com/entry/the-neoliberal-wars_b_1016328

Jabbra, N. W. (2006). Women, words and war: Explaining 9/11 and justifying U.S. military action in Afghanistan and Iraq. *Journal of International Women's Studies, 8*(1), 236–255.

Jacobson, R. (2013). Women 'after' wars. In C. Cohn (Ed.), *Women and wars* (pp. 215–241). Cambridge: Polity Press.

Jamjoom, M. (2009). War forces Iraqi mom into prostitution. *CNN*. Retrieved from http://edition.cnn.com/2009/WORLD/meast/11/02/iraq.prostitute/index.html

Jenkins, S. D. (2012). Preliminary assessment of trafficking in the Democratic Republic of Congo (DRC). Retrieved from https://iccforum.com/media/sdj_human_rights_project/2012-03_SDJ_Human_Rights_Project_at_UCLA_Report-Trafficking_in_the_DRC.pdf

John, V. M. (2016). The dangers of educated girls and women. *Education, Citizenship and Social Justice, 11*(2), 184–196.

Jones, A. (2000). Gendercide and genocide. *Journal of Genocide Research, 2*(2), 185–211.

Jones, A. (2002). Gender and genocide in Rwanda. *Journal of Genocide Research, 4*(1), 65–94.

Kaiser Family Foundation. (2019). *UNFPA funding & Kemp-Kasten: An explainer*. Retrieved from https://www.kff.org/global-health-policy/fact-sheet/unfpa-funding-kemp-kasten-an-explainer/

Kaiser, J., & Hagan, J. (2015). Gendered genocide: The socially destructive process of genocidal rape, killing, and displacement in Darfur. *Law and Society Review, 49*(1), 69–107.

Kaldor, M. (1999). *New and old wars: Organized violence in a global era*. Cambridge: Polity Press.

Kaldor, M. (2013). In defense of new wars. *Stability: International Journal of Security and Development, 2*(1). ISSN 2165-2627. Retrieved from http://eprints.lse.ac.uk/49500/

Kamp, M. (2009). Fragmented citizenship: Communalism, ethnicity and gender in Iraq. In N, Al-Ali, & N. Pratt (Eds.), *Women and war in the middle east: Transnational perspectives* (pp. 193–216). London: Zed Books.

Kanopka, G. (1966). *The Adolescent girl in conflict*. Prentice Hall: New Jersey.

Karim, S., & Beardsley, K. (2016). Explaining sexual exploitation and abuse in peacekeeping missions: The role of female peacekeepers and gender equality in contributing countries. *Journal of Peace Research, 53*(1), 100–115.

Katz, S. (2012). Thoughts on the intersection of rape and Rassenschande during the Holocaust. *Modern Judaism Online, 32*(3), 293–322.

Kelley, C. P., Mohtadi, S., Cane, M. A., Seager, R., & Kushnir, Y. (2015). Climate change in the fertile crescent and implications of the recent Syrian drought. *Proceedings of the National Academy of Sciences of the United States of America, 112*(11), 3241–3246.

Kelly, L. (1988). *Surviving sexual violence*. Cambridge: Polity Press.

Kempadoo, K. (2001). Women of color and the global sex trade: Transnational feminist perspectives. *Meridians, 1*(2), 28–51.

Kennedy, L., & Patrick, C. (2014). Introduction. In L. Kennedy & C, Patrick (Eds.), *The violence of the image: Photography and international conflict* (pp. 1-6) London: I.B.Tauris.

Khan, S. (2014). The two faces of Afghan women: Oppressed and exotic. *Women's Studies International Forum, 44*, 101–109.

Kim, B., & Merlo, A. V. (2014). Comparative/international research on women and crime: Analysis of ASC and ESC annual meeting presentations. *Feminist Criminology, 9*(4), 382–407.

Kimm, S., & Sauer, B. (2010). Discourses on forced prostitution, trafficking in women, and football: A comparison of anti-trafficking campaigns during the World Cup 2006 and the European Championship 2008. *Soccer & Society, 11*(6), 815–828.

Kirby, P. (2012). How is rape a weapon of war? Feminist international relations, modes of critical explanation and the study of wartime sexual violence. *European Journal International Relations, 19*(4), 797–821.

Kirby, P. (2015a). Acting time; or, the abolitionist and the feminist. *International Feminist Journal of Politics, 17*(3), 508–513.

Kirby, P. (2015b). Ending sexual violence in conflict: The preventing sexual violence initiative and its critics. *International Affairs, 91*(3), 457–472.

Klem, B. (2003). *Dealing with scarcity and violent conflict*. Working Paper No. 24. Retrieved from https://www.clingendael.org/sites/default/files/pdfs/20031000_cru_working_paper_24.pdf

Know Your Meme. Lynndie England Pose. (n.d). Retrieved from https://knowyourmeme.com/memes/lynndie-england-pose

Kramer, R. C., & Michalowski, R. J. (2005). War, aggression and state crime: A criminological analysis of the invasion and occupation of Iraq. *The British Journal of Criminology, 45*(4), 446–469.

Kramer, R. C., & Michalowski, R. J. (2011). Empire and exceptionalism: The Bush administration's criminal war against Iraq. In D. Rothe & C. Mullins (Eds.), *State crime: Current perspectives* (pp. 94–121). New Brunswick, NJ: Rutgers University Press.

Krause, S., Williams, H., Onyango, M. A., Sami, S., Doedens, W., Giga, N., ... Tomczyk, B. (2015). Reproductive health services for Syrian refugees in Zaatri camp and Irbid City, Hashemite Kingdom of Jordan: An evaluation of the minimum initial services package. *Conflict and Health, 9*(1), 1–10.

Kristeva, J. (1982). Powers of horror: An essay on abjection (L. S. Roudiez, Trans.). New York, NY: Columbia University Press.

Krsteva, M., Donev, D., & Iliev, K. (2018). New media content: Meme. *Yearbook – Faculty of Philology, 9*(12), 135–138.

Krylova, A. (2016). Gender binary and the limits of poststructuralist method. *Gender and History, 28*(2), 307–323.

La Capra, D. (1994). *Representing the Holocaust: History, theory and trauma*. Ithaca, NY: Cornell University Press.

Lang, J. (2010). Questioning dehumanization: Intersubjective dimensions of violence in the Nazi concentration and death camps. *Holocaust and Genocide Studies, 24*(2), 225–246.

Leatherman, J. (2011). *Sexual violence and armed conflict*. Cambridge: Polity Press.

Lee-Koo, K. (2011). Gender-based violence against civilian women in postinvasion Iraq: (Re) politicizing George W. Bush's silent legacy. *Violence Against Women, 17*(12), 1619–1634.

Leiby, M. L. (2009). Wartime sexual violence in Guatemala and Peru. *International Studies Quarterly, 53*, 445–468.

Leitner, I. (1993). Fragments of Isabella: A memoir of Auschwitz. In C. Rittner & J. Roth (Eds.), *Different voices: Women and the Holocaust* (pp. 65–68). New York, NY: Paragon House (Original work published in 1978).

Lentin, R. (1999). The rape of the nation: Women narrativising genocide. *Sociological Research Online, 4*(2). Retrieved from http://www.socresonline.org.uk/4/2/lentin.html

Levenkron, N. (2010). Death and the maidens: Prostitution, rape and sexual slavery during World War II. In S. Hedgepeth & R. Saidel (Eds.), *Sexual violence against Jewish women during the Holocaust* (pp. 13–28). Massachusetts: Brandeis University Press.

Lewis, D. A. (2009). Unrecognized victims: Sexual violence against men in conflict settings under international law. *Wisconsin International Law Journal, 27*(1), 1–49.

Linfield, S. (2012). *The cruel radiance: Photography and political violence*. London: The University of Chicago Press.

Linos, N. (2009). Rethinking gender-based violence during war: Is violence against civilian men a problem worth addressing? *Social Science & Medicine, 68*(8), 1548–1551.

Lobasz, J. K. (2008). The woman in peril and the ruined woman: Representations of female soldiers in the Iraq war. *Journal of Women, Politics and Policy, 29*(3), 305–334.

Lombroso, C., & Ferrero, W. (2004). *Criminal woman, the prostitute and the normal woman* (N. Hahn-Raftrer & M. Gibson, Trans. & Eds.). Durham, NC: Duke University Press (Original work published in 1893).

Looney, R. (2004). Neoliberalism in a conflict state: The viability of economic shock therapy in Iraq. *Strategic Insights, 3*(6), 1–11.

Luneghe, M. K. (2017). Lacking doctors, clinics, and equipment, reproductive health care scarce in North Kivu. *Global Press Journal*. Retrieved from https://globalpressjournal.com/africa/democratic-republic-of-congo/lacking-doctors-clinics-equipment-reproductive-health-care-scarce-north-kivu/

Mackenzie, M. (2010). Securitizing sex? *International Feminist Journal of Politics, 12*(2), 202–221.

Maclean, R. (2017, December 13). Congolese fighters convicted of raping young girls in landmark case. *The Guardian*. Retrieved from https://www.theguardian.com/world/2017/dec/13/congolese-fighters-convicted-raping-toddlers-young-girls-landmark-case

Maier-Katkin, D., Mears, D. P., & Bernard, T. (2009). Towards a criminology of crimes against humanity. *Theoretical Criminology, 13*(2), 227–255.

Managhan, T. (2012). *Gender, agency and war: The maternalized body in US foreign policy*. London: Rutledge.

Manjoo, R., & McRaith, C. (2011). Gender-based violence and justice in conflict and postconflict areas. *Cornell International Law Journal, 44*, 11–31.

Mantz, J. (2008). Improvisational economies: Coltan production in the eastern Congo. *Social Anthropology, 16*(1), 34–50.

Marchant, L. (2019). How do internet memes speak security? *Contemporary Voices, 1*(2), 39–62.

Marcovich, M. (2010). *Trafficking, sexual exploitation and prostitution of women and girls in Iraq*. Retrieved from http://www.catwinternational.org/Content/Images/Article/149/attachment.pdf

Mason, A. (2018). *The vital role of women in the Second World War*. Retrieved from https://www.iwm.org.uk/history/the-vital-role-of-women-in-the-second-world-war

Mason, C. (2005). The hillbilly defense: Culturally mediating U.S. terror at home and abroad. *NWSA Journal, 17*(3), 39–63.

Mason, G., & Stubbs, J. (2010). *Feminist approaches to criminological research*. Retrieved from https://www.researchgate.net/publication/228134204_Feminist_Approaches_to_Criminological_Research

Mason-Jones, A. J., & Nicholson, P. (2018). Structural violence and marginalization. The sexual and reproductive health experiences of separated young people on the move. A rapid review with relevance to the European humanitarian crisis. *Public Health, 158*, 156–162.

Masterson, A. R. (2013). *Reproductive health and gender-based violence in Syrian refugee women*. Public Health Theses. Retrieved from https://elischolar.library.yale.edu/cgi/viewcontent.cgi?referer=https://www.google.co.uk/&httpsredir=1&article=1242&context=ysphtd

Masterson, A. R, Usta, J., Gupta, J., & Ettinger, A. S. (2014). Assessment of reproductive health and violence against women among displaced Syrians in Lebanon. *BioMed Central Women's Health, 14*(25), 1–8.

Maya, M. (2012). Mobile courts in the Democratic Republic of Congo: Complementarity in Action? *American Bar Association Rule of Law Initiative*. Retrieved from https://worldjusticeproject.org/news/mobile-courts-democratic-republic-congo-complementarity-action

Mbambi, A., & Faray-Kele, M. C. (2010). *Gender inequality and social institutions in the DRC*. Retrieved from https://www.peacewomen.org/sites/default/files/hrinst_genderinequalityinthedrc_wilpf_december2010english_0.pdf

McKinnon, S. L. (2016). Gender violence as global phenomenon: Refugees, genital surgeries, and neocolonial projects of the United States. *Cultural Studies Critical Methodologies, 16*(4), 414–426.

Meger, S. (2010). Rape of the Congo: Understanding sexual violence in the conflict in the Democratic Republic of Congo. *Journal of Contemporary African Studies, 28*(2), 119–135.

Meger, S. (2015). Toward a feminist political economy of wartime sexual violence. *International Feminist Journal of Politics, 17*(3), 416–434.

Meger, S. (2016a). *Rape loot pillage: The political economy of sexual violence in armed conflict*. New York, NY: Oxford University Press.

Meger, S. (2016b). The fetishization of sexual violence in international security. *International Studies Quarterly, 60*(1), 149–159.

Merelli, A. (2017, November 22). Rohingya, Syrian, and Yemeni women are paying for Trump's ideological withdrawal of UN funds. *Quarts*. Retrieved from https://qz.com/1135083/rohingya-syrian-and-yemeni-women-are-paying-for-trumps-ideological-withdrawal-of-un-funds/

Mertens, C., & Pardy, M. (2017). 'Sexurity' and its effects in eastern Democratic Republic of Congo. *Third World Quarterly, 38*(4), 956–979.

Mertus, J. (2004). Shouting from the bottom of the well: The impact of international trials for wartime rape on women's agency. *International Feminist Journal of Politics, 6*(1), 110–128.

Micha, A., About-Atta, I., Macaud, M. C., & Barnes, S. (2011). *Karamatuna: An investigation into the sex trafficking of Iraqi women and girls*. Retrieved from https://www.peacewomen.org/assets/file/karamatuna-web_resource.pdf

Michalowski R. J., & Kramer R. C. (2007). State-corporate crime and criminological Inquiry. In H. N. Pontell & G. Geis, (Eds.), *International handbook of white-collar and corporate crime* (pp. 200–219). Boston, MA: Springer.

Milner, R. M. (2012). The world made meme: Discourse and identity in participatory media. *KU Scholar Works*. Retrieved from https://kuscholarworks.ku.edu/handle/1808/10256

Mirzoeff, N. (2011). The right to look. *Critical Inquiry, 37*(3), 473–496.

Mohanty, C. (1988). Under western eyes: Feminist scholarship and colonial discourses. *Feminist Review, 30*, 61-88.

Mookherjee, N. (2006). Remembering to forget: Public secrecy and memory of sexual violence in the Bangladesh war of 1971. *Journal of the Royal Anthropological Institute, 12*(2), 433–450.

Mookherjee, N. (2007). Available motherhood: Legal technologies, 'state of exception' and the dekinning of 'war-babies' in Bangladesh. *Childhood, 14*(3), 339–354.

Mookherjee, N. (2015). The raped woman as a horrific sublime and the Bangladesh war of 1971. *Journal of Material Culture, 20*(4), 379–395.

Motoyama, H. (2018). Formulating Japan's UNSCR 1325 national action plan and forgetting the "comfort women." *International Feminist Journal of Politics, 20*(1), 39–53.

Mourtada, R., Schlecht, J., & DeJong, J. (2017). A qualitative study exploring child marriage practices among Syrian conflict-affected populations in Lebanon. *Conflict and Health, 11*(1), 53–65.

MSF. (2016). *In Mambasa, MSF teams provide care to four new rape survivors each day.* Retrieved from https://www.msf.org/democratic-republic-congo-mambasa-msf-teams-provide-care-four-new-rape-survivors-each-day

Mudgway, C. (2017). Sexual exploitation by UN peacekeepers: The 'survival sex' gap in international human rights law. *The International Journal of Human Rights, 21*(9), 1453–1476.

Muir, J. (2017, October 17). Islamic state: Raqqa's loss seals rapid rise and fall. *BBC News*. Retrieved from https://www.bbc.co.uk/news/world-middle-east-35695648

Mullins, C. W. (2009a). "He would kill me with his penis": Genocidal rape in Rwanda as a state crime. *Critical Criminology, 17*(1), 15–33.

Mullins, C. W. (2009b). "We are going to rape you and taste Tutsi women:" Rape during the 1994 Rwandan genocide. *British Journal of Criminology, 49*(6), 719–735.

Mullins, C., & Rothe, D. (2008). Gold, diamonds and blood: International state-corporate crime in the Democratic Republic of the Congo. *Contemporary Justice Review, 11*(2), 81–99.

Murphy, A. (2007). The missing rhetoric of gender in responses to Abu Ghraib. *Journal of International Women's Studies, 8*(2), 20–34.

Mythen, G., & Walklate, S. (2006). Criminology and terrorism: Which thesis? Risk society or governmentality. *British Journal of Criminology, 46*(3), 379–398.

Mythen, G., & Walklate, S. (2008). Terrorism, risk and international security: The perils of asking what if? *Security Dialogue, 39*(2), 221–242.

Nayak, M. (2006). Orientalism and 'saving' US state identity after 9/11. *International Feminist Journal of Politics, 8*(1), 42–61.

Nduka-Agwu, A. (2009). Doing gender after the war: Dealing with gender mainstreaming and sexual exploitation and abuse in UN peace support operations in Liberia and Sierra Leone. *Civil Wars, 11*(2), 179–199.

Nordberg, J. (2014). *The underground girls of Kabul: The hidden lives of Afghan girls disguised as Boys.* London: Virago.

O'Brien, M. (2011). Sexual exploitation and beyond: Using the Rome statute of the international criminal court to prosecute UN peacekeepers for gender-based crimes. *International Criminal Law Review, 11*(4), 803–827.

O'Brien, M. (2016). "Don't kill them, let's choose them as wives": The development of the crimes of forced marriage, sexual slavery and enforced prostitution in international criminal law. *The International Journal of Human Rights, 20*(3), 386–406.

O'Connor, M. (2017). Choice, agency consent and coercion: Complex issues in the lives of prostituted and trafficked women. *Women's Studies International Forum, 62*, 8–16.

Ohambe, O. M. C., Muhigwa, J. B. B., & Wa Mamba, B. M. (2005). *Women's bodies as a battleground: Sexual violence against women and girls during the war in the Democratic Republic of Congo, South Kivu (1996-2003)*. Retrieved from https://www.international-alert.org/sites/default/files/publications/women's-bodies-as-a-english.pdf

Olivius, E. (2016a). Refugee men as perpetrators, allies or troublemakers? Emerging discourses on men and masculinities in humanitarian aid. *Women's Studies International Forum, 56*, 56–65.

Olivius, E. (2016b). Constructing humanitarian selves and refugee others. *International Feminist Journal of Politics, 18*(2), 270–290.

Olsson, O., & Siba, E. (2013). Ethnic cleansing or resource struggle in Darfur? An empirical analysis. *Journal of Development Economics, 103*, 299–312.

Onsrud, M., Sjøveian. S, Luhiriri, R., & Mukwege, D. (2008). Sexual violence-related fistulas in the Democratic Republic of Congo. *International Journal of Gynecology and Obstetrics, 103*(3), 265–269.

Onyango, M. A., Burkhardt, G., Scott, J., Rouhani, S., Haider, S., Greiner, A., ... Bartels, S. (2016). A qualitative analysis of disclosure patterns among women with sexual violence-related pregnancies in Eastern Democratic Republic of Congo. *PLoS ONE, 11*(10), 1–13.

Oosterhoff, P., Zwanikken, P., & Ketting, E. (2004). Sexual torture of men in Croatia and other conflict situations: An open secret. *Reproductive Health Matters, 12*(23), 68–77.

Orend, B. (2000). Jus post bellum. *Journal of Social Philosophy, 31*(1), 117–137.

Organization for Economic Cooperation and Development (OECD). (2015). *Mineral supply chains and conflict links in eastern Democratic Republic of Congo: Five years of implementing supply chain due diligence*. Retrieved from http://mneguidelines.oecd.org/Mineral-Supply-Chains-DRC-Due-Diligence-Report.pdf

Organization for Economic Cooperation and Development (OECD). (2017). *Gender equality and women's empowerment in fragile and conflict-affected situations: A review of donor support*. Retrieved from https://www.oecd.org/dac/conflict-fragility-resilience/docs/Gender_equality_in_fragile_situations_2017.pdf

Organization for Economic Cooperation and Development (OECD). (2019). *Social institutions gender index: DRC*. Retrieved from https://www.genderindex.org/wp-content/uploads/files/datasheets/2019/CD.pdf

Organization of Women's Freedom in Iraq (OWFI). (2010). *Prostitution and trafficking of women and girls in Iraq*. Retrieved from http://www.fondationscelles.org/pdf/prostitutionandtrafficking-OWFIreport.pdf

Owen, M. (2011). Widowhood issues in the context of united nations security council resolution 1325. *International Feminist Journal of Politics, 13*(4), 616–622.

Oxfam International. (2009). *In her own words: Iraqi women talk about their greatest challenges*. Retrieved from https://reliefweb.int/sites/reliefweb.int/files/resources/5502EC EE4FF6F3C1C1257570004373F7-Full_Report.pdf

Parker, K., & Reckdenwald, A. (2008). Women and crime in context: Examining the linkages between patriarchy and female offending across space. *Feminist Criminology, 3*(1), 5–24.

Patterson, D. (2013). The Nazi assault on the Jewish soul through the murder of the Jewish mother. In M. Goldenberg & A. Shapiro (Eds.), *Different horrors, same hell: Gender and the Holocaust* (pp. 163–176). Seattle, WA: University of Washington Press.

Pauwels, L. (2017). Key methods of visual criminology: An overview of different approaches and their affordances. In M. Brown & E. Carrabine (Eds.), *Routledge international handbook of visual criminology* (e-book version). Oxon: Routledge.

Pennington, R. (2010). Offensive women: Women in combat in the Red Army in the Second World War. *The Journal of Military History*, *74*(3), 775–820.

Perl, G. (1993). I was a doctor in Auschwitz. In C. Rittner & J. Roth (Eds.), *Different voices: Women and the Holocaust* (pp. 104–118). New York, NY: Paragon House (Original work published in 1984).

Person, K. (2015). Sexual violence during the Holocaust: The case of forced prostitution in the Warson Ghetto. *Shofar: An Interdisciplinary Journal of Jewish Studies*, *33*(2), 103–121.

Peters, T. (2006). Mad, bad, or victim? Making sense of mother-daughter sexual abuse. *Feminist Criminology*, *1*(4), 283–302.

Peterson, V. S. (2009). Gendering informal economies. In N. Al-Ali & N. Pratt (Eds.), *Women and war in the Middle East: Transnational perspectives* (pp. 35–64). London: Zed Books.

Pickles, S. (2016, December 1). *Managing the risk of illegal mining and conflict minerals in global supply chains*. Retrieved from https://blogs.thomsonreuters.com/answerson/managing-risk-illegal-mining-conflict-minerals-global-supply-chains/

Poitras, L. (2016). *Astral noise*. Retrieved from https://whitney.org/Exhibitions/LauraPoitras

Pollack, S. (2007). "I'm just not good in relationships:" Victimization discourses and the gendered regulation of criminalized women. *Feminist Criminology*, *2*(2), 158–174.

Potter, H. (2006). An argument for black feminist criminology: Understanding African American women's experiences with intimate partner abuse using an integrated approach. *Feminist Criminology*, *1*(2), 106–124.

Pratt, N. (2011). Iraqi women and UNSCR 1325: An interview with Susan Abbas, director of the Iraqi women's leadership institute, Baghdad, January 2011. *International Feminist Journal of Politics*, *13*(4), 612–615.

Pruitt, W. R. (2014). How criminology can engage in the theorizing on genocide? *International Journal of Criminal Justice Sciences*, *9*(1), 1–15.

Puechguirbal, N. (2010). Discourses on gender, patriarchy and resolution 1325: A textual analysis of UN documents. *International Peacekeeping*, *17*(2), 172–187.

Ramos, C. G., López, R. O., & Quinteros, A. C. (2015). *The FMLN and post-war politics in El Salvador from included to inclusive actor?* Retrieved from https://www.berghof-foundation.org/fileadmin/redaktion/Publications/Other_Resources/IPS/Paper-2-El-Salvador-English-final.pdf

Rasul, A., & McDowell, S. D. (2015). Images of oppression: An analysis of the coverage of Afghan women in Time and Newsweek after 9/11. *The Journal of International Communication*, *21*(1), 21–37.

Raven-Roberts, A. (2013). Women and the political economy of war. In C. Cohn (Ed.), *Women and wars* (pp. 36–53). Cambridge: Polity Press.

Reinharz, S. (2010). Foreword. In S. Hedgepeth & R. Saidel (Eds.), *Sexual violence against Jewish women during the Holocaust* (pp. ix–x). Massachusetts: Brandeis University Press.

Renzetti, C. (2013). *Feminist criminology*. London: Routledge.

Report of the United Nations Secretary General (2019). Conflict-related sexual violence. S/2019/280. Retrieved from https://www.un.org/sexualviolenceinconflict/wp-content/uploads/2019/04/report/s-2019-280/Annual-report-2018.pdf

Richani, N. (2016). The political economy and complex interdependency of the war system in Syria. *Civil Wars*, *18*(1), 45–68.

Richter-Montpetit, M. (2007). Empire, desire and violence: A queer transnational feminist reading of the prisoner 'abuse' in Abu Ghraib and the question of 'gender equality'. *International Feminist Journal of Politics*, *9*(1), 38–59.

Rigterink, A. (2013). *New wars in numbers: An empirical test of the 'new war' thesis. Discussion paper*. Retrieved from http://www.securityintransition.org/wp-content/uploads/2014/10/Rigterink.-New-Wars-in-Numbers.pdf

Riley, R. L. (2013). *Depicting the veil: Transnational sexism and the war on terror*. London: Zed Books.

Ringelheim, J. (1993). Women and the Holocaust: A reconsideration of research. In C. Rittner & J. Roth (Eds.), *Different voices: Women and the Holocaust* (pp. 374–418). New York, NY: Paragon House (Original work published in 1985).

Ringelheim, J. (1998). The split between gender and the holocaust. In D. Ofer & L. Weitzman (Eds.), *Women in the Holocaust* (pp. 340–350). New Heaven: Yale University Press.

Rittner, C., & Roth, J. (1993). Prologue. In C. Rittner & J. Roth (Eds.), *Different voices: Women and the Holocaust* (pp. 1–19). New York, NY: Paragon House.

Robertson, C., & Klein, M. A. (1997). *Women & Slavery in Africa*. Portsmouth, NH. Heinemann.

Rome Statute of the International Criminal Court. (1998). Retrieved from http://legal. un.org/ilc/texts/instruments/english/conventions/7_4_1998.pdf

Rome Statute of the International Criminal Court. (2011). *The International Criminal Court*. Retrieved from https://www.icc-cpi.int/NR/rdonlyres/ADD16852-AEE9-4757-ABE7-9CDC7CF02886/283503/RomeStatutEng1.pdf

Rothe, D. (2009). *State criminality: The crimes of all crimes*. Plymouth: Lexington Books.

Rothe, D., & Mullins, C. W. (Eds) (2011). *State crimes: Current perspectives*. Rutgers University Press.

Rothe, D., & Muzzatti, S. L. (2004). Enemies everywhere: Terrorism, moral panic, and US civil society. *Critical Criminology, 12*(3), 327–350.

Rouhani, S. A., Scott, J., Burkhardt, G., Onyango, M. A., Haider, S., Greiner, A., Albutt, K., … Bartels, S. A. (2016). A quantitative assessment of termination of sexual violence-related pregnancies in Eastern Democratic Republic of Congo. *Conflict and Health, 10* (9), 1–9.

Said, E. (1979). *Orientalism*. New York, NY: Vintage Books.

Saidel, R. (2006). *The Jewish women of Ravensbrück concentration camp*. Wisconsin: The University of Wisconsin Press.

Salih, K. O. (2008). The internationalization of the communal conflict in Darfur and its regional and domestic ramifications: 2001–2007. *Arab Studies Quarterly, 30*(3), 1–24.

Sampathkumar, M. (2017, April 4). Donald Trump defunding of UN's women's health service will cause 'millions to suffer. *The Independent*. Retrieved from https://www.independent.co.uk/news/world/americas/us-politics/donald-trump-abortion-defunding-global-mexico-city-rule-un-population-fund-a7666916.html

Save the Children. (2014). *Too young to wed: The growing problem of child marriage among Syrian girls in Jordan*. Retrieved from http://www.savethechildren.org/atf/cf/%7B9def2ebe-10ae-432c-9bd0-df91d2eba74a%7D/TOO_YOUNG_TO_WED_REPORT_0714.PDF

Save the Children. (2015). *More than half of all school attacks have been in Syria, new data shows*. Retrieved from https://www.savethechildren.org/us/about-us/media-and-news/2015-press-releases/more-than-half-of-all-school-attacks-have-been-in-syria--new-dat

Save the Children. (2018). *Education under attack*. Retrieved from https://www.savethechildren.org/content/dam/usa/reports/ed-cp/education-under-attack-2018-full-report.pdf

Schept, J. (2016). Visuality and criminology. *Oxford Research Encyclopedias: Criminology and Criminal Justice*. Retrieved from https://oxfordre.com/criminology/view/10.1093/acrefore/9780190264079.001.0001/acrefore-9780190264079-e-145?print=pdf

Schilling, J., Saulich, C., & Engwicht, N. (2018). A local to global perspective on resource governance and conflict. *Conflict, Security & Development, 18*(6), 433–461.

Schmitt, E., & Mazzetti, M. (2013, July 20). U.S. intelligence official says Syrian war could last for years. *The New York Times*. Retrieved from https://www.nytimes.com/2013/07/21/world/middleeast/us-intelligence-official-says-syrian-war-could-last-for-years.html

Schneider, G., Banholzer, L., & Albarracin, L. (2015). Ordered rape: A principal–agent analysis of wartime sexual violence in the DR Congo. *Violence Against Women, 21*(11), 1341–1363.

Schulte-Hillen, C., Staderini, N., & Saint-Sauveur, J. (2016). Why Médecins Sans Frontières (MSF) provides safe abortion care and what that involves. *Conflict and Health, 10*(19), 1–4.

Schweickart, P. (1986). Reading ourselves: Toward a feminist theory of reading. In E. Flynn & P. Schweitckart (Eds.), *Gender and reading: Essays on readers, texts and contexts* (pp. 31–62). Baltimore: The John Hopkins.

Shah, M. (2016, March 9–11). The global legal landscape: Access to safe abortion care in crisis settings. Paper presented at the 16th annual meeting of the IAWG on Reproductive Health in Crises. Dakar, Senegal. Retrieved from http://iawg.net/wp-content/uploads/2016/08/IAWG-16th-Annual-Meeting-6-21-16-FINAL.pdf

Shaheen, K. (2017, August 4). Al-Qaida-linked militants' advance throws west's Syria plans into disarray. *The Guardian.* Retrieved from https://www.theguardian.com/world/2017/aug/04/al-qaida-linked-militants-advance-throws-wests-syria-plans-into-disarray

Shangquan, G. (2000). Economic globalization: Trends, risks and risk prevention. *Economic and Social Affairs.* Retrieved from https://www.un.org/en/development/desa/policy/cdp/cdp_background_papers/bp2000_1.pdf

Shannon, L. (2011). *A thousand sisters: My journey into the worst place on earth to be a woman.* Berkeley, CA: Seal Press.

Sharkey, H. J. (2007). Arab identity and ideology in Sudan: The politics of language, ethnicity, and race. *African Affairs, 107*(426), 21–43.

Sharlach, L. (1999). Gender and genocide in Rwanda: Women as agents and objects of Genocide. *Journal of Genocide Research, 1*(3), 387–399.

Sharlach, L. (2000) Rape as Genocide: Bangladesh, the Former Yugoslavia, and Rwanda. *New Political Science, 22*(1), 89–102.

Shepherd, L. J. (2006). Veiled references: Constructions of gender in the Bush administration discourse on the attacks on Afghanistan post-9/11. *International Feminist Journal of Politics, 8*(1), 19–41.

Shepherd, L. J. (2011). Sex, security and superhero(in)es: From 1325 to 1820 and beyond. *International Feminist Journal of Politics, 13*(4), 504–521.

Sinjab, L. (2007, December 3). Prostitution ordeal of Iraqi girls. *BBC News.* Retrieved from http://news.bbc.co.uk/1/hi/world/middle_east/7119473.stm

Sivakumaran, S. (2007). Sexual violence against men in armed conflict. *European Journal of International Law, 18*(2), 253–276.

Sivakumaran, S. (2010). Lost in translation: UN responses to sexual violence against men and boys in situations of armed conflict. *International Review of the Red Cross, 92*(877), 259–277.

Sjoberg, L. (2006a). Gendered realities of the immunity principle: Why gender analysis needs feminism. *International Studies Quarterly, 50*(4), 889–910.

Sjoberg, L. (2006b). *Gender, justice and the wars in Iraq: A feminist reformulation of just war theory.* Oxford: Lexington Books.

Sjoberg, L. (2007). Agency, militarized femininity and enemy others: Observations from the war in Iraq. *International Feminist Journal of Politics, 9*(1), 82–101.

Sjoberg, L. (2011). Gender, the state, and war redux: Feminist international relations across the 'levels of analysis.' *International Relations, 25*(1), 108–134.

Sjoberg, L. (2013). *Gendering global conflict: Toward a feminist theory of war.* New York, NY: Columbia University Press.

Sjoberg, L., & Gentry, C. E. (2007). *Mothers, monsters, whores: Women's violence in global politics.* London: Zed books.

Sjoberg, L., & Gentry, C. E. (2008). Reduced to bad sex: Narratives of violent women from the bible to the war on terror. *International Relations, 22*(1), 5–23.

Sjoberg, L., & Peet, J. (2011). Targeting civilians in war: Feminist contributions. In A. J Tickner & L. Sjoberg (Eds.), *Feminism and international relations: Conversations about the past, present and future* (pp. 169–187). London: Routledge.

Sjogerg, L. (2016). *Women as wartime rapists: Beyond sensation and stereotyping.* New York, NY: New York University Press.

Skjelsbæk, I. (2001). Sexual violence and war: Mapping out a complex relationship. *European Journal of International Relations, 7*(2), 211–237.

Smeulers, A. (2015). Female perpetrators: Ordinary or extra-ordinary women? *International Criminal Law Review, 15*(2), 207–253.

Smith, D. (2011, February 11). Congolese soldiers go on trial accused of raping more than 60 women. *The Guardian.* Retrieved from https://www.theguardian.com/world/2011/feb/10/congolese-soldiers-rape-trial-gender-court

Sohl, M. (2010). *Tackling the drought in Syria.* Retrieved from https://www.natureasia.com/en/nmiddleeast/article/10.1038/nmiddleeast.2010.206

Solangon, S. & Patel, P. (2012). Sexual violence against men in countries affected by armed conflict. *Conflict, Security & Development, 12*(4), 417–442.

Sommer, R. (2010). Sexual exploitation of women in Nazi concentration camp brothels. In S. Hedgepeth & R. Saidel (Eds.), *Sexual violence against Jewish women during the Holocaust* (pp. 45–60). Massachusetts: Brandeis University Press.

Sontag, S. (1979). *On photography.* London: Penguin books.

Sontag, S. (2003). *Regarding the pain of others.* New York, NY: Picador.

Sontag, S. (2004, May 23). Regarding the torture of others. *The New York Times.* Retrieved from https://www.nytimes.com/2004/05/23/magazine/regarding-the-torture-of-others.html

Spencer, R. (2016, February 3). Nearly half a million pregnant women among displaced and refugee Syrians. *Telegraph.* Retrieved from http://www.telegraph.co.uk/news/worldnews/middleeast/syria/12139358/Nearly-half-a-million-pregnant-women-among-displaced-and-refugee-Syrians.html

Spencer, R. Usta, J., Essaid, A., Shukri, S., El-Gharaibeh, Y., Abu-Taleb, … Clark, C. J. (2015). *Gender based violence against women and girls displaced by the Syrian conflict in south Lebanon and north Jordan: Scope of violence and health correlates.* Retrieved from https://www.alnap.org/system/files/content/resource/files/main/gbv-against-women-and-girl-syrian-refugees-in-lebanon-and-jordan-final.pdf

Spens, C. (2014). The theatre of cruelty: Dehumanization, objectification & Abu Ghraib. *Journal of Terrorism Research. The Centre of the Study of Terrorism and Political Violence, 5*(3), 49–69.

Spivak, G. C. (1988). Can the subaltern speak? In C. Nelson & Grossberg, L. (Eds.), Marxism and the interpretation of culture (pp. 67–111). Basingstoke: Macmillan Education.

Stabile, C. A., & Kumar, D. (2005). Unveiling imperialism: Media, gender and the war on Afghanistan. *Media, Culture & Society, 27*(5), 765–782.

Steans, J. (2008). Telling stories about women and gender in the war on terror. *Global Society, 22*(1), 159–176.

Steans, J. (2013). *Gender and international relations: Theory, practice, and policy* (3rd ed.). Cambridge: Polity Press.

Stokes, E. (2014, May 1). Seeking justice for victims of rape in Minova, DRC. *Global Post.* Retrieved from https://www.pri.org/stories/2014-05-01/seeking-justice-victims-rape-minova-drc-video

Stokes, E., & Muyali, S. (2014, May 5). Two of 39 soldiers convicted of rape in historic DRC trial, all military officers acquitted of rape. *Global Post.* Retrieved from https://www.pri.org/stories/2014-05-05/two-39-soldiers-convicted-rape-historic-drc-trial-all-military-officers-acquitted

Stop Rape Now. (n.d.). Retrieved from http://www.stoprapenow.org/

Storr, W. (2011, July 17). The rape of men: The darkest secret of war. *The Guardian*. Retrieved from https://www.theguardian.com/society/2011/jul/17/the-rape-of-men

Stoter, B. (2015, September 9). After mass rape by the Islamic state, Yazidi women still struggle to break the silence. *Al-monitor*. Retrieved from http://www.al-monitor.com/pulse/originals/2015/09/yazidi-women-rape-slave-islamic-state.html

Sullivan, B. (2003). Trafficking in women: Feminism and the new international law. *International Feminist Journal of Politics*, 5(1), 67–91.

Sutton, T., Daniels, J. P., & Maclean, R. (2017, August 1). Insult to injury: How Trump's 'global gag' will hit women traumatized by war. *The Guardian*. Retrieved from https://www.theguardian.com/global-development/2017/aug/01/insult-to-injury-trump-global-gag-will-hit-women-traumatised-by-war?CMP=share_btn_link

Sylvester, C. (2002). Feminist arts of international relations. In C. Sylvester (Ed.), *Feminist international relations: An unfinished journey* (pp. 267–286). Cambridge: Cambridge University Press.

Syrian Network for Human Rights. (n.d.). *Civilian death toll*. Retrieved from http://sn4hr.org/blog/2018/09/24/civilian-death-toll/#

Syrian Network for Human Rights. (2013). *The destruction of schools and its consequences*. Retrieved from http://sn4hr.org/public_html/wp-content/pdf/english/The_Destruction_Of_Schools_And_its_Consequences_en.pdf

Taguba, A. (2004). *Article 15-6 investigation of the 800th military police brigade*. Retrieved from https://fas.org/irp/agency/dod/taguba.pdf

Takai, A. (2011). Rape and forced pregnancy as genocide before the Bangladesh tribunal. *Temple International and Comparative Law Journal*, 25, 393–422.

Takševa, T. (2015). Genocidal rape, enforced impregnation, and the discourse of Serbian National Identity. *Comparative Literature and Culture*, 17(3), 2–8.

Tappis, H., Freeman, J., Glass, N., & Doocy, S. (2016). Effectiveness of interventions, programs, and strategies for gender-based violence prevention in refugee populations: An integrative review. *PLOS Currents*, 19, 1–19.

Tec, N. (2003). *Resilience and courage: Women, men and the Holocaust*. New Haven, CT: Yale University Press.

Teo, T. (2014) Epistemological violence. In T. Teo (Eds.) *Encyclopedia of critical psychology*. New York, NY: Springer.

Tétreault, M. A. (2006). The sexual politics of Abu Ghraib: Hegemony, spectacle, and the global war on terror. *The National Women's Studies Association Journal*, 18(3), 33–50.

The Convention on the Prevention and Punishment of the Crime of Genocide. (2014). Retrieved from http://www.oas.org/dil/1948_Convention_on_the_Prevention_and_Punishment_of_the_Crime_of_Genocide.pdf

The Freedom Fund. (2016). *Struggling to survive: Slavery and exploitation of Syrian refugees in Lebanon*. Retrieved from https://d1r4g0yjvcc7lx.cloudfront.net/uploads/Lebanon-Report-FINAL-8April16.pdf

The International Center for Transnational Justice (ICTJ). (2018). *We didn't think it would hit us': Understanding the impact of attacks on schools in Syria*. Retrieved from https://www.ictj.org/sites/default/files/Report_Save_Syrian_Schools_English_Web.pdf

The International Criminal Court DRC. (n.d.). Retrieved from https://www.icc-cpi.int/drc

The International Criminal Court. (2011). *Elements of crimes*. Retrieved from https://www.icc-cpi.int/NR/rdonlyres/336923D8-A6AD-40EC-AD7B-45BF9DE73D56/0/ElementsOfCrimesEng.pdf

The International Rescue Committee. (2013). *Syria: A regional crisis. The IRC commission on Syrian refugees*. Retrieved from http://utra.sa.utoronto.ca/files/2013/10/IRCReportMidEast20130114.pdf

The New Humanitarian. (2009). *Drought driving farmers to the cities*. Retrieved from http://www.thenewhumanitarian.org/feature/2009/09/02/drought-driving-farmers-cities

The New Humanitarian (2013). *Armed groups in the DRC*. Retrieved from http://www.
   thenewhumanitarian.org/news/2013/10/31/armed-groups-eastern-drc
The Syrian Centre for Policy Research (SCPR). (2015). *Syria: Confronting fragmentation.
   Impact of Syrian crisis report*. Retrieved from https://www.undp.org/content/dam/
   syria/docs/Framework/SCPR-report-Confronting-fragmentation-2015-EN%20(1).
   pdf
The Week (2019, April 24). Isis: How a global terror network was born. *The Week*.
   Retrieved from https://www.theweek.co.uk/islamic-state/59001/what-is-isis-and-
   can-the-terror-group-be-stopped
Themnér, L., & Wallensteen, P. (2013). Armed conflicts, 1946–2012. *Journal of Peace
   Research, 50*(4), 509–521.
Touquet, H., & Gorris, E. (2016). Out of the shadows? The inclusion of men and boys in
   conceptualizations of wartime sexual violence. *Reproductive Health Matters, 24*(47),
   36–46.
Tousaw, E., Moo, S. N. H. G, Arnott, G., & Foster, A. M. (2017). It is just like having
   a period with back pain: Exploring women's experiences with community-based
   distribution of misoprostol for early abortion on the Thailand-Burma border.
   Contraception, 97(2), 122–129.
Trenholm, J., Olsson, P., Blomqvst, M., & Ahlberg, B. M. (2013). Constructing soldiers
   from boys in Eastern Democratic Republic of Congo. *Men and Masculinities, 16*(2),
   203–227.
True, J. (2010). The political economy of violence against women: A feminist international
   relations perspective. *Australian Feminist Law Journal, 32*(1), 39–59.
True, J. (2012). *The political economy of violence against women*. Oxford: Oxford University
   Press.
Tucker, B., & Triantafyllos, S. (2008). Lynndie England, Abu Ghraib, and the new imperial-
   ism. *Canadian Review of American Studies, 38*(1), 83–100.
Turshen, M. (2016). *Gender and the political economy of conflict in Africa*. London:
   Routledge.
U.S. Department of State. (2012). *Trafficking in persons report – Iraq*. Retrieved from http://
   www.refworld.org/docid/4fe30cbf32.html
United Nations (UN). (2007). *The United Nations and Darfur*. Retrieved from http://www.
   unis.unvienna.org/pdf/UN-Darfur_fact_sheet.pdf
United Nations (UN). (2017). *Civilians in Darfur still under threat, as proliferation of weapons aggravates situation, peacekeeping chief tells security council*. Retrieved from
   https://www.un.org/press/en/2017/sc12678.doc.htm
United Nations (UN). (2018a). *Group of experts on the DRC*. Retrieved from https://
   reliefweb.int/sites/reliefweb.int/files/resources/N1812836.pdf
United Nations (UN). (2018b). *Report of the secretary-general on conflict-related sexual
   violence*. S/2018/250. Retrieved from https://www.un.org/sexualviolenceinconflict/
   wp-content/uploads/report/s-2018-250/SG-REPORT-2017-CRSV-SPREAD.pdf
United Nations Assistance Mission for Iraq. (2008). *Human rights report, July 1–December
   31*. Retrieved from https://www.ohchr.org/Documents/Countries/IQ/UNAMI_
   Human_Rights_Report_July_December_2008_EN.pdf
United Nations Children's Education Fund (UNICEF). (2014). *A study on early marriage
   in Jordon*. Retrieved from https://reliefweb.int/report/jordan/study-early-marriage-
   jordan-2014
United Nations DRC. (2019). *Sexual violence in conflict*. Retrieved from https://www.
   un.org/sexualviolenceinconflict/countries/democratic-republic-of-the-congo/
United Nations General Assembly. (1981). *Convention on the elimination of all forms of
   discrimination against women (CEDAW)*. Retrieved from http://www.ohchr.org/
   Documents/ProfessionalInterest/cedaw.pdf

United Nations General Assembly. (1993). *Declaration on the elimination of violence against women*. Retrieved from https://www.un.org/en/genocideprevention/documents/atrocity-crimes/Doc.21_declaration%20elimination%20vaw.pdf

United Nations General Assembly. (2013a). *Report of the special rapporteur on violence against women, its causes and consequences, Rashida Monjoo. A/HRC/17/26*. Retrieved from http://www.ohchr.org/Documents/HRBodies/HRCouncil/Regular Session/Session23/A_HRC_23_49_English.pdf

United Nations General Assembly. (2013b). *Report of the independent international commission of inquiry on the Syrian Arab Republic 22nd session, 5th February U.N. Doc. A/HRC/22/59*. Retrieved from https://www.ohchr.org/Documents/HRBodies/HRCouncil/ColSyria/A.HRC.22.59_en.pdf

United Nations General Assembly. (2015). *Report of the independent international commission of inquiry on the Syrian Arab Republic, 27th session, 5th February U.N. Doc. A/HRC/28/69*. Retrieved from https://documents-dds-ny.un.org/doc/UNDOC/GEN/G15/019/37/PDF/G1501937.pdf?OpenElement

United Nations General Assembly. (2016). *Child, early and forced marriage: Report of the Secretary-General*. Retrieved from https://www.refworld.org/topic,50ffbce4c9,50ffbce4e7,57cd39584,0,UNGA,,.html

United Nations High Commissioner for Refugees (UNHCR). (1997). *Guidelines on policies and procedures in dealing with unaccompanied children seeking asylum*. Retrieved from https://www.unhcr.org/3d4f91cf4.pdf

United Nations High Commissioner for Refugees (UNHCR). (2003). *Sexual and gender-based violence against refugees, returnees and internally displaced persons: Guidelines for prevention and response*. Retrieved from https://www.unhcr.org/3f696bcc4.pdf

United Nations High Commissioner for Refugees (UNHCR). (2015). *Woman alone: The fight for survival by Syria's refugee women*. Retrieved from http://www.unhcr.org/ar/53bb8d006.pdf

United Nations High Commissioner for Refugees (UNHCR). (2016). *Global trends: Forced displacement in 2016*. Retrieved from https://www.unhcr.org/globaltrends2016/

United Nations Human Rights Office of the High Commissioner. (2010). *Protocol to prevent, suppress and punish trafficking in persons*. Retrieved from https://www.ohchr.org/en/professionalinterest/pages/protocoltraffickinginpersons.aspx

United Nations Office for the Coordination of Humanitarian Affairs. (n.d.) *Syrian Arab Republic*. Retrieved from https://www.unocha.org/syrian-arab-republic/about-ocha-syria

United Nations Office for the Special Representative of the Secretary-General on Sexual Violence in Conflict (UN SRSG-SVC). (2013). *Report of workshop on sexual violence against men and boys in conflict situations*. Retrieved from https://ifls.osgoode.yorku.ca/wp-content/uploads/2014/01/Report-of-Workshop-on-Sexual-Violence-against-Men-and-Boys-Final.pdf

United Nations Office for the Special Representative of the Secretary-General on Sexual Violence in Conflict (UN SRSG-SVC). (2015). *United Nations special representative welcomes unanimous adoption of security council resolution on the peace process in Syria and urges all parties to take immediate steps to ensure the protection and participation of women*. Retrieved from https://www.un.org/sexualviolenceinconflict/statement/united-nations-special-representative-welcomes-unanimous-adoption-of-security-council-resolution-on-the-peace-process-in-syria-and-urges-all-parties-to-take-immediate-steps-to-ensure-the-protection-an/

United Nations office on genocide prevention and the responsibility to protect: Crimes against humanity. (n.d). Retrieved from https://www.un.org/en/genocideprevention/crimes-against-humanity.shtml

United Nations office on genocide prevention and the responsibility to protect: War crimes. (n.d). Retrieved from https://www.un.org/en/genocideprevention/war-crimes.shtml

United Nations Population Fund (UNFPA). (2015). *Five years of saving lives.* Retrieved from https://www.unfpa.org/sites/default/files/resource-pdf/UNFPA_Annual_Report_E.compressed.pdf

United Nations Population Fund (UNFPA). (2017a). *Statement by UNFPA on U.S. decision to withhold funding.* Retrieved from https://www.unfpa.org/press/statement-unfpa-us-decision-withhold-funding

United Nations Population Fund (UNFPA). (2017b). *Voices from Syria 2018: Assessment findings of the humanitarian needs overview.* Retrieved from https://www.humanitarianresponse.info/sites/www.humanitarianresponse.info/files/documents/files/2017-12_voices_from_syria_2nd_edition.pdf

United Nations Population Fund. (n.d). *FAQ.* Retrieved from https://www.unfpa.org/frequently-asked-questions

United Nations Population Fund. (n.d.). *About us.* Retrieved from https://www.unfpa.org/about-us

United Nations Secretary General's Bulletin. (2003). *Special measures for protection from sexual exploitation and sexual abuse.* Retrieved from https://www.refworld.org/docid/451bb6764.html

United Nations Security Council (UNSCR). (2000). *Resolution 1325.* Retrieved from https://documents-dds-ny.un.org/doc/UNDOC/GEN/N00/720/18/PDF/N0072018.pdf?OpenElement

United Nations Security Council (UNSCR). (2002). *Resolution 1146. Final report of the Panel of Experts on the Illegal Exploitation of Natural Resources and Other Forms of Wealth of the Democratic Republic of the Congo.* Retrieved from https://www.securitycouncilreport.org/atf/cf/%7B65BFCF9B-6D27-4E9C-8CD3-CF6E4FF96FF9%7D/DRC%20S%202002%201146.pdf

United Nations Security Council (UNSCR). (2003). *Report of the panel of experts on the illegal exploitation of natural resources and other forms of wealth of the Democratic Republic of Congo.* S/2003/1027.

United Nations Security Council (UNSCR). (2003). *Resolution 1483.* Retrieved from http://www.unesco.org/culture/laws/pdf/resolution1483_iraq_en.pdf

United Nations Security Council (UNSCR). (2008). *Resolution 1820.* Retrieved from https://www.securitycouncilreport.org/atf/cf/%7B65BFCF9B-6D27-4E9C-8CD3-CF6E4FF96FF9%7D/CAC%20S%20RES%201820.pdf

United Nations Security Council (UNSCR). (2009a). *Resolution 1888.* Retrieved from http://unscr.com/files/2009/01888.pdf

United Nations Security Council (UNSCR). (2009b). *Resolution 1889.* http://unscr.com/files/2009/01889.pdf

United Nations Security Council (UNSCR). (2010). *Resolution 1960.* Retrieved from http://unscr.com/files/2010/01960.pdf

United Nations Security Council (UNSCR). (2013a). *Resolution 2106.* Retrieved from https://undocs.org/en/S/RES/2106(2013)

United Nations Security Council (UNSCR). (2013b). *Resolution 2122.* Retrieved from http://unscr.com/en/resolutions/doc/2122

United Nations Security Council (UNSCR). (2015). *Resolution 2242.* Retrieved from http://unscr.com/files/2015/02242.pdf

Universal Periodic Review. (2016). *Human rights violations against women and girls in Syria. Submission to the United Nations universal periodic review of the Syrian Arab republic.* Retrieved from: https://www.madre.org/sites/default/files/PDFs/Syria%20UPR%20submission%20Final.pdf

USAID (n.d.) *Responsible minerals trade fact sheet*. Retrieved from https://www.usaid.gov/democratic-republic-congo/fact-sheets/usaiddrc-fact-sheet-responsible-minerals-trade

van der Mensbrugghe, C. (2016, August 16). *Respect rape victims right to abortions in Syria*. [Blog post]. Retrieved from http://globaljusticecenter.net/blog/526-respect-rape-victims-right-to-abortions-in-syria

Vojdik, V. K. (2014). Sexual violence against men and women in war: A masculinities approach. *Nevada Law Journal, 14*(3), 923–952.

Von Uexkull, N. (2014). Sustained drought, vulnerability and civil conflict in Sub-Saharan Africa. *Political Geography, 43*, 16–26.

Vujnovic, M. (2017). *Hypercapitalism*. Retrieved from https://onlinelibrary.wiley.com/doi/abs/10.1002/9780470670590.wbeog278.pub2

Walklate, S. (2017). Mediated suffering. In M. Brown & E. Carrabine (Eds.), *Routledge international handbook of visual criminology* (e-book version). Oxon: Routledge

Waller, J. (2012). Rape as a tool of 'othering' in genocide. In C. Rittner & J. Roth (Eds.), *Rape: Weapon of war and genocide* (pp. 83–100). St Paul Minnesota: Paragon.

Weitzer, R. (2005). Flawed theory and method in studies on prostitution. *Violence Against Women, 11*(7), 934–949.

Weitzman, L. & Ofer, D. (1998). Introduction. In D. Ofer & L. Weitzman (Eds.), *Women in the Holocaust* (pp. 1–18). New Haven, CT: Yale University Press.

Wesely, J. K. (2006). Considering the context of women's violence: Gender, lived experience and cumulative victimization. *Feminist Criminology, 1*(4), 303–328.

West, L., Isotta-Day, H., Ba-Break, M., & Morgan, R. (2016). Factors in use of family planning services by Syrian women in a refugee camp in Jordan. *Journal of Family Planning, Reproductive Health Care, 73*(2), 96–102.

Whyte, D. (2007). The crimes of neo-liberal rule in occupied Iraq. *British Journal of Criminology, 47*(2), 177–195.

Wikimedia.commons.org. (2003a). Retrieved from https://commons.wikimedia.org/wiki/File:Sabrina-Harman.jpg

Wikimedia.commons.org. (2003b). Retrieved from https://commons.wikimedia.org/wiki/File:AbuGhraibDogs03.jpg

Wilcox, L. (2015). *Bodies of violence: Theorizing embodied subjects in international relations*. Oxford: Oxford University Press.

Willemse, K. (2007). "In my father's house": Gender, Islam and the construction of a gendered public sphere in Darfur, Sudan. *Journal for Islamic Studies, 27*, 73–115.

Willemse, K. (2009). Masculinity and the construction of a Sudanese national identity. In S. M. Hassan & C. E. Ray (Eds.), *Darfur and the crisis of governance in Sudan: A critical reader* (pp. 213–232). New York, NY: Cornell University Press.

Wirtz, A., Pham, K., Glass, N., Loochkartt, S., Kidane, T., Cuspoca, D., ...Vu, A. (2014). Gender-based violence in conflict and displacement: Qualitative findings from displaced women in Colombia. *Conflict and Health, 8*(10), 1–14.

Wolfe, L. (2013, April 3). Syria has a massive rape crisis. *The Atlantic*. Retrieved from https://www.theatlantic.com/international/archive/2013/04/syria-has-a-massive-rape-crisis/274583/

Women on Waves. (n.d.). *Women in Syria need more than guided missiles*. Retrieved from https://www.womenonwaves.org/en/page/4555/women-in-syria-need-more-than-guided-missiless

Women's International League for Peace and Freedom (WILPF). (2016). *Violations against women in Syria and the disproportionate impact of the conflict on them. NGO summary report. Universal periodic review of the Syrian Arab republic*. Retrieved from https://wilpf.org/wp-content/uploads/2016/06/WILPF_VAW_HC-2016_WEB-ONEPAGE.pdf

Women's Media Centre (WMC). (n.d.). *Bangladesh*. Retrieved from http://www.womensmediacenter.com/women-under-siege/conflicts/bangladesh

Women's Refugee Commission (WRC). (2016). *A girl no more: The changing norms of child marriage in conflict*. Retrieved from https://www.womensrefugeecommission.org/girls/resources/1311-girl-no-more

Wood, E. J. (2009). Armed groups and sexual violence: When is wartime rape rare? *Politics and Society*, *37*(1), 131–162.

Wood, E. J. (2014). Conflict-related sexual violence and the policy implications of recent research: Sexual violence in armed conflict. *International Review of the Red Cross*, *96*(894), 457–478.

Work, C. (2018). Climate change and conflict: Global insecurity and the road less travelled. *Geoforum*, *102*, 222–225.

World Health Organization (WHO). (2004). *Clinical management of rape survivors: Developing protocols for use with refugees and internally displaced person*. Retrieved from http://www.unhcr.org/403a0b7f4.pdf

Young, A. (2014). From object to encounter: Aesthetic politics and visual criminology. *Theoretical Criminology*, *18*(2), 159–175.

Zoepf, K. (2007, May 29). Desperate Iraqi refugees turn to sex trade in Syria. *New York Times*. Retrieved from http://www.nytimes.com/2007/05/29/world/middleeast/29syria.html?pagewanted=all&_r=0.

Zubriggen, E. L. (2010). Rape, war, and the socialization of masculinity: Why our refusal to give up war ensures that rape cannot be eradicated. *Psychology of Women Quarterly*, *34*(4), 538–549.

Index

Note: Page numbers followed by "*n*" indicate notes.